For more information:

www.gmathacks.com

Also by the author:

Total GMAT Math

GMAT Math Challenge

GMAT Math Fundamentals

Total GMAT Verbal

GMAT 111: Tips, Tricks, and Tactics

Forthcoming, Summer 2011:

GMAT Verbal Challenge

Total GMAT Verbal

Total GMAT Verbal

Jeff Sackmann / GMAT HACKS

May 2011

Contents

CONTENTS

CONTENTS

CONTENTS

CONTENTS

1 Introduction

If you're reading this book, you don't need me to tell you how important the GMAT is. Your test scores are one of the key ingredients in a successful business school application. Not only is the test a pressure-packed experience, it pits you against thousands of other highly-motivated test-takers. All of this means that it's harder than ever to get a high GMAT score.

For many people, the difference between the score they've got and the score they want is the Verbal portion of the test. It's one thing to learn a pile of formulas and shortcuts to master the Quantitative section, but the Verbal half of the test can be much more intractable. The patterns that underlie verbal questions are subtler, and test items require a more nuanced grasp of the English language.

No book can teach you how to master the English language in three easy steps, but the goal of Total GMAT Verbal is to make that mastery less important. In this book, you'll learn about what to expect on the Verbal section of the GMAT and how to attack each and every question type you'll encounter. Along the way, you'll be exposed to a variety of patterns that the test-maker uses to create this material. Understanding those patterns will make Verbal questions that much more accessible.

As you'll soon learn, the GMAT Verbal section is best understood as two or three different test sections. While there is a fair amount of overlap between the skills needed to master Critical Reasoning and Reading Comprehension, they have little in common with the skills needed to become proficient with Sentence Correction. Accordingly, this book is separated into three main sections, one for each of the three major question types.

In each of the three sections, you'll start by discovering the basic structure of the question type. You'll move on to some general categorizations that will help you narrow down your approach on any given question. Then, as the chapters proceed, you'll find they get more and more detailed, focusing on specific nuances of GMAT Verbal questions. Think of it like the hierarchy of a large corporation. Right now, we're discussing this at the "upper management" level, taking in the big picture. The introduction to each question type is a little lower down the chain, perhaps a division manager. As you continue, you'll find that you need to approach the GMAT from a variety levels, all the way from the CEO down to the mailroom. This book will help you accomplish that.

Finally, a note about me, the author of Total GMAT Verbal. I've been helping people improve their GMAT scores for nearly a decade now. I've seen the Verbal curricula used by nearly every GMAT prep company in existence. There are plenty of good ideas out there, but they are rarely grouped together into one well-organized resource. That's what led me to create this book. It's certainly valuable to use additional practice materials (for more details, see the chapter on "Further Resources"), but as far as skills, strategy, and tactics, I've put everything you need into this book. These are the approaches I've been teaching my students for years, finally assembled in one place.

By purchasing this book, you've taken an important first step toward success on the GMAT Verbal section. Turn to the next chapter to keep that momentum going!

2   How to Use This Book

The key to any successful GMAT training regimen, whether you're aiming for a 450 or a 750, is consistency. Too many students try to cram their studying into weekends, or the week before the test, or their occasional days off. Preparation of that sort is better than nothing, but it is far inferior to doing things the right way.

I've written extensively on my website about how to make the most of your study time. I won't recap all of that here; instead, I encourage you to browse www.gmathacks.com for more information. But I will review one simple concept: quality is more important than quantity. Too many students think their goal should be to do as many practice problems as possible, often numbering in the thousands. That is simply wrong.

Much better is to really learn from every practice problem you do. The GMAT not only tests your content knowledge, it tests how quickly you can recognize question types and deploy that knowledge. So, if you can't do a question correctly, or you can't complete it in two minutes or so, you might as well have gotten it wrong. Your preparation should reflect that. If you get a question right, but it takes you five minutes (even three!) you aren't done with that question. It should go on a list for review the next day.

In that vein, I often tell people that if they do (and understand, and can complete in two minutes) every question in The Official Guide to GMAT Review, they'll be ready for the test, and will likely score in the 80th percentile or higher. I've rarely been wrong. 300+ verbal questions is more than enough. Similarly, if you understand all the content and can comfortably and speedily complete the 100+ practice questions in this book, you'll be well on your way to being ready for the GMAT Verbal section.

As I've suggested already, consistency is the name of the game. It's better to spend an hour a day for an entire week than to spend twelve hours on the weekend. With that in mind, do everything you can to carve out a bit of study time every single day (at worst, every other day). If you don't, you'll find yourself stressing out, spending a great deal of your study time catching up, and not making as much progress as you'd like. Trust me: I've watched it happen to too many people.

No matter how busy your life is, I'm convinced that you can carve out a half-hour or an hour a day for the GMAT. If you can do that, your test preparation shouldn't take longer than two or three months. It may mean sneaking away from the office during lunch, or setting the alarm thirty minutes earlier, but if you really care about getting into the business school of your choice, you can make that sacrifice. If you do that consistently, you will reach your goal.

And that, in a nutshell, is how to work through this book. Pay particular attention to the explanations. I've put a lot of time into creating useful, extensive explanations, and much of the value of the book is contained in them. When you find a question that gives you trouble the first time around, mark it and return to it the following day. You can do a lot of work in an hour a day. In fact, I suspect that many of the sections of this book–including both the content review and the GMAT-like problems–can be completed in about an hour.

There's no magic bullet to GMAT success, but this book is designed to help you make your consistent study time that much more efficient.

3 GMAT Verbal Basics

The GMAT Verbal section is made up of 41 questions, which you are expected to answer in 75 minutes or less. Of those 41 questions, you'll see a nearly equal number of Critical Reasoning, Reading Comprehension, and Sentence Correction questions. (There are a few more SC questions than the others.)

Critical Reasoning questions provide short passages, then ask logic-related questions about them. For instance, you might be asked to select passage's underlying assumption, to explain a paradox in the passage, or to determine which of five statements is supported by the passage. Some passages are based on hypothetical countries, regions, or firms; others are factual, covering topics such as business, economics, and various sciences.

Reading Comprehension questions start with longer (usually 2-4 paragraph) passages, and the test asks multiple questions about each passage. These passages are generally academic in tone, and cover similar topics to the ones that Critical Reasoning passages touch on. However, all RC passages are factual. They are written directly for the GMAT (they are not excerpts from other sources), but they should not contradict knowledge you may have. RC questions ask for things like the main idea of the passage, specific details from the passage, and inferences one might logically make from the passage.

Sentence Correction questions give you a sentence with all or part of the sentence underlined. The five choices present five ways that the underlined part might be corrected. It's also possible that the sentence is correct as is. Choice (A) is always identical to the original sentence, so if the sentence is correct as written, select (A). The GMAT tests standard English grammar, though sentences are often long and awkward. You don't need to have a thorough knowledge of technical grammar rules, but a good grasp of English grammar helps quite a bit.

Of course, most of this book is devoted to elaborating on what I've said so far. In the sections below, you'll find each type of question broken down much further, and you'll have a chance to work through dozens of examples of each. Before getting there, though, there are some general strategic concepts to discuss.

Getting Through the Verbal Section

One of the hardest things about the GMAT Verbal section is that it just isn't very interesting.

The content is uninteresting and unfamiliar, the arguments are flawed, the sentences are ungrammatical (even the right ones aren't very good sometimes), and you've got to focus on all those details for more than an hour. It's like reading a bad in-flight magazine, only with the expectation of a detailed quiz when you land.

Unfortunately, there's nothing I can tell you to really solve these problems: Reading Comprehension will always use topics that you don't know much about; Sentence Correction answers will always be objectionable; and Critical Reasoning passages will require you to switch gears every couple of minutes. But there are a couple of ways to deal with the drudgery.

First, remember to breathe. It's that simple. I didn't discover this until I had taken the test several times. What makes the GMAT Verbal section so stressful is that you must change gears from question to question, and there's no logical transition. That's not how you operate in real life, so it isn't how you should operate during the exam, either.

Instead, try this. After you click an answer choice and hit "confirm" to move on, close your eyes, take a breath, count to three, and then–only then–open your eyes and look at the next question. Like I said, it's simple. But if it works for you as well as it works for me, you won't believe the difference.

In case you're worried about using so much time to do something other than answer questions, do the math. Three seconds times forty breaks (one between each question) is two minutes. I guarantee you that you'll save that time by being that much more refreshed when you look at each question.

Additionally, since the test is presented on a computer screen, it's important to give yourself short breaks from staring at that screen. I'm a big proponent of doing as much scratchwork as you can–in other words, move the problem off the screen and onto your scratch paper. That isn't really possible on Verbal, at least not to the same extent that it is for math. However, there is one way you can get your eyes off the screen for another moment or two.

Each question, after you take a short breather, don't look right back at the screen. Instead, turn your focus to your scratch paper, where you'll write the number of the question, and "A B C D E." That way, if the question turns out to be tricky, and you want to keep track of which answer choices you can eliminate, you can cross them off on your scratch paper.

This is a great way to stay focused, and it also helps you keep track of which choices you've evaluated, and which conclusions you've arrived at.

Content and Complexity

The GMAT is an adaptive test: The questions you see depend on how well you are doing. If you answer a lot of questions right, you'll see harder problems. If you are going to get a high score on the Verbal section, you need to be able to handle more difficult problems. It may not be obvious how Verbal questions get harder, so it's worth taking a look at that now.

In short, GMAT Verbal difficulty boils down to two issues: content and complexity. Let's look at each one.

First, content. One of the more frustrating things about verbal content on any standardized test is that you have to read and absorb material you have virtually no interest in. To make questions more difficult, the GMAT takes that to the next level. If you've been studying for long, you know that some of the most challenging GMAT Verbal questions are based on science content–the sort of thing most potential MBA candidates never give a second thought to.

For instance, what would you rather read about: differing opinions as to the cause of the Great Depression, or differing theories as to why a rare South American bird evolved with a clipped left wing? If you chose the latter, consider yourself lucky–you're not in the majority.

Content difficulty is not limited to Reading Comprehension. While most Critical Reasoning questions follow a few basic argument structures, the topic of the question can add difficulty. Many of the toughest GMAT problems in the question pool are based on biology: genetics, disease, and drug effectiveness. Because those are more complicated subjects than invented scenarios involving Company X, those questions are often longer, as well.

There are, however, ways to deal with difficult content. Most of all, figure out a way to stay focused. The previous section in this chapter offers several solutions.

Also, remember that the GMAT is never testing you on prior knowledge, so whatever you need to answer the question is right there on the screen. Especially in Reading Comprehension, read actively: take notes, make an outline, think about what you're reading.

The second way in which Verbal questions become more difficult is through complexity.

There's nothing worse than reviewing a Critical Reasoning question and discovering that you got the wrong answer because you missed one tiny concept– sometimes nothing more than a single word. Especially when you are starting out, this is going to happen; it's a big part of why you need to spend so much time preparing for the test.

As GMAT Verbal questions get harder–and this applies to all three question types–the difference between the right answer and the wrong ones get smaller. It may be as little as one word, or a slight shift in scope. In Sentence Correction, two answers might be equally awkward, but one of them will have some tiny grammatical flaw that you might miss the first time through.

In Reading Comprehension, this can be the most frustrating of all. Given as many as 350-400 words, you're expected to notice these details, even when you're already trying to keep track of multiple arguments.

Thankfully, there are ways of dealing with complexity. Students often ask me whether they should skim Reading Comprehension passages. No! You have more than enough time to read each passage once, carefully. The more difficult the passage, the more likely that skimming will cause you to miss an important detail, whether it's a fact that alters the meaning of the passage, or a key word that signals the distinction between two differing viewpoints.

The same rule goes for Critical Reasoning–only more so. Because CR passages are shorter, you probably aren't tempted to skim them. But take that one step further: comb over those passages like your score depends on your reading every word. As they get harder, that becomes true: your GMAT score does hinge on you noticing every last detail.

Reading more carefully can take a lot of time, and you are limited to 75 minutes for all 41 questions. To avoid taking too long, the key is to read thoroughly–once. Many test-takers see a RC passage, skim it, and then skim the passage again for each question. It's much more efficient to read the passage carefully one time than to skim through it five times.

It may take practice–both on RC and CR–to read the passage so effectively that you don't need to go back (except to confirm details). But that's what your preparation time is for–train yourself to read the passage once even if, at first, it takes you far longer than the 3-4 minutes you should be spending on each Reading Comprehension passage.

There are plenty of ways the GMAT makes Verbal questions more difficult, but if you read the questions and passages carefully and recognize the sorts of answer choices that trick you on a regular basis, you should be able to get those questions right. It's a lot like math: there are rules, but once you learn them, every question is within your grasp.

4 GMAT Verbal Scratchwork

Scratch work is easy on the GMAT Quantitative section. You write down your work, just like you always have when completing math problems. (That isn't to say you can't improve your math scratchwork, but that's outside the scope of this book!)

Most people, though, don't have a good idea of how to maximize their scratchwork on the GMAT Verbal section. I'll admit, it's not as easy, and there's not as much advantage to be gained with better scratchwork. Finding the best approach is more personal, as well.

Reading Comprehension Scratchwork

Every test-prep company has some particular method they'd like you to use to take notes through GMAT reading passages. I don't put too much stock in any of them; what matters isn't exactly how you take notes, but that you do jot something down, and that it doesn't take too much of your time.

In fact, that's worth emphasizing further. The idea isn't to force you into thinking about every passage the same way. Writing down an outline, or a few key points, is all that matters, whether you do so briefly or exhaustively.

The main benefit of note-taking is that it requires that you maintain your focus. Especially with passages that don't interest you at all, it's easy to zone out and lose time. If you force yourself to write something down at the conclusion of every paragraph, you're much less likely to do that.

Thus, the idea is to jot down a note every few sentences, focusing on general ideas and structure. In a perfect world, you'd be able to state the "primary purpose" of the passage once you've finished reading it, whether the GMAT gives you that question or not.

Critical Reasoning Scratchwork

It's much less important to jot down notes in CR questions. That's mainly because there's so much less to read–it's harder to lose concentration during a CR question. However, if you find that you do have trouble maintaining focus for the minute or so it should take you to read the prompt, try taking a note or two to break the task into smaller pieces.

Where scratchwork can be helpful in CR is noting causal relationships. A large number of CR questions involve some sort of causation. When they do, especcially if the question is an assumption, strengthen, or weaken, that relationship will play a key part in the correct choice.

This doesn't have to be complicated: you might just write "changing climate –> new food-gathering techniques" or "threat of patent law reversal –> different publication method."

You can also use your scratchwork to track answer choices, which applies to all three types of Verbal questions. I'll discuss that in the next section.

Sentence Correction Scratchwork

When I take the GMAT, I do one thing before every single Verbal question. I take a second, force myself to look away from the screen (thus giving myself a much-needed, though brief, break) and jot down "A B C D E" on my scratch paper. For some questions, especially SC, that's all I write down. (Writing down those five letters is a good way to maintain focus, as noted in the previous chapter, and it can be helpful on all types of Verbal questions, not just SC.)

Since each answer choice requires a fresh thought and sometimes a new angle on the question, you don't want to track your progress in your head. Instead, use the scratch paper to record which choices you've eliminated, and which ones are possibilities.

To do that, I mark each choice in one of three ways:

An "X" through the choice means "This couldn't possibly be right."

A "?" next to the choice means "I don't think this is right, but if nothing better comes along, it's not so awful that I couldn't select it."

An underline ('_') beneath the choice means "This is probably right. I'll look at the other choices, though."

It doesn't matter whether you adopt my method or not; what is important is that you consistently use a method that works for you, and that method helps you keep track of the work you've already done. Unless you struggle with the English language, I'm convinced that you should be able to complete the GMAT Verbal section in much less than the allotted 75 minutes. People who don't usually spend much of their time daydreaming or re-reading passages they didn't focus on the first time.

Effective scratchwork is often the difference between struggling to get through all 41 questions and comfortably finishing the section with plenty of time to spare.

5   Introduction to Critical Reasoning

Critical Reasoning makes up about one-third of the GMAT Verbal section. To be more precise, there are usually 13 CR questions among the 41 problems on the Verbal portion of the test.

Each CR question consists of three parts:
A brief, paragraph-long passage;
A question;
Five answer choices.

Here's a sample passage:
Until recently, the scholarly consensus was that few marine species are approaching extinction. Closer examination of marine species near the island of Tasmania, however, revealed many factors, such as climate change and fishing, that may be contributing to the extinction of species thought to be safe. The rate of extinction of marine species may be just as high as that of non-marine species, but the lack of systematic sampling has disguised the trend.

Remember I used the word "unfamiliar" before to refer to the content? I wasn't kidding around. On all three types of Verbal questions, the makers of the GMAT are including more and more technical topics, often science-related, that you are unlikely to have much exposure to.

(This passage, along with most of the others used as examples in this book, is part of one of the sample questions included in the book.)

While the passage is the first thing you'll see on a CR question, that doesn't mean you should read it first. Consider the passage you just read: Do you have any idea what you should do with it? What you were reading for?

Instead, start with the question. The question related to the passage above is as follows:
Which of the following is most strongly supported by the statements given?

If you had known that, you'd have been able to focus your reading efforts that much more. So every time you see a CR question, start with the question, then read the passage.

Types of CR Questions

Almost all Critical Reasoning questions are somehow related to the construction of arguments. In the item above, you're looking for a statement that is logically supported by the passage. That isn't the most common question type, though it does come up regularly.

Here are some common types of questions in CR:

> Which of the following, if true, would most strongly support the consultants' proposal?
>
> Which of the following, if true, most seriously weakens the argument in the advertisement?
>
> Which of the following is an assumption on which this argument depends?
>
> Which of the following, if true, would best explain the apparent discrepancy described above?

Almost all of these types of questions demand that you identify the assumption–the unstated evidence–underlying the argument. There's no hard and fast rule governing how you'll identify the assumption, but it will always be there. The assumption is not stated, but it is necessary in order for the conclusion to be true.

As you practice GMAT Critical Reasoning questions, you'll see plenty of variations on those question types. Some even explicitly test your awareness of evidence, assumptions, and conclusion, though such questions are rare. When you are confronted with an unfamiliar type of question, remember that the skills tested aren't new. Such items will always hinge on these same concepts.

How This Section Works

We'll start by breaking down Critical Reasoning passages into two basic types. We'll discuss how to treat each type, as well as some of the common passage structures you'll encounter. After that, there are nine chapters on individual question types. Finally, the last two chapters discuss common patterns and pitfalls in Critical Reasoning answer choices.

6 CR: Types of Passages

If you skim through pages of sample Critical Reasoning questions, all the passages will look more or less the same. However, it's useful to start by classifying passages into two categories, based on the type of question asked about them:
> Passages for assumption-based questions
> Passages for inference-based questions

Since the type of passage is based on the question that goes with it, it's important to read the question first. You won't always be able to tell, simply by reading the passage, which type of question it goes with. Some are obvious; others could go with an assumption-based question or an inference-based question. Let's look at the differences.

Passages for assumption-based questions

These passages represent complete arguments. They might not be correct or logical arguments, but they have a conclusion and some evidence that supports that conclusion. In the next chapter, we'll discuss the many types of questions that the GMAT will ask regarding this sort of passage. For now, let's focus on what to do with it.

First, identify the conclusion. There are some conclusion keywords that sometimes make this easier, such as "thus," "therefore," and the particularly straightforward "in conclusion." Not every conclusion has such a keyword, but it wouldn't sound wrong if it did have one. If you're not sure which sentence (or part of a sentence) is the conclusion, look instead for the main point. If you had to distill the passage to one of its sentences, that summary would probably be the conclusion. Usually that sentence takes a position for or against something.

Next, look for subtle shifts. Perhaps the passage talks about something that happened last year, and then it draws a conclusion that forecasts the future. Maybe it cites data from a neighboring country, then concludes that the same data apply in a different country. What you are looking for are holes in the argument. No CR passage will represent a perfect, unassailable argument. The more flaws you can identify before you start analyzing the answer choices, the easier it will be to eliminate clearly wrong choices.

This focus, on shifts and flaws in the passage, is what sets apart successful CR students from less successful ones. (Also, you may not be surprised to learn that law students and lawyers arc typically very, very good at this question type.) Beyond doing lots of Critical Reasoning questions, there are a few ways you can practice. One source for sample arguments, all of which are flawed–and many of which are flawed in multiple ways–are the sample GMAT Analysis of Argument essay topics. You can find more of them than you'll ever need at the mba.com website.

Another way to start thinking like this more often is to be more skeptical in your day-to-day reading. There are many unstated assumptions in nearly every newspaper article, internal memo, and magazine feature. Whenever you see an author drawing a conclusion, take a step back and see if you can find a flaw in the reasoning. There's usually some kind of problem if you look for it.

Passages for inference-based questions

The passages associated with inference questions (more on those in a few chapters!) sometimes represent entire arguments, but often do not. They certainly don't need to. Inference questions are asking for a conclusion–an inference is, by definition, something that can logically be concluded from the information given.

Thus, if you want to think of inference passages in the same way as assumption-based passages, you can consider the entire passage as evidence for the conclusion, which will be one of the answer choices. This eliminates a whole lot of the work associated with assumption-based questions. It's still important, however, to look for shifts. The language used in GMAT passages is very precise. If a term comes up twice, the passage is emphasizing that it is referring to the same exact thing. If a slightly different term is used, it may be referring to something else. That's one kind of shift that will come up in all sorts of passages.

Also take note of parts of the passage that seem a bit off-topic. It is rare that a GMAT passage has any superfluous content. If something does appear to be unnecessary, consider how it might fit in. Further, keep it in mind when you start analyzing the answer choices–that part of the passage might end up providing the connection between the correct answer and a more central part of the passage.

I realize that some of this chapter is a little vague. The specifics of Critical Reasoning questions hinge on the questions themselves, and that's what we'll turn to next.

7 CR: Types of Assumption-Based Questions

Roughly three-quarters of the Critical Reasoning questions you'll see on your GMAT will be assumption-based. They come in many flavors, from the simple and obvious to the convoluted and obscure.

The three most common types of questions like this are:
Assumption
Strengthen
Weaken

Assumption questions are the most clear-cut. They ask for the argument's underlying assumption, and that's it. (As with the other question types, there is an entire chapter on this sort of question below.)

Strengthen and weaken questions are extremely common, and sometimes they are a bit harder to spot. Here's one example of a weaken question (without the passage):

In light of the situation, which of the following, if true, most strongly argues that adopting the proposal would be an ineffective way of achieving the goal?

Clearly, you won't know much about the proposal and the goal until you read the passage. But from the phrase "ineffective way," you should recognize that the question is asking you to undermine the argument, or in this case, show why the proposal may fail. Not every strengthen and weaken question contains a plan or proposal, but many do, and you'll get plenty of practice propping up (on strengthen questions) and undermining (on weaken questions) various proposals in items like this one.

In all of these questions, you're looking for the subtle shifts I discussed in the previous chapter. (More specific patterns are discussed in the following chapter.) Focus on the conclusion, or main point, of the argument. If there is a plan or proposal, make sure you understand the exact scope of that plan. As you practice, err on the side of spending too much time understanding the passage, rather than spending more time picking apart the answer choices. If you have a firm grasp of the passage, you should be able to quickly eliminate at least two or three wrong answer choices per question.

There are several other related question types that appear with assumption-based passages:
Explanation
Paradox
Flaw
Evidence

Explanation and paradox questions are very similar. In fact, they are grouped together in a chapter below. Explanation questions are usually worded something like this:

> Which of the following, if true, most helps to explain the
> apparent discrepancy?

Not every explanation question will include the word "discrepancy," but most will. In other words, most of these items have a passage that doesn't quite make sense. Explanation questions, then, require that you do a little more work to identify an assumption. The assumption is usually somewhat counterintuitive–it explains what didn't quite make sense in the passage.

Paradox questions are almost the same thing. Instead of asking you to resolve the apparent discrepancy, the question will ask you to identify, or resolve, the paradox. In questions like this, there will be a discrepancy, but it will be more blatant than the ones in explanation questions.

Flaw questions are just a type of weaken question. Rather than asking you to identify the choice that weakens the argument (or shows why the plan won't work), the question will ask you to identify the flaw in the argument. Often, there will be little or no difference in the types of answer choices provided. As with weaken questions, you'll identify the conclusion, look for an assumption, and find a choice that causes the argument to fall apart.

Evidence questions are the trickiest of these less-common question types. They are typically worded something like this:

> Which of the following would it be most useful to establish in
> order to evaluate the argument?

The answer choices usually start with "Whether." The choices don't make assertions (as they do in strengthen and weaken questions), they offer points that may or may not be true. The correct choice will be the one that, depending on the answer, could either strengthen or weaken the argument. This isn't the easiest CR concept to get your head around, and we'll delve into it further when we give evidence questions their own chapter.

Before we get into more details of each question type, the next chapter continues to focus on the general concepts of passages that accompany this whole range of assumption-based questions.

8 CR: Patterns in Assumption-Based Questions

The most common pattern in assumption-based Critical Reasoning passages is one of cause and effect. Such an argument asserts that one thing causes another. Often these arguments are very convincing; others are counterintuitive and may have obvious flaws.

Let's start by looking at a short example. Consider the following argument:

> Of the 75 bicyclists who were injured riding their bicycles last month, 54 of them regularly wear bicycle helmets. Therefore, wearing a helmet makes it more likely that a bicyclist will be injured while riding their bicycle.

Does that sound right to you? I'm guessing it doesn't. As it turns out, this argument has two common Critical Reasoning flaws. Let's take them one at a time, starting with the one I mentioned above, related to causality.

The argument concludes with a statement that suggests that one thing causes another:

(wearing a helmet) $\rightarrow$ (injury)

In more general terms, the argument claims that x causes y. This suggestion of causality is the assumption made by the argument. To weaken such an argument, we attack the assumption. After all, we can't attack the things that are stated as facts: either 54 bicyclists were injured, or they weren't. So we focus on what is left unstated.

The flaw here is a common one, and it stems from conflating "correlation" with "causation." Simply because two things happen simultaneously (they correlate) doesn't mean that one causes the other (causation). Sometimes they do–when it's raining outside, more people carry umbrellas–they carry umbrellas because it is raining. But if more people wear purple clothing when it's raining outside, odds are that the two things are not related.

In terms of answering a Critical Reasoning question like this one, there are many ways to attack an argument based on causation. The following are claims that could weaken such an argument:

x does not cause y

y causes x

z causes both x and y

Consider how each of those claims would be phrased as they relate to the bicycle example:

"Studies show that bicyclists wearing helmets are less likely to be

injured in accidents than those who do not wear helmets."
"When a bicyclist is injured, he or she becomes more likely to
    regularly wear a helmet in the future."
"Bicyclists who ride more than 100 miles per week are less likely to
    wear helmets and more likely to suffer a bicycle-related injury."

There are surely other ways of representing all three, but those examples are presented to give you an idea of some of the ways you might attack a causal argument.

Numbers and Percents

Let's take another look at the bicyclist example and isolate another possible flaw in the reasoning:

> Of the 75 bicyclists who were injured riding their bicycles last month, 54 of them regularly wear bicycle helmets. Therefore, wearing a helmet makes it more likely that a bicyclist will be injured while riding their bicycle.

The idea that one group is "more likely" to be injured is not quite the same as saying more people are injured. A phrase like "more likely" really means that the odds of any one person making a certain choice (like wearing or not wearing a helmet) and experiencing a certain outcome (getting injured or remaining unhurt) are higher or lower.

In other words, we care about percents (or probabilities), not numbers. If we wanted to strengthen this argument, we'd say that an equal number of bicyclists wear helmets and do not wear helmets. If the number of total bicyclists making each choice is the same, then the 54 who wear bicycle helmets represent a larger percent than the 21 who do not.

If we wanted to weaken the argument, we'd also translate the numbers to percents, but we'd aim for different percents. If 90% of bicyclists wear helmets and about 70% of those injured regularly wear helmets, then any given bicyclist would seem to be less likely to be injured while wearing a helmet. By contrast, if 10% of bicyclists do not wear helmets, and that group represents 30% of the injuries, we could conclude something opposite to what the argument claims.

Any time you see absolute numbers in a passage, especially if the question is an explanation or paradox question, consider the possibility that the numbers are misleading, and percents would be better.

Sample Sizes

Many Critical Reasoning passages refer to surveys and studies. Any survey or study necessarily relies on a sample, and this sample is where you should focus. Let's consider another example:

> 60% of those surveyed in a recent poll said they would vote for Candidate X in the upcoming election. Therefore, Candidate X is likely to win the election.

Simple enough, right? We read something like that (albeit with a little more detail) in the newspapers all the time. However, this is a common trap on the GMAT. There are many ways such an argument could be weakened:

> Only some of those surveyed are likely voters.
> The sample of those surveyed is too small.
> The sample is large enough, but it is not representative of the population (perhaps all of those surveyed were small-business owners, or all were women).
> The election is still months away.

This is not quite as general of a pattern as causality and numbers/percents, but it does appear on a number of GMAT items. When you see it, focus on the sample.

9 CR: Types of Inference-Based Questions

Inference-based questions make up a much smaller fraction of Critical Reasoning items than assumption-based questions, and there are correspondingly few types of questions, as well.

The main type of question is, simply, the inference question. You're given a series of statements, and you're asked for a logical conclusion. In the chapter on this question type, you'll see several different ways in which the GMAT will ask this question, but identifying them is rarely very difficult.

The other common type of question is what I call the "Fill-In-the-Blank." Instead of three or four sentences of evidence, followed by a question, the FITB question adds a half sentence at the end followed by some blank space. Here's what it might look like (minus the first several sentences):
"Given this state of affairs, it seems most likely that _____."

The few words that precede the blank will always be very suggestive. This example is almost indistinguishable from an inference question: you're looking for what can logically be deduced from the previous sentences. In other FITB questions, the blank will be preceded by the word "because," so you'll be providing a bit more evidence that supports the conclusion.

FITB questions don't test any unique skills–if you can handle the range of assumption, strengthen, weaken, and inference questions, you'll be fine with the logical aspect of this question type. The only real challenge is that the presentation is a little different, and many of the most common practice resources (such as The Official Guide) don't have very many items like this.

10   CR: Assumption Questions

Finally, it's time to delve into each individual question type. As you've already seen, assumptions are extremely important in Critical Reasoning, as they underpin a wide variety of questions. As I noted above, about three-quarters of CR passages are assumption-based.

Despite this, assumption questions are not the most common question type. They make up approximately 10% of the pool, meaning that you're likely to see one or two of them when you take the GMAT.

Assumption questions are rarely difficult to identify. Here are a few examples of questions that signal an assumption question:

> Which of the following is an assumption on which this argument depends?
>
> The explanation offered above assumes that
>
> Which of the following is an assumption made in drawing the conclusion above?
>
> John's argument relies on the assumption that
>
> The conclusion drawn above is based on the assumption that

You get the idea. Once you've identified the item as an assumption question, you know to read the passage, looking for the conclusion, trying to identify unstated, underlying assumptions, and hunting for subtle shifts in the argument. Let's take a look at an example so we can discuss this is more concrete terms.

> Most airlines use some form of "tiered pricing," a strategy that involves selling similar seats for different prices depending on factors such as the type of customer and the number of days between the purchase and the flight. Generally, business customers and customers purchasing tickets at the last minute pay more than average price for a seat. Air Macaria, however, sells all seats for the same price. Therefore, when traveling routes served by Air Macaria and an airline that uses tiered pricing, business travelers purchasing tickets at the last minute save money by flying Air Macaria.
>
> Which of the following is an assumption on which the argument depends?

The conclusion is easy to spot: It's at the end of the passage, and is signaled by the word "therefore." Next, identify shifts in the focus of the argument. The argument features a common type of shift: from one comparison to another.

The background information in this passage compares two things: the price of an average ticket on an airline that uses tiered pricing, and the price paid by business customers and those purchasing tickets at the last minute. Air Macaria isn't even mentioned until the second-to-last sentence. The conclusion compares a different set of prices: those paid by the business traveler on a tiered-pricing airline (which is more than the average price on that airline), and the prices paid on Air Macaria.

The passage doesn't provide any information to compare the price range of tickets on Air Macaria to the price range of tickets on any other airline, but the argument changes focus to include this. This is what I mean by a "scope shift," or a "subtle shift in focus." If this argument is going to hold up, the assumption needs to fill in this gap we've identified. You'll have a chance to answer this question several chapters from now, but in the meantime, jot down your prediction as to what the assumption underlying this argument will be.

Assumptions = Jigsaw Puzzles

Notice how, in the preceding example, the argument was missing a connection. For the argument to make sense, it needed another piece that fit together the range of prices of a tiered-pricing airline and on Air Macaria. While the assumption in such a question will not always follow this exact pattern, it will often follow a more general one.

In almost every assumption-based CR passage, the argument will take a little bit of a turn midway through. In this case, it goes from talking about tiered-pricing airlines to Air Macaria. Train yourself to notice that shift. In this case, the fact that such a shift is present means that the argument has weaknesses.

A completely valid argument, however, will have no such shifts. The presence of a shift simply means that a step is missing. In this case, it needs to be stated that the average price of a ticket on Air Macaria is equal to the average price of a ticket on the airline that uses tiered-pricing. Then there are more steps in the argument, but all of the steps logically follow from one another, closing the loopholes that would allow someone to attack the argument.

As the title of this section suggests, it's useful to think of arguments as jigsaw puzzles. The assumption, in this case, is the exact puzzle piece, one side of which fits into the evidence supporting the conclusion, and another side of which fits into the conclusion. Just like in a real-world jigsaw puzzle, there will be pieces (assumptions) that don't fit perfectly, or that might look like they fit until you try them. Look for that assumption that fits neatly into each of the other parts of the argument.

As we'll see, identifying assumptions is one of the most important skills in the GMAT Verbal section. Not only do assumptions play a big role in assumption questions, they factor in strengthen, weaken, explanation, paradox, and evidence questions. That list makes up nearly 80% of the Critical Reasoning questions you'll encounter on the GMAT.

11 CR: Assumption: Practice

Note: Answers and explanations to these questions (along with all of the other questions in the book) make up the final chapters of the book. Check the Table of Contents for exact page numbers.

1.   FoodMart, a grocery store in Palmont, offers special discounts to customers who sign up for a FoodCard. Between 1990 and 1995, the number of FoodMart locations in Palmont increased from 3 to 16. However, since the number of customers who had FoodCards was about the same in 1995 as in 1990, the number of Palmonters taking advantage of special discounts from FoodMart probably did not increase significantly.

Which of the following is an assumption on which the argument depends?

(A)   Few if any of the additional FoodMart locations that opened between 1990 and 1995 served customers who signed up for FoodCards.

(B)   In 1995 most Palmonters who lived within 10 miles of a FoodMart did not have a FoodCard.

(C)   Offering discount programs such as the FoodCard does not decrease the profit margin of a grocery store.

(D)   In 1995 Palmonters who did not have FoodCards usually chose to shop at grocery stores other than FoodMart locations.

(E)   The discounts offers to FoodCard holders in 1995 were not the same at all FoodMart locations.

2.   Last year, AutoSafe sold a large number of new automobile
insurance policies and luxury cars were stolen at a particularly
high rate, resulting in a record number of theft-related insurance
claims submitted to AutoSafe. This year, Autosafe will no longer
sell insurance policies to owners of luxury cars. Therefore,
unless Autosafe sells a record number of policies to owners of
non-luxury cars, fewer theft-related claims will be submitted
this year.

Which of the following is an assumption on which the
argument relies?

(A)   Each year, luxury cars are stolen at a higher rate than
are non-luxury cars.

(B)   Customers who purchased policies last year are no
more likely to have their cars stolen this year than they
were last year.

(C)   This year, the theft rate of non-luxury cars will not be
substantially higher than the theft rate of non-luxury
cars last year.

(D)   This year, the number of stolen cars recovered by
AutoSafe policyholders will be greater than the
number of stolen cars recovered by policyholders
last year.

(E)   The number of automobile thefts that affected AutoSafe
policyholders last year was not nearly as high as the
number of thefts that affected non-policyholders.

3.   To prevent its tenants from relocating their offices, a building
      management company has hired a customer service employee
      who monitors tenant satisfaction. When the new employee
      determines that a tenant may be considering relocation, the
      management company offers the tenant benefits, such as
      reduced rent, to induce the tenant to stay. Since hiring the new
      employee, the management company has cut in half the number
      of its tenants who have relocated. The new employee, therefore,
      is increasing the management company's profits by reducing
      tenant turnover.

      Which of the following is an assumption on which the argument
      depends?

      (A)   The presence of the new employee increases the
             satisfaction of all tenants, not just those who may be
             considering relocation.
      (B)   The costs of the new employee and the benefits offered
             to induce tenants to stay do not outweigh the financial
             benefit of reducing tenant turnover.
      (C)   The new employee was hired on the recommendation
             of a consultant who has consistently increased the profits
             of other building management companies.
      (D)   The new employee was hired before the summer months,
             when most companies choose to relocate their offices.
      (E)   The cost of refurbishing an empty office before seeking a
             new tenant outweighs the cost of providing benefits that
             induce a current tenant to stay.

12   CR: Strengthen Questions

Strengthen questions are more common that assumption questions, making up about 15% of the CR item pool. That means most test-takers will see two of them per exam.

Since strengthen questions are related to assumption questions, the passages they accompany are very similar to the ones you've seen in the assumption section. In fact, even the answers to strengthen questions are often very similar to the answers to assumption questions.

Here are some examples of strengthen questions:
Which of the following, if true, is further evidence that [doing x] will help [y] achieve their goal?
Which of the following, if true, provides the strongest support for [x's] contention?
Which of the following, if true, most strongly support's the researchers' hypothesis?

Let's turn back to the Air Macaria example presented in the previous chapter:

> Most airlines use some form of "tiered pricing," a strategy that involves selling similar seats for different prices depending on factors such as the type of customer and the number of days between the purchase and the flight. Generally, business customers and customers purchasing tickets at the last minute pay more than average price for a seat. Air Macaria, however, sells all seats for the same price. Therefore, when traveling routes served by Air Macaria and an airline that uses tiered pricing, business travelers purchasing tickets at the last minute save money by flying Air Macaria.

A chapter ago, we identified that the passage assumes that the average price of tickets on Air Macaria is equal to the average price of tickets on the competing airline. To strengthen this, or any, argument, we affirm the assumption. In other words, we move the assumption from the realm of the unstated to the realm of the concrete. Once the assumption is stated, it makes the argument more valid.

Plans and Proposals

Some strengthen questions ask you to identify a choice that makes a plan or proposal more likely to succeed. These are very similar to other strengthen questions, but the argument isn't quite as thoroughly stated. Consider a plan described like this:

The Mayor of City X is concerned about the increasing amount of litter on City X sidewalks. To address the problem, he has proposed that anyone caught littering be levied a $50 fine.

The question might be phrased as follows:
> Which of the following, if true, would increase the likelihood that
> the Mayor's proposal will have the desired effect?

Essentially, the conclusion of the passage is shifted into the question. A proposal isn't a conclusion, but it does imply one. Here's how you can rephrase that passage and question to make it look more like other types of strengthen questions:
> The Mayor of City X is concerned about the increasing amount of litter on City X sidewalks. To address the problem, he has proposed that anyone caught littering be levied a $50 fine. **The proposal is likely to have the desired effect.**
>
> Which of the following, if true, most strongly supports the argument above?

See the difference? Now the conclusion is explicitly included in the passage. After you handle a few plans and proposals, you may not need to go through that step to understand the argument. But as you get started, it's a good way to make all of these passages and questions follow a similar structure.

Except Questions

You may have noticed that a large number of Critical Reasoning questions use the phrase "which of the following." If you haven't already, you'll probably start to ignore that phrase, as it appears so often. There is one variation worth discussing, however.

A handful of questions don't look for the one correct answer, they ask you to find the one wrong answer. These questions are worded like this:
> Each of the following, if true, strengthens the prospects that the
> plan will succeed EXCEPT:

Aside from the fact that instead of one answer that strengthens the argument, you'll see four, you can analyze the passage and choices the same way. The four "correct" choices will all be similar to correct answers on other strengthen questions–they will affirm one of the passage's underlying assumptions.

There is one trap to be aware of on this sort of question. Because strengthen and weaken are opposites, it may be tempting to look for the one choice that weakens the argument. After all, if a choice weakens the argument, it doesn't strengthen the argument, and it must be correct! However, there are plenty of answer choices that don't strengthen OR weaken the argument. On "except" questions, the correct answer will probably not be the opposite of strengthen; instead, it will probably have no effect. In other words, no choices will weaken the argument.

You'll occasionally see the "except" phrasing on weaken and other types of assumption-based questions, but it most commonly arises on strengthen questions.

13 CR: Strengthen: Practice

11. When a laptop computer needs maintenance, it is often shipped to a central location for service, then shipped back when the service is complete. In order to reduce the risk of additional problems caused by jostling in transit, MP Tech has hired part-time technicians to provide maintenance service on MP Tech laptops in cities across the country. Providing local technicians costs MP Tech approximately the same amount as paying for shipping as well as employing a large centralized staff.

    Which of the following, if true, is further evidence that using local technicians will help MP Tech achieve its goal?

    (A) Moving maintenance services away from a centralized location makes it less economical to provide phone support.

    (B) Customers who take their laptop computers to local technicians pack their computers extremely carefully to avoid causing further problems in transit.

    (C) MP Tech laptop computers are unique, so their technicians require special training.

    (D) Purchasers of MP Tech laptop computers tend to use their machines more than average, and they require more frequent service than purchasers of other computer brands.

    (E) Many of the local technicians MP Tech has hired have experience working as technicians at MP Tech's centralized location.

12. The government of Defastena is planning to introduce additional
     income taxes on corporations with 500 or more employees. Large
     corporations in Defastena have complained that the additional
     taxes will provide a disincentive for companies to grow, and thus
     limit the number of jobs available to Defastena residents.
     Nevertheless, the government contends that the taxes will
     ultimately result in more jobs for Defastena residents.

     Which of the following, if true, provides the strongest support for
     the government's contention?

     (A)   The government will spend the revenue from the tax to
           subsidize small companies, which hire new employees
           at a faster rate than do large companies in Defastena.
     (B)   Most of the corporations in Defastena that have more
           than 500 employees have at least 1,000 employees.
     (C)   The additional taxes will have no have effect on education
           and job-training programs that the Defastena government
           currently offers with the goal of reducing unemployment.
     (D)   The tax rate on large corporations will be set at a level
           such that corporations with 500 or more employees will
           be unlikely to lay off employees so that they are not
           subject to the taxes.
     (E)   Compared to the seven countries that share a border with
           it, Defastena already has the highest corporate tax rate,
           yet it has one of the lowest unemployment rates.

13. Although the pesticides used in nearby fields are the primary cause of pollution in the Ellenville River, researchers believe that increased automobile traffic in the immediate vicinity is a contributing cause, since nearly all water samples taken from the river show signs of contamination from vehicular emissions. Such emissions are not typically considered a major source of water pollution, but researchers hypothesize that vehicular emissions are the source of more pollution in the Ellenville River than are pesticides.

Which of the following, if true, most strongly supports the researchers' hypothesis?

(A) Research has shown that there is more pollution from vehicular emissions in the Ellenville River than in any other river within a 500 miles radius.

(B) The water filtration system that produces drinking water for Ellenville is specifically designed to protect against the pesticides used in nearby fields.

(C) Water samples from the Ellenville River taken fifty years ago show evidence of pollution from vehicular emissions.

(D) In laboratories without the most sophisticated diagnostic tools, it is difficult to differentiate between types of water pollutants.

(E) The diseases caused by the different forms of water pollution cause different health problems, and the illnesses caused by vehicular emissions are much more prevalent in Ellenville than are those caused by pesticides.

14.   In the past year the National Broadcasting Network (NBN) has lost nearly 30 percent of its advertising revenue. Most of the advertisers who ended their association with NBN did so in the month following the network's broadcast of a controversial political program. Industry analysts believe that the controversial program led to NBN's loss of so much revenue.

Each of the following, if true, provides additional support for the analysts' belief EXCEPT:

(A)   Many of the advertisers that left NBN have strong political positions and prefer not to financially support those who disagree with them.

(B)   Another network that broadcast the controversial program experienced a similar drop in advertising revenue.

(C)   Most of the drop in advertising revenue resulted from advertisers cutting down their number of advertisements, not ceasing to advertise completely.

(D)   Many of the advertisers who left NBN also advertise on competing networks, and these other networks did not experience drops in advertising revenue when NBN did.

(E)   The month following the broadcast of the controversial program is typically one in which networks experience an increase in advertising revenue.

14   CR: Weaken Questions

Weaken questions are the backbone of the GMAT Critical Reasoning section. Of the 13 CR questions you're likely to see when you take the GMAT, as many as five of them could be weaken questions. They are more than twice as common as any other individual question type, and more common than all inference-based questions combined.

Thankfully, you've already done most of the work in developing an approach to weaken questions. Weaken items, like strengthen items, are closely related to assumption questions, and the passages they refer to are indistinguishable. Here are some sample weaken items:

> Which of the following, if true, most threatens the plan's likelihood of success?
> Which of the following, if true, could present the most serious disadvantage for [x] in [doing y]?
> Which of the following, if true, would most undermine [x's] conclusion?
> Which of the following, if true, most seriously weakens the argument?
> The argument is vulnerable to criticism on the grounds that it gives reason to believe that it is likely that

After you've worked on assumption and strengthen questions, the strategy for weaken questions is relatively simple. Instead of stating the assumption (as in an assumption question) or affirming it (in a strengthen question), the object of a weaken question is to contradict it. For instance, in the Air Macaria example discussed in the previous two chapters, a weaken choice could say, "The average ticket price on Air Macaria is higher than rates charged to business and last-minute travelers on airlines that used tiered pricing." That may not be the only possible answer that would weaken the argument, but it's the one that addresses the assumption we've been focusing on.

Note again, that we're focusing on the assumption–the unstated, but necessary, part of the argument. The correct answer won't contradict the evidence or conclusion: it doesn't make sense to say something directly opposite of what the passage already states. Instead, focus on what the argument assumes.

Strengthen/Weaken Questions

Just when you think you've seen it all, the GMAT will hand you something like this:

> Which of the following, if true, would support one of the two hypotheses and undermine the other?

In other words, the passage has two conclusions (believe it or not, I've seen a practice question with *three*!), and the correct answer will strengthen one and weaken the other. Making matters even more complicated, you don't know which conclusion will be strengthened and which weakened.

There's no easy way to handle a question like this. I mostly include it here so that you won't be surprised if you encounter one on the exam. Unlike most Critical Reasoning items, it might be best to start with the answer choices, rather than working on assumptions, strengtheners, and weakeners for both of the conclusions. The skills you use are the same as what we've been discussing for three chapters now, but you have to deploy them much more thoroughly.

Flaw Questions

Flaw questions are more common than strengthen/weaken questions, but not by much. They make up less than 2% of CR questions, meaning there's about a one in five chance you'll encounter one on your exam. Here's a sample question:

> Which of the following, if true, would point to a possible flaw in [x's] plan?

In terms of strategy, treat a flaw question as a weaken question. If you looked hard enough, you could find some subtle differences between flaw answer choices and weaken answer choices, but given the rarity of this question type, it isn't worth it. If you approach it as a weaken question, you should be able to handle the challenges it presents.

15 CR: Weaken: Practice

21. Carnigan International Airport was once the busiest airport in the region, but two major airlines have relocated to nearby airports, reducing the number of flights in and out of Carnigan by more than half. The gates at Carnigan were built more than thirty years ago and cannot accommodate the largest modern aircraft. In an effort to bring in more business, Carnigan officials plan to build dozens of gates to accommodate modern aircraft and offer reduced-rate leases to airlines willing to make long-term commitments.

Which of the following, if true, most threatens the plan's likelihood of success?

(A) Most of the airlines operating out of nearby airports have long-term leases on gates at the other airports.

(B) The existing gates at Carnigan rent at rates that are, on average, much lower than the proposed rates for the new gates to be built there.

(C) Because of highway congestion and changing development patterns that make Carnigan inconvenient to access, airline customers prefer to depart from other airports.

(D) Of the 18 airlines that serve Carnigan or nearby airports, none serve more than one airport in the area.

(E) If the proposed addition is completed, Carnigan will be the largest airport, as measured both by gates and square footage, in the region.

22.   Situation: Geologic evidence strongly suggests that at some point in the next decade, the La Maria volcano will erupt. News of the potential eruption is likely to cause tourists to stay away from destinations in La Maria County.

    Goal: The La Maria Chamber of Commerce wishes to maintain the present high rate of tourism in La Maria County.

    Proposal for consideration: Develop an advertising campaign that emphasizes the safety of La Maria destinations in the case of a volcano eruption.

    In light of the situation, which of the following, if true, most strongly argues that adopting the proposal would be an ineffective way of achieving the goal?

(A)   Tourists who visit La Maria County rate safety as one of their top priorities in choosing a vacation destination.

(B)   All over the world, there are active volcanoes near areas whose economies depend on tourism.

(C)   Very few visitors to La Maria County participate in volcano-related activities such as camping and hiking.

(D)   Most potential vacationers to La Maria County are not aware that the volcano is active, and would discover that it is through advertisements that emphasize the area's safety.

(E)   Compared to tourist destinations that are not near active volcanoes, La Maria County is an inexpensive place for a family to vacation.

23.　At present Satellex Radio provides only music stations. However, many Satellex subscribers listen to talk radio stations as well, and they would prefer that Satellex offered talk radio as well. Moreover, subscribers to radio services that provide talk radio usually subscribe for longer periods of time than those who subscribe to music-only services. Therefore, if Satellex added talk radio stations, its profits would increase.

The argument is vulnerable to criticism on the grounds that it gives reason to believe that it is likely that

(A)　Satellex's large subscriber base would appeal to talk radio hosts, making it easy for Satellex to hire quality talent for its talk radio stations.

(B)　most talk radio hosts broadcast on advertiser-supported radio stations that listeners can access without paying a subscription fee.

(C)　Satellex's costs would rise by adding several talk-radio stations, while many of the listeners who want talk radio are already Satellex subscribers.

(D)　talk radio listeners generally spend more time on a single radio station than do listeners to music radio.

(E)　if Satellex added talk radio stations, many of Satellex's music radio hosts would switch to talk-radio stations, making the music stations less appealing.

24.   At a start-up company, hiring is often done by the company's
       founder. Since founders are often experts in fields far removed
       from the expertise they are looking for in employees, hiring
       decisions in early-stage start-ups can result in poor matches
       between the company and the employee. Enough poor matches
       can make it nearly impossible for such a company to succeed
       in the marketplace.

       Which of the following, if true, points to the most serious flaw of
       a start-up founder's plan to outsource hiring to a firm that
       specializes in matching employees and early-stage start-up
       companies?

       (A)   It is not well understood why founders often make poor
              choices when selecting new employees for their
              companies.

       (B)   If a founder is successful in hiring an employee that is a
              good match for his company, he or she will not necessarily
              be successful the next time a new employee must be hired.

       (C)   While founders tend to make decisions quickly, firms that
              handle hiring decisions for start-up companies interview
              more candidates and take longer to select an employee.

       (D)   Firms that handle hiring decisions for start-ups rarely use
              interviewers who have the expertise that a start-up
              company is looking for in a given employee.

       (E)   The average starting salary paid to employees selected
              by outside firms is considerably higher than the average
              starting salary paid to employees hired directly by a
              start-up's founder.

16   CR: Explanation and Paradox Questions

As we continue our tour of assumption-based questions, we now turn to explanation and paradox questions, both of which could be considered variations of the strengthen question. Between them, these two question types make up about 10% of the CR question pool, and most of that 10% is represented by explanation questions. Paradox questions are about as rare as flaw questions.

The only difference between explanation/paradox questions and strengthen questions (besides the wording of the question itself) is the apparent logic of the passage. The passages for assumption, strengthen, and weaken questions usually appear sensible. You might spot a problem here and there, but those questions are often difficult because the argument doesn't seem to need your help. In explanation and paradox questions, there is usually an inconsistency (at least an *apparent* inconsistency) or an unexpected result.

Here are a couple of sample questions of this type:
Which of the following, if true, most helps to explain the apparent discrepancy?
Which of the following, if true, would best help explain how [x] might produce [y]?

To best approach these questions, don't look at the answer choices until you understand what it is you are trying to explain. If you're not confident about what constitutes the "apparent discrepancy" or "unexpected effect," re-read the passage looking for it. The correct answer will address that discrepancy very specifically.

Essentially, the answer choice that explains the apparent discrepancy *strengthens* the argument. If a paradox is resolved, there is no longer a discrepancy, so the argument appears to be more valid. To get a better idea of what these questions entail, turn to the practice questions in the next section.

17 CR: Explanation/Paradox: Practice

31. In Manila, Phillipines, one of the largest shopping malls in the world, the recently-opened SM Mall of Asia, is threatening the viability of other "super-malls" in Manila, but its appearance has had a positive effect on many small businesses in the area. The SM Mall o f Asia has few of the same attractions as other Manila super-malls, but it has become of the largest tourist destinations in the Phillipines.

    Which of the following contributes most to an explanation of the difference between the SM Mall of Asia's effect on other super-malls and small businesses?

    (A) Tourists often visit the Phillipines because of the wide variety of shopping opportunities.

    (B) The locations of super-malls, including the SM Mall of Asia, are carefully chosen to limit competition between super-malls.

    (C) The SM Mall of Asia is home to the only Olympic-sized ice skating rink in the Phillipines.

    (D) The opening of a new super-mall has increased the number of weekend tourists visiting Manila, and these tourists typically visit only one super-mall.

    (E) The success of a super-mall is often dependent on the major retailers chosen as "anchor stores," and the SM Mall of Asia has more anchor stores than other Manila super-malls.

32.   At Allied Consulting, an employee receives a raise at the end
        of her first year with the company if she has reached a certain
        sales target and has received satisfactory reviews from two
        managers. Even though being assigned to a rural region makes
        the sales target more difficult to reach, a higher percent of first-
        year employees assigned to such regions receive raises than
        first-year employees assigned to non-rural regions.

        Which of the following, if true, most helps to explain the apparent
        discrepancy?

        (A)   Managers are aware of the challenges involved in
                reaching sales targets in rural regions, and are more
                likely to give satisfactory reviews to first-year employees
                assigned to such regions.

        (B)   The average first-year employee at Allied Consulting
                reaches higher sales figures than the average first-year
                employee at Allied's competition.

        (C)   Once an employee has stayed with the company for six
                months, she typically has more contacts in the industry,
                making it easier for her to reach her sales target.

        (D)   Managers at Allied Consulting give satisfactory reviews
                to the majority of first-year employees.

        (E)   Employees assigned to rural regions typically make more
                sales per customer than employees assigned to non-rural
                regions.

33.   A study separated all of the Saradian firms in a certain industry
into two groups. The first group consisted of firms that have the
largest proportion of clients outside of Saradia, and the second
consists of those with the smallest proportion of such clients.
The first group showed a much larger increase in sales over the
five-year span in which in the firms were studied. The effect was
attributed to the weakness of the Sarade, the currency of Saradia.

Which of the following, if true, would best help explain how the
weakness of the Sarade might result in the observed effect?

(A)   Each year in the five-year span, the Sarade got weaker
relative to the Euro.

(B)   When a country's currency is weak, goods sold by firms
in that country are relatively inexpensive to customers
who reside in countries with stronger currencies.

(C)   The weakness of the Sarade caused Saradia's national
bank to raise interest rates, making it more expensive
for Saradian firms to raise money to fund expansion.

(D)   The Sarade is the main currency of the region, so
fluctuations in exchange rates affect several neighboring
countries in addition to Saradia.

(E)   The firms involved in the study were not notified that the
study was taking place until after the five-year span was
complete.

34.   In Country Y, universities have produced so few graduates with degrees in finance that many firms have struggled to attract qualified candidates. SimInc, a company in need of employees with finance training, opted instead to hire recent graduates with degrees in other fields and then design a fully-paid, one-year training program for their new hires in order to provide them the necessary finance education.

SimInc's strategy will require a substantial initial investment, but will ultimately save the company money. Which of the following, if true, is the best basis for an explanation of how this could be so?

(A)   The shortage of qualified employees has made it more expensive to hire graduates with finance degrees than to provide a year of training to graduates in other fields.

(B)   Companies that hire graduates with degrees in mathematics and physics are also finding that the number of qualified candidates has decreased substantially.

(C)   The first year that SimInc's strategy was in effect, the company's average productivity per employee was nearly 10 percent lower than it had been the previous year.

(D)   Firms that are not as well capitalized as SimInc would not have the ability to undertake a strategy such as SimInc's.

(E)   To ensure that their competition would not take advantage of their training program, SimInc required that new hires commit to a five-year contract with the company in addition to signing an agreement by which they would not work in the industry for two years after that.

18 CR: Evidence Questions

Evidence questions are the final assumption-based question type, and they aren't very common. About 5% of CR questions are of this type, meaning that you won't see more than one on your exam, and you might not see any.

In strengthen and weaken questions, you look for a choice that has a specific effect on the argument. An evidence question is similar, only the answer choices don't make any claims. Instead of presenting additional points that might support or undermine the argument, the answer choices in an evidence question suggest things that might or might not be true, and which would–if true or false–have an effect on the argument.

Here's a sample evidence question:
> Which of the following would it be most useful to establish in
> order to evaluate the argument?

Answer choices typically begin with the word "whether," indicating the non-committal nature of these choices. To return once more to the Air Macaria example, here's what an answer choice might look like if the Air Macaria passage were coupled with an evidence question like the example given here:
> Whether the average price of a ticket on Air Macaria is the same
> as the average price of a ticket on a competing airline

Note that the answer choice doesn't say that the average price *is* the same (or greater or lower), just that this is something that would be useful to know. To relate this more closely to strengthen and weaken questions, note that an answer choice beginning in "whether" could result in two different findings:
> The average price of a ticket on Air Macaria *is* the same as the
> average price of a ticket on a competing airline.
> The average price of a ticket on Air Macaria *is not* the same as
> (or "is higher than," or "is lower than") the average price of a
> ticket on a competing airline.

The first finding would strengthen the argument, while the second would weaken it. That's a sign you've found the correct choice. If the possible findings suggested by an evidence answer choice do not strengthen or weaken the argument, the choice isn't sufficiently relevant to the argument.

19 CR: Evidence: Practice

41. Over the last five years, demand for introductory-level philosophy courses at Inagua College has increased significantly, as has the number of students across the country who choose to major in philosophy. These trends are projected to continue for the next several years. In response, Inagua College is considering a plan to stop hiring professors in other fields and hire only philosophy professors in order to attract more students to the college.

Which of the following would it be most useful for Inagua College to know in evaluating the plan it is considering?

(A) Whether the number of philosophers awarded doctorates is expected to grow in the next several years

(B) Whether availability of philosophy courses has an effect on potential students' decisions regarding where they will attend college

(C) Whether demand for post-secondary education in Inagua is likely to increase in the near future

(D) Whether the increased demand for philosophy courses, if met, is likely to lead to an increase in the demand for courses in related fields, such as logic

(E) Whether, on average, newly-hired philosophy professors are as highly-rated by students as the professors currently teaching philosophy classes at Inagua College

42. Regulations in Guravia dictate that commercial aircraft are subject to government inspection and maintenance at least once per week. A proposed law would allow airlines to opt out of the required inspection and maintenance. Opponents object that the airlines may attempt to cut costs and perform inadequate safety procedures. But since airlines are accountable to their customers, and air travelers consistently rate safety their first priority in choosing an airline, airlines would follow safety procedures at least as thorough as those currently undertaken by government inspectors and maintenance workers.

Which of the following would it be most useful to establish in order to evaluate the argument?

(A) Whether shifting the safety procedures to the airlines themselves would reduce the cost and time required for sufficient inspection and maintenance

(B) Whether safety regulations in other countries grant airlines more responsibility in keeping their aircraft at or above a certain standard of airworthiness

(C) Whether government inspectors and maintenance workers would be hired by the airlines to perform tasks similar to their current assignments

(D) Whether airlines that are not known for their safety records would suffer financially as a result of the proposed law

(E) Whether airline customers would have a way to determine which airlines followed safety procedures at or above the standard established by government inspectors and maintenance workers

20 CR: Inference Questions

Finally, we shift gears from assumption-based questions to inference-based questions. There aren't as many inference-related items, but we're still looking at 20-25% of Critical Reasoning, so it deserves a good portion of your time. Inference questions, specifically, make up about 10% of the question pool, so you'll probably see one of them on test day.

Note, also, that inference skills are relevant to Reading Comprehension, as well. More than one quarter of RC questions are inference-based. There are some differences between CR and RC inference questions, but you don't need to worry about that now. I'll discuss how the two question types compare when we get to the Reading Comprehension section of the book.

One definition of inference is, "A position arrived at by reasoning from premises." That's a reasonable summary of what you're doing on a CR inference question. Unlike assumption-based questions, in which the passage includes evidence and a conclusion, the passages of inference-based questions may not have a conclusion. Instead, you should treat them as a block of evidence or, in terms of that definition, a series of premises. The correct answer will be the most logical conclusion drawn from them.

Here are a few examples of inference questions:
> If the statements above are true, which of the following is most strongly supported by them?
> Which of the following hypotheses is best supported by the statements given?
> Which of the following conclusions can properly be drawn from the information above?
> Which of the following can properly be inferred regarding [x]?
> [x's] argument is structured to lead to which of the following as a conclusion?

There are many ways inference questions can be phrased, but the idea behind them is always the same.

The most important concept in inference questions is that of scope. In a three-sentence passage, you get very little information. Some of the details might fit together, and others might appear irrelevant. The correct answer will follow from the limited information you're given, but it won't rely on any other information. More wrong answer choices in inference questions are wrong because they are off-topic than any other reason.

Similarly, note the tone of a typical inference question. (The examples in the following section will give you a good idea of this.) Passages rarely use strong language, such as "all," "never," or "every.": If the evidence uses a measured, academic tone with no absolutes, the logical conclusion (that is, the correct answer) will also steer clear of absolutes. For this reason, the "safe" choice is often the right one. If an answer choice seems so innocuous that it couldn't possibly be false, you may have found your answer.

21 CR: Inference: Practice

51.   Frobnia's economy relies on two major industries. The oil fields
       in south Frobnia allow the country to export petroleum and the
       natural landmarks in the north attract hundreds of thousands of
       tourists each year. Tourism employs more than one-third of
       working Frobnians, and the oil fields employ less than half as
       many. However, about half of the population of Frobnia lives in
       the south.

       The information given, if accurate, most strongly supports which
       of the following?

       (A)   To remain fully staffed, tourism-related companies in
              Frobnia must recruit in the south.
       (B)   Most of the people in Frobnia who are not employed
              live in the south.
       (C)   Many employed Frobnians in the south work for
              petroleum-related companies apart from the oil fields,
              such as refineries.
       (D)   A higher proportion of Frobnians working in the north
              work in one of Frobnia's two major industries than the
              proportion of Frobnians in the south who do.
       (E)   Frobnia's oil fields are not a major tourist attraction, but
              a small number of visitors include the oil fields as part
              of their travel.

52.   Among firms that transport their goods via truck, some hire
        drivers directly, whereas others contract transportation to outside
        firms. Firms that transport food items are twice as likely as other
        firms to hire drivers directly. Firms that transport perishable food
        items , which must be delivered in a timely manner, are more than
        five times more likely than other firms to hire drivers directly, while
        firms that transport non-perishable food items are only slightly
        more likely than other firms to do so.

        The information above provides the most support for which of the
        following hypotheses?

        (A)   A firm's decision to hire drivers directly depends in part on
                whether goods must be delivered in a timely manner.
        (B)   It is usually more expensive to hire drivers directly than to
                contract transportation to outside firms.
        (C)   Firms that hire drivers directly are unlikely to do business
                with firms that contract transportation to outside firms.
        (D)   Firms that provide truck transportation usually carry non-
                food items.
        (E)   Between one-fifth and one-half of firms that transport their
                goods via truck contract transportation to outside firms.

53. Until recently, the scholarly consensus was that few marine species are approaching extinction. Closer examination of marine species near the island of Tasmania, however, revealed many factors, such as climate change and fishing, that may be contributing to the extinction of species thought to be safe. The rate of extinction of marine species may be just as high as that of non-marine species, but the lack of systematic sampling has disguised the trend.

Which of the following is most strongly supported by the statements given?

(A) There are many marine species near Tasmania that are nearing extinction.

(B) Scholars who analyze the possible extinction of non-marine species rely on systematic sampling to determine which species are endangered.

(C) If systematic sampling were a more common practice in marine environments, there would likely be more evidence supporting the hypothesis that many marine species are approaching extinction.

(D) The threat to marine species near Tasmania is more severe than the threat to marine species whose habitats are elsewhere.

(E) If the rate of climate change were arrested and fishing were curtailed, the rate of extinction of marine species would fall to a level far below that of non-marine species.

22 CR: Fill-In-the-Blank Questions

Fill-In-the-Blank questions (FITBs) are often inference questions, just presented in a different way. Sometimes they are more similar to assumption-based questions, looking for a piece of evidence instead of a logical conclusion. About 5% of CR questions are Fill-In-the-Blanks, so you may see one–but probably not more–on your exam.

As you might guess from the name, these questions have blanks (underlined blocks) in the passage, and your task is to find the answer that most properly fills that blank. The blank is always at the end of the passage, and there is always a key word or two right before the blank that signals what kind of answer you're looking for. We can classify FITB questions into two categories:

Inference FITBs

Some FITBs give you key words that signal that a conclusion is coming right before the blank. For instance:

Because of this trend, it is likely that _____.

The researchers' findings suggest that it is reasonable to
conclude that _____.

There is little difference between inference FITBs and inference questions. The only distinction is that the conclusion is grammatically built into the passage instead of separated as a free-standing sentence.

Evidence/Assumption FITBs

Other FITBs, like most of the examples you'll see in the following section, use key words that suggest the passage will conclude with a final piece of evidence. Here are some examples of concluding sentences:

The plan is likely to succeed because _____.

The scientists consider the technique worthy of further study,
since _____.

The words "because" and "since" signal that what follows will support the preceding phrase, which is usually a conclusion. If you've read through the Critical Reasoning section in order, you've already been exposed to some of the techniques you need to handle these questions. If you can identify an unstated assumption in the passage, that might be what should fill in the blank. You may have to look at the answer choices and consider each one, but the logical relationships of evidence and conclusion are the same for a FITB as they are for the whole range of CR assumption-based questions.

23   CR: Fill-In-the-Blank: Practice

61.   Which of the following most logically completes the argument?

A common approach to algae cultivation involves covering a pond with a greenhouse, instead of leaving the pond uncovered. Because there is a practical limit on the size of a greenhouse, this method limits the extent of the algae-growing system. Nevertheless, covering the pond results in a much higher algae yield because _____.

(A)   the greenhouse prevents contamination from invasive bacteria, which can destroy entire species of algae.

(B)   the greenhouse changes the quality of sunlight that reaches the algae, causing more frequent genetic mutations.

(C)   leaving the pond uncovered is an acceptable solution depending on the species of algae being cultivated.

(D)   covered ponds better mimic the artificial environment of a photobioreactor, which is the most effective tool to preserve certain threatened types of algae.

(E)   the limited available space makes it more likely that only one species will be cultivated in a given pond.

62.   Which of the following most logically completes the passage?

Both silvicultural clearcutting and commercial clearcutting involve removing a high percentage of trees from a forested area. Silvicultural clearcutting involves removing nearly every tree from the area in order to create an environment suitable for a species to regenerate after the trees are removed. However, commercial clearcutting is usually not as extensive, because _____.

(A)   removing all the trees from an area does not always create an environment in which a species can regenerate.

(B)   other forested areas are subject to the silvicultural method, ensuring that species will regenerate in other locations.

(C)   commercial clearcutting typically takes place in much larger areas, and is more common in developing countries.

(D)   forested areas that are commercially clearcut are not home to species that are as environmentally important as those in areas that are silviculturally clearcut.

(E)   the goal of commercial clearcutting is to remove only commercially valuable trees, and not every tree fits that description.

63.   Which of the following most logically completes the passage?

For the past several years, cellular phone service has not been available in Volsinia, despite service being available in neighboring Rolisica. Recently two companies, Cyberdyne and Noratech, have each established the infrastructure necessary to provide cellular service to Volsinia residents. Although the services offered by the companies are similarly priced and are equally easy to use, Cyberdyne's product is likely to dominate the market, because _____.

(A)   Cyberdyne has a much larger share of the international cellular service market than Noratech does.

(B)   the number of Volsinia residents who will purchase cellular service is likely to double over the next few years.

(C)   Noratech's infrastructure is better designed to accommodate population growth in Volsinia.

(D)   both Cyberdyne and Noratech sell mobile phones in addition to cellular service.

(E)   Cyberdyne is the only cellular service provider with a substantial presence in Rolisica, and many Volsinia residents frequently travel between the two countries.

24   CR: Boldface Questions

There's no Critical Reasoning question type that inspires the same kind of fear that this one does. For whatever reason, many test-takers think that boldface Critical Reasoning questions are their worst enemy.

Part of the problem is a lack of familiarity. There are very few boldface CR questions in the common practice materials. In part, that should cause you to worry less–if there aren't very many in the practice materials, such as the Official Guide, there aren't going to be very many on the test. It would be an extremely rare GMAT exam in which you saw more than two of these, and on average, you probably won't see more than one. They make up less than 5% of the question pool, so you're not even guaranteed to see one of them.

These questions don't fit neatly into the categories of assumption-based or inference-based items. Instead of finding an assumption or evidence, you are asked to analyze the argument at a different level. As you'll see in the Reading Comprehension section of the book, they are somewhat related to RC structure-based questions.

Let's look at an example:

> Plant scientists have used genetic engineering on seeds to produce crop plants that are highly resistant to insect damage. **Unfortunately, the seeds themselves are quite expensive, and the plants require more fertilizer and water to grow well than normal ones.** Thus, for most farmers the savings on pesticides would not compensate for the higher seed costs and the cost of additional fertilizer. **However, since consumer demand for grains, fruits, and vegetables grown without the use of pesticides continues to rise, the use of genetically engineered seeds of this kind is likely to become widespread.**
>
> In the argument given, the two portions in **boldface** play which of the following roles?

The wording of the question is usually very similar to this, though it's possible you'll encounter something a little different, along the lines of, "The first boldface statement has what relationship to the second boldface statement?"

It may be tempting to take a shortcut, but don't just read the bold. The other sentences are just as important as the boldface ones. In this example, the conclusion is is the sentence between the two boldface statements. If you just read the two bolded statements and look for the relationship between them, you'll never figure this question out. In a sense, the bold font is actively distracting you.

In almost any GMAT CR argument, the conclusion is the most important sentence. Everything else centers on that. You certainly can't identify something like the assumption, or a piece of evidence, without knowing what the conclusion is.

So, take apart the passage as if you didn't have the answer choices in front of you. (You'll want to do the same on the test.) Identify the conclusion. In this case it's not bolded, but it might be on another example. Then analyze how the bolded statements relate to the conclusion. In our example, the first bold statement is a piece of evidence supporting the conclusion, and the second is a piece of evidence seems to contradict the conclusion.

Answer Choices

Each answer choice in a boldface question will offer a characterization of each boldface statement. Here's a sample answer choice:

> The first and the second are both evidence offered by the
> argument as support for its main conclusion.

You'll also see statements characterized as some of the following:

> initial conclusion
> revised conclusion
> assumption
> a development the argument seeks to explain
> a problem
> a judgment

The list could go on and on. As I noted above, these are similar to Reading Comprehension structure questions, and once you've read my chapter on that question type, you may find you have an even better grasp of the possibilities in boldface questions. Certainly, RC will give you lots of practice reading for structure, which is what this question type is testing.

25 CR: Boldface: Practice

71.   In the past five years, Peak Production's profits from recorded
music sales has steadily declined. **Peak cannot increase the
number of recordings it releases, so it cannot increase
revenue that way.** Therefore, Peak has decided to drastically cut
back on the number of recordings it releases. It will save on costs
by only releasing recordings by its most popular artists. **Thus,
because the most popular artists bring in the most
revenue on a per-recording basis, Peak's plan is
likely to increase its annual profits.**

In the argument above, the two portions in **boldface** play which
of the following roles?

(A)   The first and the second are both evidence offered by
the argument as support for its main conclusion.

(B)   The first presents a problem a response to which the
argument assesses; the second is the judgment
reached by that assessment.

(C)   The first is the position the argument seeks to
establish; the second is a judgment the argument
uses to support that position.

(D)   The first is a development that the argument seeks to
explain; the second is a prediction the argument makes
in support of the explanation it offers.

(E)   The first presents a development whose likely outcome is
at issue in the argument; the second is a judgment the
argument uses in support of its conclusion about that
outcome.

72.   A cancer drug that shows positive results in early laboratory tests can generate a great deal of interest from cancer patients. **Because of this interest, and the desire to make a profit early in the development cycle, many pharmaceutical companies rush the new drug to market as quickly as possible.** But positive early results are often misleading, meaning that the effort to bring the drug to market was largely wasted. **Consequently, the strategy to maximize long-term profit from a new cancer drug is to bring the drug to market only after its positive effects are more thoroughly tested and established.**

In the argument above, the two portions in **boldface** play which of the following roles?

(A)   The first is a consideration that has been raised to argue that a certain strategy is counterproductive; the second presents an alternative strategy.

(B)   The first is a consideration raised to support the strategy that the argument recommends; the second presents that strategy.

(C)   The first is a consideration raised to explain the appeal of a certain strategy; the second presents an alternative strategy.

(D)   The first is an assumption, rejected by the argument, that has been used to justify a course of action; the second presents that course of action.

(E)   The first is a consideration that has been used to justify pursuing a goal that the argument rejects; the second presents a course of action that has been adopted in pursuit of that goal.

26 CR: Other Question Types

In the preceding chapters, I've tried to be exhaustive as possible. I've discussed question types as rare as flaw and paradox, both of which are so uncommon that there's only about a 20% chance you'll see them on the exam at all. However, the makers of the GMAT are always experimenting with slightly different question types. For that reason, you may encounter something unfamiliar. Just a few years ago, no test-prep materials even mentioned boldface questions.

If you do see an unfamiliar CR question type, first take a moment and see if it relates to one of the question types we've discussed here. There are dozens of ways of phrasing weaken questions, and probably a dozen ways a CR question could be constructed to test your knowledge of a passage's structure, as boldface questions do. Between your preparation for CR and RC, you'll probably be able to figure out a reasonable approach even to an unfamiliar question type.

27 CR: Basic Logic and the Contrapositive

Before we get into common types of wrong answer choices, let's talk about one specific, important topic. On the GMAT, you don't need to know as much formal logic as is required for other standardized tests such as the LSAT. However, a small amount will prove useful.

As we've seen, one of the most common passage structures in Critical Reasoning is the implied causal relationship–if A, then B. We've discussed how to strengthen and weaken that argument. To become better prepared for those questions, and their answer choices, let's look more carefully at the nuts and bolts of causal relationships.

Here's a sample if-then statement:
If it is raining, then I carry an umbrella.
Logicians might abbreviate that, "if r then u."
If all you know about me is the information in that statement, consider what deductions you can make. What if it is not raining? Do you know whether I carry an umbrella? What if I am carrying an umbrella? Do you know whether it is raining?
That's where logic comes in.

The *converse* of the above statement is:
If I am carrying an umbrella, then it is raining.
In logic terms: "if u then r."
Is that a reasonable deduction? No! It might be true, but it might not. Converses are often tempting (after all, if I'm carrying an umbrella, it's more than likely that it is raining), but are not airtight.
Let's look at the *inverse*:
If it is not raining, then I do not carry an umbrella.
Or in the logic abbreviation: "if not r, then not u."
How about that–a reasonable deduction? Again, no! It's possible, but it cannot be logically inferred from the original claim. Our first statement only told us what happens when it is raining. Maybe I carry an umbrella all the time!

Finally, the *contrapositive*:
If I am not carrying an umbrella, then it is not raining.
In logic terms: "if not u, then not r."
This one is a valid deduction. Consider the other possibility. If I am not carrying an umbrella and it is raining, then we know from the initial statement that I am carrying an umbrella. That's a contradiction.

The contrapositive of any true if-then statement is also true. The converse and inverse might be true, but without additional information, it is not a logical inference.

Next time you hear an if-then statement ("If I get out of work before 6 tonight, I'll go to the gym straight from the office.") think about what deductions are valid. As with any underlying skill, the more you internalize the knowledge, the more you'll be able to rely on it when you take the GMAT.

28 CR: Common Wrong Answer Choices

Let's start by spending a moment discussing how you can best study wrong answer choices.

The key to getting better at GMAT Critical Reasoning is understanding what makes wrong answers wrong. It's less important to know what makes right answers right. As you study, you may sometimes find it difficult to describe why a correct answer is correct. However, you should always be able to see (and explain) why each wrong answer is wrong.

Your goal on every CR question should be as follows. For each wrong answer choice, you should be able to complete the sentence:
　　This choice is wrong because...

Sometimes that's easy; sometimes it's extremely difficult. But the difference between test-takers who ace the CR and those who flounder, consistently picking the "second best" answer, is this study tip. It forces you to understand the choices better, and in doing so, think with more focus about the CR question itself.

To help you on your way to that goal, here are several categories of common CR wrong answer choices:

Off-Topic

The scope of each passage is very narrow, whether it's an assumption-based question or an inference-based question. This sort of wrong answer choice takes some tidbit from the passage and acts as if that tidbit were the main focus. It might be appealing for a moment, but if you consider the conclusion of the passage, or the scope of the premises, you'll realize that such a choice can't possibly relate to the entire passage.

Irrelevant Comparison

Many questions rely on the relationship between two things. For instance, the Air Macaria example we've turned to throughout this section has a conclusion that is based on the relationship between Air Macaria's prices and a competitor's prices. Wrong answer choices of this sort reflect the fact that the correct choice will include a comparison, but gets at least half of the comparison wrong.

Several chapters ago, I compared an assumption to a piece in a jigsaw puzzle. The correct answer fits on every side, but this sort of incorrect choice only fits on one side. The side that fits might make it a tempting choice, but it's more important to focus on what might make an answer wrong.

Strong Language

On inference-based questions especially, the wording of the passages is not very strong. The tone is academic and few broad generalizations are made. The same should be true of the correct answer. Words like "all," "none," and "never" will almost never appear in a correct answer choice. The one exception to this rule is when the passage itself contains such extreme language. If the premises make broad generalizations, it might be reasonable to draw a conclusion that uses strong language.

Wrong Question

As you've discovered, many types of CR questions are closely related. Strengthen and weaken, for instance, are opposites, but the strategies you'll use to answer those questions are very similar. Frequently, at least one wrong answer choice is on topic, comparing the right things, but answers the wrong question! It sounds simple, but beware of choices that strengthen the argument on a weaken question, and vice versa.

29 CR: Mixed Review 1

81.   Most airlines use some form of "tiered pricing," a strategy that involves selling similar seats for different prices depending on factors such as the type of customer and the number of days between the purchase and the flight. Generally, business customers and customers purchasing tickets at the last minute pay more than average price for a seat. Air Macaria, however, sells all seats for the same price. Therefore, when traveling routes served by Air Macaria and an airline that uses tiered pricing, business travelers purchasing tickets at the last minute save money by flying Air Macaria.

Which of the following is an assumption on which the argument depends?

(A)   Customers who purchase tickets more than three weeks in advance spend less, on average, per ticket, than customers who purchase tickets less than three weeks in advance.

(B)   Airlines that use tiered pricing serve many more routes than airlines that do not.

(C)   When flying a route that includes both Air Macaria and an airline that uses tiered pricing, a traveler is subject to the different pricing strategies of the airlines for each portion of the trip.

(D)   The average price of a ticket on any given route on Air Macaria is equal to the average price on the same route of a ticket offered by an airline that uses tiered pricing.

(E)   More business travelers fly on airlines that used tiered pricing than on airlines that do not.

82.   Environmentalist: It is true that the tiny population of grey wolves in the southern part of the country have much in common with the larger population in the north. Based on these similarities, government officials are claiming that the distinct population in the south is not endangered. The claim is mistaken. The wolf population in the south has no contact, and is incapable of breeding with the population in the north, so it should be considered a distinct species, and thus an endangered one.

Which of the following, if true, provides the strongest support for the environmentalist's claim?

(A)   Historical data suggests that the wolf population in the south descends from a separate population that lived in the north less than a century ago.

(B)   The two wolf populations have genetic differences that are more substantial than the differences that cause two populations of red wolves to be categorized as distinct species.

(C)   There are currently no wolf species categorized by the government as endangered.

(D)   The environmentalist previously worked for the government in a capacity that allowed him to help classify certain species as endangered.

(E)   There are large numbers of grey wolves in captivity throughout the country.

83.   Which of the following most logically completes the argument?

In the last two years, Kaiba Corporation, an electronics manufacturer, has laid off more than 20% of its workforce as its competitors cut into Kaiba's market share. A popular new line of products just released by Kaiba promises to increase profits and allow the company to expand into other markets. However, it would be premature to conclude that Kaiba's expansion will result in an increase in its workforce, because _____.

(A)   the electronics industry is unlikely to undergo any major changes over the next several years.

(B)   the company's success has largely been a result of relying on contractors instead of in-house employees for production and marketing.

(C)   Kaiba's popular new product line was a joint venture with one of the company's competitors.

(D)   most of the employees that Kaiba laid off in the last two years have moved on to other industries and would not seek employment at the company again.

(E)   Kaiba considers that its current workforce is at least as productive on a per-employee basis as its workforce two years ago.

84. Primatech Corporation has told its regular customers that a short-term materials shortage affecting one of its suppliers prevents the company from taking any orders at this time. Some of the customers have learned, however, that Primatech accepted a substantial order from the federal government. So the customers concluded that Primatech's real reason for not accepting their orders is to shift its focus to the more lucrative government market.

Which of the following, if true, would most undermine the customers' conclusion?

(A) Most of Primatech's regular customers also do business with the federal government.

(B) Almost all of Primatech's employees have received raises in pay during the last year.

(C) A recent memorandum from the president of Primatech requested that all employees familiarize themselves with the published guidelines for companies doing business with the federal government.

(D) Most of Primatech's regular customers order the company's products in bulk and receive discounts for doing so.

(E) The order placed by the federal government with Primatech does not require delivery for more than a year, while orders are typically placed for delivery within one month.

30 CR: Difficult Wrong Answer Choices

The wrong answer choices discussed in the previous chapter are a good way to eliminate three choices. This chapter focuses on getting rid of that fourth wrong answer choice, even on the trickiest questions.

The key concept, as always, in CR questions is that of scope. If an answer choice is too general or too specific, it is usually easy to spot as such. It's trickier when the scope is wrong, but not because it's too local or too global–it's just subtly shifted from the scope of the question. For example, the scope might shift from the effect of rainfall on the health of a certain species to the effect of rainfall on the growth of a certain plant that the species feeds on.

Find Assumptions, Don't Make Them

When the scope shifts, it's perfectly natural to fill in the gaps for yourself. In the example above, you might think, "of course, if rainfall means that there's a more ample supply of this plant, then the species will have more food and be healthier." Depending on the question, though, that's the kind of rationale that gets you in trouble. Your job on CR questions isn't to devise justifications, it's to recognize them.

The difference is slight, but it's crucial. GMAT Critical Reasoning questions are very carefully written and designed. If a question means to say something, it will. Wrong answer choices are planned with equal care: there are no accidents in these questions. Both assumption-based and inference-based questions expect you to understand the argument precisely. That means that all the information you need is right there in the question, and if you start making assumptions of your own, you're probably doing something wrong.

It's hard to adjust to reading this way. Most writing, from almost any source, is sloppy, and requires you to fill in the gaps by making assumptions. The GMAT doesn't. You will, over the course of your Critical Reasoning practice, make this mistake at least a handful of times–I guarantee it. But those mistakes are opportunities waiting for you to embrace them.

Through those mistakes, try to "watch" your own thought process so that you can catch yourself before you make another assumption. It is a distinct step in your mental process: you read the answer choice, you try to understand it, you see if it makes sense as the answer, and–perhaps–then try to figure out a way it *could* be the answer. That final step is where most people go astray: if you bring in explanatory material from outside the question, you've probably just made a mistake.

As with all other types of questions, when you get one wrong, carefully read the explanation and try to isolate what you did incorrectly. If you find yourself making assumptions, going beyond the scope of the question in Critical Reasoning, pay closer attention to your thinking as you analyze those answer choices that are "close, but not quite right." Usually, if it's not quite right, it's just plain wrong–you just need to recognize the shift in scope, or the leap in your own thought process.

31 CR: Mixed Review 2

91. Western Agriculture farms millions of acres of land in Alpastia, a wheat-farming region that receives extremely high amounts of rainfall. Western Agriculture's profit margins depend on taking advantage of the economies of scale resulting from their large holdings, so it is planning to purchase another two million acres of farmland in Alpastia. If the purchase is completed, over 70% of Western Agriculture's land would be devoted to wheat farming in Alpastia.

Which of the following, if true, could present the most serious disadvantage for Western Agriculture in purchasing an additional two million acres of farmland in Alpastia?

(A) Because of Western Agriculture's presence in Alpastia, farming an additional two million acres would require less manpower per acre than its current holdings.

(B) The price of wheat is expected to increase over the next decade.

(C) The heavy rainfall in Alpastia limits the number of other crops that Western Agriculture could cultivate on its land.

(D) None of Western Agriculture's competitors own more than one million acres of land in Alpastia.

(E) In regions with heavy rainfall, wheat yields are highly variable, resulting in inconsistent profits on wheat cultivation in such regions.

92. Neither extensive experience in a field nor access to exhaustive industry data, by itself, establishes an executive's ability to make appropriate decisions. Both are required simultaneously since experience can blind one to logical conclusions drawn from data, and exhaustive data is almost always, by definition, a way of measuring past trends that may or may not continue.

If the facts stated in the passage above are true, a proper test of an executive's ability to make appropriate decisions is its ability to

(A) use knowledge gained from experience to determine which trends are likely to continue.

(B) use knowledge gained from experience to direct data-collection efforts.

(C) amass data that competitors are not collecting so that knowledge gained from experience can be set aside.

(D) establish technical infrastructure to collect data that supports the conclusions drawn from extensive experience.

(E) hire middle managers who can maintain the appropriate balance between experience-based and data-based decision-making.

93.   Industry analysts feel that Bluecorp paid far too much to acquire
       rival firm Strickland. While doing so limited competition they face
       in the marketplace, this approach cannot be profitable in the long
       run. Once two rival firms merge in order to increase profits, the
       higher prices would only provide other competitors an opportunity
       to enter the field at a lower price, cutting into Bluecorp's profits
       and making the acquisition of Strickland an expensive mistake.

       Which of the following, if true, most seriously weakens the
       argument?

       (A)   In some countries it is legal for two companies to merge
              even if the resulting entity would nearly monopolize the
              market.

       (B)   The combination of Bluecorp and Strickland creates an
              entity whose size allows it to produce items at a far lower
              cost than could any smaller enterprise.

       (C)   In addition to eliminating competition, Bluecorp's
              acquisition gives it a much more substantial presence
              in urban areas.

       (D)   As a result of the acquisition, the new corporate entity
              will create two smaller entities to operate as independent
              suppliers to Bluecorp.

       (E)   When two large companies in the same field combine,
              entrepreneurs tend to shy away from the field due to the
              single entity's perceived dominance.

32 Introduction to Reading Comprehension

GMAT Reading Comprehension is somewhat similar to GMAT Critical Reasoning in that you read a passage and answer some questions about it. However, both the nature of the passages and the types of passages are very different.

There are two main differences between CR and RC. The first is obvious: RC passages are longer. They vary in length quite a bit, but you can expect to see passages between about 150 and 400 words. Some will consist of one or two long paragraphs; others will be broken up into four or five short paragraphs.

Because the passages are longer, they can be quite a bit more involved. The shorter CR passages can use unfamiliar, technical language, but there's very little to understand in a three-sentence argument. In Reading Comprehension, however, you can be thrown into an unfamiliar topic and be expected to answer complicated questions about anything from physics to archaeology to the history of economics.

Types of Questions

The fact that the passage is longer and more involved influences the other main difference between RC and CR: the types of questions. In Critical Reasoning, the questions are almost always focused on some aspect of an argument. You'll see that in RC, too, but not nearly as much.

In fact, there's a wide variety of questions on Reading Comprehension passages. There are a number of ways they can be broken down, but I'll offer four categories:

Scope: This is the old standard, "What is the main idea of the passage?" The GMAT has numerous ways of asking this–you'll come across at least a half-dozen. The key is to find the answer choice that not only matches the topic (say, the excavation of Mayan ruins), but also the specific focus of the passage (perhaps a controversy about proper excavation methods).

Detail: These usually come with the phrase, "According to the passage," or something similar. The answer is just a reworded version of something in the passage. Here, the GMAT is testing whether you read the passage and understood the structure well enough to find a specific detail that you may not have remembered.

Inference: There aren't very many assumption and strengthen/weaken questions in RC, but there are plenty of inference questions. Often, the GMAT expects you to grasp the differences between different viewpoints on the same issue, or determine which parts of the passage are the author's opinion and which parts are factual.

Structure: These are less common but don't fit into any of the other three paragraphs. You might be asked how a certain sentence functions, or what the purpose of one of the paragraphs is. RC Structure questions are not too far removed from the boldface items in Critical Reasoning.

General Strategies

Nearly everyone finds it beneficial to take notes while reading RC passages. Exactly how you do that will depend on what works best for you. I prefer to jot down a sentence or two at the end of each paragraph, if only to keep myself focused and prevent my mind from wandering. (These topics aren't exactly thrilling!)

Pay particular attention to structure and scope. The structure gives you clues to the author's argument, and his or her method of establishing it. Is she describing two theories only to reject both? Defending a position and holding off competitors? The structure of RC passages is usually quite plain in this regard.

"Scope" refers to the passage's specific focus. The GMAT will never use the word "scope," but the concept will come up in the form of at least one general question on nearly every passage. Make sure you understand not only what the author has chosen to address, but what she has chosen to leave out. There's only so much you can write in four or five paragraphs, so GMAT passages are typically very focused.

Time Management

When timing your progress through GMAT Reading Comprehension passages, it's important that you consider separately the time it takes to read the passage and the time you spend answering the questions.

Usually, when people take too long on Reading Comprehension, it's because they spend too much time reading the passage. Or, as is sometimes the case, blankly staring at the passage thinking they are reading it, but really losing focus. (This is common enough when the passage is on paper, and the computer-based test makes it even easier.) The key to moving more quickly through passages is to eliminate, or at least minimize, the time you spent unfocused.

You should spend 3-4 minutes reading each Reading Comprehension passage. That's a very general rule for such a wide range of and passage lengths and topics, but it has served my students well. Unless you have a hard time reading English, you should have no problem getting through even the most difficult passages in four minutes.

In fact, if you eliminate time spent blanking out, glazing over, and re-reading, you can probably read the longest, most difficult passages in three minutes. Fortunately, the standard isn't that high.

Maintaining Focus

Every GMAT prep company has some particular approach to Reading Comprehension passages, and some of them are very involved. There's no need to follow a strict formula, or to write down exact characteristics of every passage.

(For instance, one large company suggests you jot down "topic," "scope," and "purpose," along with a paragraph-by-paragraph outline.)

What is important is that you write *something* down. It doesn't matter whether you outline the structure of the passage, rephrase each paragraph's topic sentence, or scribble down some key details that you think will come up in the questions. Whatever it is that comes easily to you, do it.

In my experience, I rarely refer back to my notes. However, that doesn't mean that taking those notes was a waste of time. The purpose of the note-taking isn't to create a replacement for the passage, it's to keep you focused. If you force yourself to write something down at least once per paragraph, it's much more difficult to glaze over and spend a minute or more staring at the screen, accomplishing nothing.

How to Practice RC

As with every aspect of GMAT preparation, make your practice as test-like as possible. If you're working out of a book, prop it up against your desk or a wall, so that it simulates working off a computer screen. Don't even think about underlining the passage. If you're doing the practice passages in this book, take advantage of the PDF format and read them off of a computer screen.

Tinker with my suggestions above: for one passage, try writing something down at the beginning of each paragraph; for another, at the end; for another, write things down whenever they seem important. There's no one write way to take notes to GMAT Reading Comprehension passages, and there's no way I'll be able to tell you which one is most practical for you.

You'll know that you're improving when two things happen:
  You're reading faster–no more than four minutes per passage.
  You spend less time re-reading the passage when confronted
     with questions.

If you find yourself skimming the entire passage for every question, you aren't getting enough out of the passage when you read it the first time. Re-reading is fine–in fact, it's absolutely necessary on many Reading Comprehension questions–but you never want to re-read more than one paragraph (at most!) for any one purpose.

I'm sure you know how important it is to manage your time wisely on the GMAT Verbal section. If you can control the amount of time you spend working through Reading Comprehension passages, you'll be in a much better position to do that.

How This Section Works

The structure of this section is very similar to that of the Critical Reasoning section. We'll start by analyzing the types of structures of passages, with special focus on the challenges presented by science passages. Next, the discussion turns to each specific type of question you're likely to see, following by patterns in RC answer choices.

33   RC: Passage Topics

There are a variety of topics that the GMAT likes to cover in its Reading Comprehension passages. Some are considered more difficult than others; for instance, it's a rare GMAT test-taker who is excited to see a biology passage.

While the range of potential subjects is wide, it is somewhat predictable. It's yet another reason why practicing with realistic materials–namely, The Official Guide and the Verbal supplement–is so important. The mix of content areas in those books very closely approximates what you can expect when you sit for the GMAT.

Science Passages

On both Reading Comprehension and Critical Reasoning, the GMAT loves biology. I don't know exactly why that is; perhaps the test-makers want you to take over a biotech company after getting your MBA. Regardless of the reason, biology is by far the most common branch of science covered in GMAT passages.

Other common topics are physics (particularly astronomy) and–again, I can't explain this one–archaeology. With the exception of astronomy passages, the emphasis is generally on things having to do with people. For instance, a biology passage might focus on life-saving pharmaceuticals, or an archaeology passage may be about what a recently uncovered civilization has to say about human nature.

For many test-takers, science passages present unique challenges; for that reason, the next chapter is devoted solely to science passages.

Business and Economics Passages

While science passages are considered difficult, I think most test-takers don't worry too much about business-oriented topics. After all, you probably have some interest in the corporate world if you're applying to MBA programs!

However, don't let that attitude seep into related economics passages. Many people think they understand economics better than they actually do, and GMAT passages often discuss multiple ways of addressing the same problem. In an economics passage, be especially careful to answer questions based on the content in the passage (not other things you've read) and be clear on the differing opinions that the passage presents.

Social Sciences Passages

These passages include a mix of history and political science. Occasionally, though, you'll also see topics such as ethnic studies and literature.

For me, these are the easiest: one of my majors in college was in the liberal arts, so handling academic-style writing is a breeze. But therein lies the trap for many people: Just because the content might be seen as "lightweight" (compared to denser science passages) doesn't mean it will be easy for you.

Academics in the liberal arts–the people who write, or at least inspire, the passages in this category–develop specialized vocabularies of their own, and they don't hesitate to use them. Like science passages, social science passages define their terms, but that means you have to pay just as close of attention to unfamiliar language in this type of content than with physics or biology.

What To Expect

The passages on the GMAT are, roughly speaking, evenly split between the three categories described in this chapter. If you are doing well on the Verbal section, you will see more difficult passages, and in many cases those are science passages. But that's no more than a rule of thumb. You'll typically have four or five passages per section, and there's a degree of randomness to every aspect of the test.

Supplemental Reading

One thing that will help you improve your Reading Comprehension skills is to do more reading. Preferably, you should read things that are similar to GMAT passages.

That's easier said than done. However, if you've practiced much Reading Comp, you know that many passages fit into the same patterns:

A theory is described and criticized;

Competing ideas are offered and compared;

A discovery or scientific phenomenon is explained.

You'll consistently find reading material that follows those patterns (without requiring too much of your time!) in the book review section of a newspaper or serious magazine such as The New Yorker or The New York Review of Books. If you are particularly concerned about science passages, you might consider a publication like Scientific American.

What To Read For

As with an actual GMAT passage, read for structure. What's the argument? How is it developed? What's the author's perspective? All of those things will be present in book reviews. Pay close attention to how the reviewer is evaluating the book in question, as well as how the review develops his or her own ideas.

When you are reading these articles, don't get hung up on the details. The GMAT doesn't expect you to be conversant in microbiology or physics; it only expects that you'll be able to follow the thrust of an argument and track a few key ideas. The details are there so that you can look them up later.

Book reviews are great practice for this, because the reviewer will often differ from the author of the book under consideration in a general way. The argument may hinge on details, but you'll want to read for the more general differences in arguments. No matter how many details and technical definitions you see, the focus should always be on the overall structure of the piece.

Of course, no number of book reviews will replace the value of actual GMAT practice. But there are only so many actual GMAT Reading Comprehension passages available to you, and sometimes you might want to read something that's legitimately interesting. A single issue of The New York Times Book Review could keep you busy during your commute or lunch break all week long.

34   RC: Science Passages

There's nothing on the Verbal portion of the GMAT that scares test-takers more than Reading Comprehension passages dealing with science. If you have a science background, you probably aren't worried about them (and rightly so); if you don't, my guess is that you tense up a little bit upon the first reference to molecules, chromosomes, or alluvial deposits.

It doesn't have to be that way. There are three main reasons why you have nothing to fear from science passages:
1. They are structured exactly the same way as non-science passages.
2. They are short. The scientific detail is superficial; in other words, you don't really have to understand it.
3. Most GMAT test-takers don't know very much science. If it's hard for you, it's probably a challenge for others, too.

A Sample Passage

To illustrate my point, let's look at an example. (This is from one of the passages you'll be working with in the practice sections.) If you prefer the humanities, the first paragraph alone contains enough to give you pause:

> Since the early 1990s, cancer researchers have recognized the role of **heat shock proteins (HSPs) in "chaperoning" peptides** and assisting the immune system in its constant effort to recognize and destroy diseased cells. Unlike the many illnesses that take advantage of weakened immune systems, cancerous tumors can "trick" an immune system because their cells are derived from normal cells and thus do not elicit a response. It is the task of researchers, then, to identify and isolate **unique cancer cell antigens** that are more likely to stimulate immune systems to take action. It turns out that members of the **HSP60, HSP70, and HSP90 families carry peptides generated within cells**; when those HSPs are taken from infected cells, the peptides they carry have similar properties and can spur an immune system into action.

It's a mouthful, alright. The phrases I've bolded are the ones that tend to pop out at the science-phobic. In order to answer some questions, you'll need to know where to find those details, but you won't need much in the way of understanding. Rather than focusing on what you don't immediately grasp, turn your attention to what you've seen before:

> **Since the early 1990s, cancer researchers have recognized the role of** heat shock proteins (HSPs) in "chaperoning" peptides and

assisting the immune system in its constant effort to recognize and destroy diseased cells. **Unlike the many illnesses that** take advantage of weakened immune systems, cancerous tumors can "trick" an immune system **because their cells are derived from normal cells and thus do not elicit a response. It is the task of researchers, then, to** identify and isolate unique cancer cell antigens that are more likely to stimulate immune systems to take action. It turns out that members of the HSP60, HSP70, and HSP90 families carry peptides generated within cells; when those HSPs are taken from infected cells, **the peptides they carry have similar properties and can spur an immune system into action.**

Note the shift in focus. The second time around, I've bolded phrases that emphasize distinctions and characteristics that even the science-phobic can understand.

Reading the Rest of the Passage

GMAT passages very reliably signpost their intentions: often you can determine the outline of the passage just from the first paragraph. That isn't the case in this example, but some of the questions that are based on this passage do not delve very far into the scientific details in this first paragraph. Once you read the first sentence of the second paragraph, you'll have a good idea of most of the paragraph's structure. (This passage, as it turns out, is only two paragraphs long.)

In other words, you've already done much of the grunt work. From here, you can expect to see more details, but it does get a bit easier:

> **In contrast to** the cancer vaccines that rely on antigen-presenting peptides in HSPs, **viral vector vaccines are manufactured in the laboratory.** Such a vaccine involves manipulating a gene similar to the targeted tumor and injecting it into the patient in an attempt to trigger the immune system to attack not only the manufactured cells, but also the cancerous cells already present in the body. **Both approaches rest on the assumption** that each patient's tumor is unique and that the vaccine must be created specifically to induce an immune system response. **While the first method is better established, the second may turn out be both more cost-effective and easier to use in treating large numbers of patients.**

So much of GMAT Verbal is about comparisons. Even if you could barely follow the first paragraph, the second gives you plenty of information you can understand. There's a second type of vaccine that differs from the first; the two have one thing in common (each patient's tumor is unique), and you're given some general information about the advantages and disadvantages of each. You might not be ready to handle difficult inference questions, but you have enough information to determine the passage's primary purpose, or to answer questions about the structure of the passage.

How Science Differs

Science passages are often packed with detail. Unlike humanities passages, they are more likely to explain a phenomenon or detail two competing proposals than to present an argument or defend a position. For this reason, there will be less theory and more detail. Don't fall into the trap, however, of spending every last second on the passage, trying to memorize all those details.

In fact, the best approach is precisely the contrary. The more difficult the details of a passage, the less time you should spend on them. If you don't grasp the idea by the second reading or so, you're not going to grasp it in another two passes. Better to make sure you understand the structure of the passage and return to the difficult sections if and only if a question forces you to.

The GMAT only shows you one question at a time, so there's no way to scan all of the questions before you read the passage. But even with that limitation, you don't have to understand a detail if the test doesn't ask you about it. There's a strong possibility that, for any given passage, you'll only have to answer three questions, so the odds you'll have to master the subtleties of a specific part of the passage are quite low.

35   RC: Common Passage Structures

As with just about anything in a standardized test, GMAT Reading Comprehension passages follow predictable patterns. In fact, there are three general templates, and nearly every RC passage fits into one of them. I call them:

> The explanatory passage
> The competing theories passage
> The position passage

The Explanatory Passage

Some GMAT passages–particularly shorter passages–focus on explaining a concept. The author usually doesn't take a position. The passage chooses a very narrow topic and provides a couple hundred words of exposition.

Explanatory passages are common ways of presenting scientific material. They'll be packed with detail, but you don't have to worry about keeping track of multiple viewpoints or the purported problems with certain arguments. Often, if an explanatory passage has two paragraphs, the first paragraph will be somewhat general, and the second paragraph will expand on one particular detail mentioned in the first paragraph.

These passages can be tricky when the GMAT breaks out of the template. A fair number of passages look like standard explanatory passages, presenting detail after detail until the end, and then offering a final sentence in which the author takes a position. As with any passage, be extra careful with the first and last sentences in each paragraph: this is where the author relays his topic and, in the passages where there is one, his argument.

The Competing Theories Passage

In the previous chapter on science passages, you saw a competing theories passage. In that example, the first paragraph explained one type of cancer vaccine, while the second presented a description of another type of vaccine. In these passages, the author may or may not choose a side, but make sure you know whether or not she does! As in explanatory passages, sometimes the indication that the author has an opinion is limited to one sentence, and that one sentence may be the last one of the passage.

The most important aspects of a competing theories passage are the differences between the theories. It's also key to track who holds which position. That isn't relevant in a passage like the cancer vaccine discussion, but in some passages of this sort, each theory will be assigned to a scholar, or a school of thought. When the passage does that, expect nearly every question to focus on what one group or the other thinks, or the difference between the positions.

Competing theories passages are most common for science topics and business/economics topics. The structure of the passage provides an excellent outline of the arguments, as the GMAT usually gives you very clear topic sentences. As in the cancer vaccine passage, you can understand some of the key differences between the theories without delving too far into the details of each theory.

The Position Passage

The author might argue for one position or theory in any type of GMAT passage, but in a position passage, the structure is defined by the author's argument. If you had to write argumentative essays in high school or university, you are probably familiar with this style. The author will present an argument in the first paragraph or shortly thereafter, and much of the remainder of the passage will be devoted to defending that position.

One variation of the position passage is what I call the attack passage. The typical position passage is defined by the author's argument; the attack passage is defined by a different argument that the author is trying to dismantle. In that case, the author's position might not become clear until a little later in the passage, because it takes a few sentences to fully describe the objectionable argument. There isn't a clear line of demarcation between the position passage and the attack passage; in either type, the GMAT may give you plenty of details about both the author's position and a position the author chooses to attack.

In this type of passage, details tend to be a bit more important. If the position is made clear in the first paragraph, the following paragraphs might present very different types of evidence for that position. By asking you detail-oriented questions, the GMAT is testing to see if you know what sort of evidence will support which sort of position. Once again, we're talking about structure. Regardless of the sort of passage, focus relentlessly on positions, perspectives, and topic sentences. You can skim a passage to find a detail, but you can't skim a passage to understand how it is assembled.

36   RC: Scope-Based Questions

Almost every passage has a scope question. Scope, if you aren't familiar with the word, is similar to the idea of subject or topic. I use the word "scope" because it implies the more specific range of the passage. RC passages can be complicated, but because of their length, they usually stick to a very narrow topic. Instead of looking for the general topic ("Jane Austen," "cancer vaccines," or "unemployment theory"), it's better to aim for something more precise.

Here are several ways in which the GMAT will ask you this general question:
Which of the following best summarizes the main point of the passage?
Which of the following best describes the content of the passage?
Which of the following best expresses the central idea of the passage?
The author's main point is
The author of the passage is primarily concerned with
The passage is primarily concerned with
The primary purpose of the passage is to

These are all fairly similar, and their correct answers would be, as well. We can break them down into two categories, though.

Some scope-based questions are concerned with what the author is *saying*, while others are more concerned with what the author is *doing*. In the list above, the questions at the top fall into the "saying" category, while the ones at the bottom are better fits in the "doing" category. It isn't a black and white distinction, but there is a noticeable difference between the "main point" and "primary purpose."

In "primary purpose" questions, each answer choice will often begin with a verb. That initial verb is sometimes enough to eliminate two, three, or even four choices. Here's an example of the five initial verbs in the choices of one scope-based question:
(A)   explaining
(B)   emphasizing
(C)   suggesting
(D)   arguing
(E)   suggesting

These aren't different enough to settle on an answer without looking at more than the first word in each choice (even if I did show you the passage!). But you should consider the distinctions nonetheless. "Explaining" sounds appropriate for an explanatory passage. "Arguing" would be better for a position passage. "Emphasizing" isn't a great verb for a "primary purpose," as one typically emphasizes something rather narrow. I wouldn't eliminate the answer altogether, but the initial verb doesn't bode well.

I don't mean to suggest that you should ignore all but the first word of the choices in a "primary purpose" question, but I do mean to emphasize, once again, the importance of structure in GMAT RC questions. If you correctly recognize the structure and the passage type, you'll have a head start on this question. If you understand the relationship of the various topic sentences in the passage, you could probably answer most scope-based questions without reading the details at all.

37   RC: Scope-Based: Practice

Questions 101-102 refer to the following passage:

Thanks to her inclusion in Alexander Pope's mock epic poem "The Dunciad" as a vacuous figure willing to write (and perhaps do) anything for financial recompense, Eliza Haywood was long regarded as of marginal importance in the literary history of the "long" 18th century. Many of her best-known novels have been described as "amatory fiction," a genre not considered central to the British novel tradition. Thus, until recently, even her supporters had little to say for her style, often emphasizing the historical importance of her journalism.

A closer examination of Haywood's novels indicates that disregarding her fiction in such a manner would be a mistake. Even if works such as the early "Love in Excess" and the late "The History of Miss Betsy Thoughtless" did not influence 19th-century novelists to the extent that more famous novels such as Richardson's "Pamela" and Fielding's "Tom Jones" did, they reveal a prose writer presenting both structural innovations and a surprisingly forward-looking view of society. Her shifting attitudes regarding class, courtship, and marriage are reflected in a noticeable change from her early novels to her more mature works, suggesting that she ought to be considered as more than a simple polemicist.

In fact, as Paula Backscheider has shown, Haywood's substantial corpus had more of an impact on the British novel tradition than was previously suspected. Haywood's "Anti-Pamela," a satire of Richardson's didactic novel, was as widely read as Fielding's parody of the same, and "Betsy Thoughtless" can be seen as the beginning of a tradition of novels of marriage, which culminated in Bronte's "Jane Eyre." Most importantly, the 18th-century novel was largely concerned with domestic issues hinging on the role of women, and Haywood's dozens of works are among the best representations we have of a female perspective on such topics.

101.   The author's main point is that

   (A)   next to parodies such as "The Dunciad" and "Anti-Pamela," novels of marriage were much more crucial to the development of the novel.

   (B)   it is a mistake to treat Haywood's polemical journalism as more than a historical curiosity.

   (C)   Haywood's novels are valuable in more ways than were thought by previous generations of scholars.

   (D)   18th-century novels by women such as Haywood deserve more attention that novels by men, such as Richardson and Fielding, on women's topics.

   (E)   "amatory fiction" influenced many important novelists writing in the 19th century.

102.   The primary purpose of the passage is to

    (A)   offer sociohistorical explanations for the prevalence of female novelists in the 18th century

    (B)   examine how one novelist has been viewed by scholars throughout history

    (C)   show why an underrated novelist should be taken more seriously

    (D)   propose a new ranking of prose writers in the 18th century to reflect more modern literary preferences

    (E)   outline specific distinctions between well-known novelists that have long been considered equals

Questions 103-104 refer to the following passage:

While it may seem simple and unobjectionable to non-specialists, one of the many issues that illustrates the divergence of post-Keynesian economics from mainstream economics is the idea of time. Most models of neoclassical economics utilize the notion of "logical time," in which markets (whether they be capital, goods, or labor markets) return to equilibrium after a disturbance is introduced and then overcome. While few economists object to this general model, post-Keynesians try to shift focus away from the "long run"-level analysis and analyze instead events in "historical time," emphasizing the real-world effect of deviations from equilibrium.

However, post-Keynesian economics cannot be understood simply as a reaction to, or adjustment of, the ideas of Keynes. In fact, because many post-Keynesians believe that the movement known as Keynesianism actually represents a severe divergence from the ideas of Keynes, they are in the position of both resuscitating and updating his theories. One example of this phenomenon is the labor market, on which traditional Keynesians follow the classical theory (that is, pre-Keynesian) of unemployment. While traditional and post-Keynesians both support [deficit spending] (known as "pump-priming") as a solution to short- and medium-term inefficiencies in the labor market, traditional Keynesians believe that, so long as wages and prices are perfectly flexible, those inefficiencies will disappear. That is the extent of the story for the traditional Keynesian, but viewed through the lens of "historical time," such inefficiencies are problems worthy of the economist's further study.

103.   The passage is primarily concerned with

    (A)   using a standard concept in neoclassical economics
            to illustrate a characteristic of a different view

    (B)   evaluating competing explanations of equilibrium in
            the labor market

    (C)   comparing the notion of "historical time" with that of
            "logical time" as they apply to economics

    (D)   clarifying the positions of a misunderstood field of
            economics by explaining a key difference with another
            field

    (E)   suggesting that "long run"-level analysis leads to economic
            misunderstandings and poor policy

104.   Which of the following best summarizes the main point of
        the passage?

    (A)   The importance of time in economic theories has long
            been understated, and its inclusion sheds new light on
            possible methods to curtail unemployment.

    (B)   The appearance of the post-Keynesian school of
            economics allowed mainstream economists to abandon
            their reliance on traditional theories such as the classical
            theory of unemployment.

    (C)   The ideas of Keynes remain among the most crucial in
            contemporary economic thought, but traditional
            Keynesians have long misrepresented them.

    (D)   Traditional Keynesians and post-Keynesians share some
            views, but the way each group approaches the idea of time
            causes them to pursue different paths of study.

    (E)   The labor market is a controversial subfield of economics,
            one in which Keynesians have little to contribute.

38 RC: Detail-Based Questions

In addition to a scope-based question, most GMAT Reading Comprehension passages come with at least one detail-based question. In fact, you are likely to see more detail-based questions than any other type of RC item. They will probably represent four of your twelve RC questions.

Detail-based questions are very literal. They ask for specific information from the passage, and the correct choice is usually very similar to what you'll find in the passage itself. Here are some of the ways detail-based questions are phrased:

> According to the passage, which of the following is a concern...
>
> Which of the following best characterizes...as described in the passage?
>
> The author cites which of the following as a disadvantage of...

Every detail-based question can be summarized as either, "What did the author say?" or, "What did the passage say?"

Your task with this sort of question is to find the specific reference in the passage. Usually, the question will point you to a single paragraph, if not a specific sentence. If you skimmed the passage, or misunderstood some of the details, you may need to spend some time re-reading until you make sure you're in the right place.

Once you are sure you've found the right location in the passage, expect to find an answer choice that is very similar to the relevant phrase in the passage. Occasionally a detail-based answer will be almost comically easy; the choice will restate a sentence from the passage almost word for word. It's generally not a good idea to second-guess yourself if an answer seems too easy–that's particularly important advice on detail-based questions.

39 RC: Detail-Based: Practice

Questions 111-113 refer to the following passage:

Thanks to her inclusion in Alexander Pope's mock epic poem "The Dunciad" as a vacuous figure willing to write (and perhaps do) anything for financial recompense, Eliza Haywood was long regarded as of marginal importance in the literary history of the "long" 18th century. Many of her best-known novels have been described as "amatory fiction," a genre not considered central to the British novel tradition. Thus, until recently, even her supporters had little to say for her style, often emphasizing the historical importance of her journalism.

A closer examination of Haywood's novels indicates that disregarding her fiction in such a manner would be a mistake. Even if works such as the early "Love in Excess" and the late "The History of Miss Betsy Thoughtless" did not influence 19th-century novelists to the extent that more famous novels such as Richardson's "Pamela" and Fielding's "Tom Jones" did, they reveal a prose writer presenting both structural innovations and a surprisingly forward-looking view of society. Her shifting attitudes regarding class, courtship, and marriage are reflected in a noticeable change from her early novels to her more mature works, suggesting that she ought to be considered as more than a simple polemicist.

In fact, as Paula Backscheider has shown, Haywood's substantial corpus had more of an impact on the British novel tradition than was previously suspected. Haywood's "Anti-Pamela," a satire of Richardson's didactic novel, was as widely read as Fielding's parody of the same, and "Betsy Thoughtless" can be seen as the beginning of a tradition of novels of marriage, which culminated in Bronte's "Jane Eyre." Most importantly, the 18th-century novel was largely concerned with domestic issues hinging on the role of women, and Haywood's dozens of works are among the best representations we have of a female perspective on such topics.

111.   According to the passage, which of the following was a primary issue in the 18th-century novel?

    (A)   The function of women in society
    (B)   Class distinctions in industrialized London
    (C)   Feminist perspectives of journalism
    (D)   Satirical treatments of other prose works
    (E)   The importance of financial gain

112.   According to the passage, which of the following works
        influenced "Jane Eyre?"

        (A)   Love in Excess
        (B)   Tom Jones
        (C)   The History of Miss Betsy Thoughtless
        (D)   The Dunciad
        (E)   Anti-Pamela

113.   The author of the passage states that Haywood had which
        of the following in common with Fielding?

        (A)   Her novels are often read for their structural innovations.
        (B)   She penned a parody of Richardson's "Pamela."
        (C)   She was a target of Pope's in "The Dunciad."
        (D)   Her novels were preoccupied with domestic issues.
        (E)   Her most popular works were as well-known as "Pamela."

Questions 114-115 refer to the following passage:

While it may seem simple and unobjectionable to non-specialists, one of
the many issues that illustrates the divergence of post-Keynesian economics
from mainstream economics is the idea of time. Most models of neoclassical
economics utilize the notion of "logical time," in which markets (whether they
be capital, goods, or labor markets) return to equilibrium after a disturbance
is introduced and then overcome. While few economists object to this general
model, post-Keynesians try to shift focus away from the "long run"-level analysis
and analyze instead events in "historical time," emphasizing the real-world effect
of deviations from equilibrium.

However, post-Keynesian economics cannot be understood simply as a reaction to, or adjustment of, the ideas of Keynes. In fact, because many post-
Keynesians believe that the movement known as Keynesianism actually represents a severe divergence from the ideas of Keynes, they are in the position
of both resuscitating and updating his theories. One example of this phenomenon is the labor market, on which traditional Keynesians follow the classical
theory (that is, pre-Keynesian) of unemployment. While traditional and post-
Keynesians both support [deficit spending] (known as "pump-priming") as a solution to short- and medium-term inefficiencies in the labor market, traditional
Keynesians believe that, so long as wages and prices are perfectly flexible, those
inefficiencies will disappear. That is the extent of the story for the traditional
Keynesian, but viewed through the lens of "historical time," such inefficiencies
are problems worthy of the economist's further study.

114. Which of the following best characterizes the difference between the way traditional Keynesians and post-Keynesians view inefficiencies in the labor market, as described in the passage?

    (A) Post-Keynesians differ from traditional Keynesians by studying practical effects of inefficiencies in the labor market.

    (B) Traditional Keynesians differ from post-Keynesians in that they consider short-term inefficiencies less important than medium-term inefficiencies.

    (C) Post-Keynesians and traditional Keynesians both accept the accuracy of the classical theory of unemployment and diverge only in the details of its interpretation.

    (D) Traditional Keynesians differ from post-Keynesians in that each group had a substantial effect on the history of economic thought at different points in the 20th century.

    (E) Both post-Keynesians and traditional Keynesians consider both "historical time" and "logical time" in evaluating the most important topic of study within the field of unemployment.

115. According to the passage, "logical time" is

    (A) an aspect of most models of neoclassical economics
    (B) now considered less useful than "historical time"
    (C) irreconcilable with "long run"-level analysis
    (D) a key tenet of post-Keynesian theory
    (E) the mechanism by which markets return to equilibrium

40 RC: Inference-Based Questions

This isn't the first chapter in the book on inference questions–inference questions are also relatively common in Critical Reasoning. However, there are some key differences.

For one thing, of course, the passages are longer. In CR inference questions, it's important to consider every detail in the short passage to make sure you haven't missed some connection between a sentence and an answer choice. With a full-length RC passage, that's just not practical. In a sense, then, a Reading Comprehension inference question is about halfway between a CR inference question and detail-based RC question.

> RC inference questions use the same keywords as CR inference questions:
> It can be inferred from the passage that...
> The passage suggests which of the following...
> Information in the passage suggestions that the author would be
>   most likely to agree with...

Some inference-based questions are barely distinguishable from detail-based questions, except for the wording of the questions. If they ask for something very specific, the process of answering the question might in fact be similar to the detail-based approach of finding the appropriate reference in the passage. The only difference is that, in an inference-based question, it's much less likely that an answer choice will be an almost word-for-word replica of a phrase in the passage.

Other inference-based questions require more work. This is particularly true when they delve into general concepts in position passages and competing theories passages. When the author provides multiple viewpoints, you can expect at least one inference question to require that you differentiate between the viewpoints, perhaps explaining how two perspectives are different. These more general questions may give you no hint at all about where in the passage to research; in those cases, it might be more efficient to start with the answer choices, eliminating two or three that you know are wrong, then checking the passage to confirm the accuracy of the remaining choices.

When the questions are more general, they shift from being similar to detail-based questions to having much in common with scope-based questions. In this regard, remember the differences between CR and RC inferences. RC inferences are much more approximate. You don't have to worry about every detail, and the correct answer may not be as logically precise as a correct answer on a CR question. While there is nothing wrong with these more approximate answers, recognize what the GMAT is testing: It is trying to determine if you can sort out the competing viewpoints, approaches, perspectives, or methods described in a lengthy passage.

41 RC: Inference-Based: Practice

<u>Questions 121-122 refer to the following passage:</u>

Since the early 1990s, cancer researchers have recognized the role of heat shock proteins (HSPs) in "chaperoning" peptides and assisting the immune system in its constant effort to recognize and destroy diseased cells. Unlike the many illnesses that take advantage of weakened immune systems, cancerous tumors can "trick" an immune system because their cells are derived from normal cells and thus do not elicit a response. It is the task of researchers, then, to identify and isolate unique cancer cell antigens that are more likely to stimulate immune systems to take action. It turns out that members of the HSP60, HSP70, and HSP90 families carry peptides generated within cells; when those HSPs are taken from infected cells, the peptides they carry have similar properties and can spur an immune system into action.

In contrast to the cancer vaccines that rely on antigen-presenting peptides in HSPs, viral vector vaccines are manufactured in the laboratory. Such a vaccine involves manipulating a gene similar to the targeted tumor and injecting it into the patient in an attempt to trigger the immune system to attack not only the <u>manufactured cells</u>, but also the cancerous cells already present in the body. Both approaches rest on the assumption that each patient's tumor is unique and that the vaccine must be created specifically to induce an immune system response. While the first method is better established, the second may turn out be both more cost-effective and easier to use in treating large numbers of patients.

121. It can be inferred from the passage that the first type of vaccine described has which of the following drawbacks?

    (A)   Cells can generate only a limited number of peptides, which limits their ability to stimulate an immune system response.

    (B)   It is unknown how many different types of cancers can be prevented with this type of vaccine.

    (C)   Weakened immune systems are not always able to respond appropriately to the antigen-presenting peptides introduced by vaccines.

    (D)   It may be more difficult to use in vaccinating large numbers of patients.

    (E)   HSPs in the HSP60, HSP70, and HSP90 families are not always present in the cells of a patient, preventing their usage in cancer vaccines.

122.   The passage suggests which of the following about the
         manufactured cells mentioned in the underlined text?

    (A)   They are introduced into the patient's body to further
         weaken the patient's immune system.

    (B)   They are identical to cancerous cells already present
         in the patient's body.

    (C)   They rely on HSPs to "chaperone" peptides into a
         position that will stimulate a response from the
         patient's immune system.

    (D)   They are created in a laboratory specifically for each
         individual cancer patient receiving a viral vector vaccine.

    (E)   Their peptides are different from those created by the
         patient's body in that they operate independently of HSPs.

Questions 123-125 refer to the following passage:

While it may seem simple and unobjectionable to non-specialists, one of
the many issues that illustrates the divergence of post-Keynesian economics
from mainstream economics is the idea of time. Most models of neoclassical
economics utilize the notion of "logical time," in which markets (whether they
be capital, goods, or labor markets) return to equilibrium after a disturbance
is introduced and then overcome. While few economists object to this general
model, post-Keynesians try to shift focus away from the "long run"-level analysis
and analyze instead events in "historical time," emphasizing the real-world effect
of deviations from equilibrium.

However, post-Keynesian economics cannot be understood simply as a reaction to, or adjustment of, the ideas of Keynes. In fact, because many post-
Keynesians believe that the movement known as Keynesianism actually represents a severe divergence from the ideas of Keynes, they are in the position
of both resuscitating and updating his theories. One example of this phenomenon is the labor market, on which traditional Keynesians follow the classical
theory (that is, pre-Keynesian) of unemployment. While traditional and post-
Keynesians both support [deficit spending] (known as "pump-priming") as a solution to short- and medium-term inefficiencies in the labor market, traditional
Keynesians believe that, so long as wages and prices are perfectly flexible, those
inefficiencies will disappear. That is the extent of the story for the traditional
Keynesian, but viewed through the lens of "historical time," such inefficiencies
are problems worthy of the economist's further study.

123.   The passage suggests which of the following about the
        deficit spending mentioned in the highlighted text?

(A)   To a traditional Keynesian, it is a way to eliminate
       inefficiencies in the labor market.

(B)   To a post-Keynesian, it solves all of the problems
       associated with inefficiencies in the labor market.

(C)   To both traditional and post-Keynesians, it is a key
       aspect of the classical theory of unemployment.

(D)   To a traditional Keynesian, it is a way to turn attention
       away from "long run"-level analysis.

(E)   To a post-Keynesian, it is a superior strategy to that
       of "pump-priming."

124.   The author of the passage would be most likely to agree with
        which of the following statements about the idea of time
        mentioned in the first sentence of the passage?

(A)   It underlies the most trenchant critiques of the classical
       theory of unemployment.

(B)   It applies most directly to theories of the labor market,
       which has long been misunderstood by economists.

(C)   It represents the most serious problem with the
       positions held by post-Keynesians.

(D)   It is the leading cause of the inefficiencies that
       wreak havoc with economic theories.

(E)   It illustrates an important distinction between streams
       of economic thought.

125.   It can be inferred from the passage that which of the following
        is true about traditional Keynesians?

(A)   When studying the labor market, they are mainly
       concerned with eliminating short- and medium-term
       inefficiencies.

(B)   In criticizing the classical theory of unemployment,
       they understate the importance of "pump-priming."

(C)   They favor the notion of "historical time" to that of
       "logical time."

(D)   They support more of the theories of Keynes than do
       post-Keynesian economists.

(E)   As neoclassical economists, they study the real-life
       impact of inefficiencies that appear in the capital, goods,
       and labor markets.

42   RC: Structure-Based Questions

Compared to scope-, detail-, and inference-based Reading Comprehension questions, structure-based questions are not nearly as important. In fact, they represent less than 10% of RC items, which means you probably won't see more than one on your exam. But you will probably see one.

I've noted many times in the preceding chapters how important it is that you focus on the structure of the passage, both as a way to avoid getting mired in detail and a way to understand the general themes of the passage. As you might imagine, grasping the structure of a passage also comes in handy in a structure-based question.

Here are some examples of this question type:
> Which of the following best describes the function of the third paragraph of the passage?
>
> Which of the following best describes the relationship of the second paragraph to the first paragraph?
>
> Which of the following best describes the overall content of the second paragraph of the passage?

Answer choices tend to be technical, using non-specific language to characterize theories, viewpoints, and arguments. For instance, these are a couple of choices for the second of the three questions listed above:
> It presents contrasting explanations for a phenomenon presented in the first paragraph.
>
> It provides information that qualifies a claim presented in the first paragraph.

If you needed any more encouragement to prioritize your understanding of the passage's structure when you first read it, this question type ought to push you over the edge.

43   RC: Structure-Based: Practice

Questions 131-133 refer to the following passage:

Thanks to her inclusion in Alexander Pope's mock epic poem "The Dunciad" as a vacuous figure willing to write (and perhaps do) anything for financial recompense, Eliza Haywood was long regarded as of marginal importance in the literary history of the "long" 18th century. Many of her best-known novels have been described as "amatory fiction," a genre not considered central to the British novel tradition. Thus, until recently, even her supporters had little to say for her style, often emphasizing the historical importance of her journalism.

A closer examination of Haywood's novels indicates that disregarding her fiction in such a manner would be a mistake. Even if works such as the early "Love in Excess" and the late "The History of Miss Betsy Thoughtless" did not influence 19th-century novelists to the extent that more famous novels such as Richardson's "Pamela" and Fielding's "Tom Jones" did, they reveal a prose writer presenting both structural innovations and a surprisingly forward-looking view of society. Her shifting attitudes regarding class, courtship, and marriage are reflected in a noticeable change from her early novels to her more mature works, suggesting that she ought to be considered as more than a simple polemicist.

In fact, as Paula Backscheider has shown, Haywood's substantial corpus had more of an impact on the British novel tradition than was previously suspected. Haywood's "Anti-Pamela," a satire of Richardson's didactic novel, was as widely read as Fielding's parody of the same, and "Betsy Thoughtless" can be seen as the beginning of a tradition of novels of marriage, which culminated in Bronte's "Jane Eyre." Most importantly, the 18th-century novel was largely concerned with domestic issues hinging on the role of women, and Haywood's dozens of works are among the best representations we have of a female perspective on such topics.

131.   Which of the following best describes the function of the third paragraph of the passage?

(A)   It attempts to reconcile conflicting views presented in the previous paragraphs.

(B)   It presents examples intended to undermine the argument presented in the second paragraph.

(C)   It provides evidence that supports the position taken in the first sentence of the second paragraph.

(D)   It describes the importance of the works mentioned in the second paragraph.

(E)   It suggests that the claims reported in the first paragraph are still valid.

132.   Which of the following best describes the relationship of the
        second paragraph to the first paragraph?

        (A)   It presents contrasting explanations for a phenomenon
               presented in the first paragraph.
        (B)   It discusses an exception to a general principle outlined
               in the first paragraph.
        (C)   It provides an argument to counter the position described
               in the first paragraph.
        (D)   It presents an example that strengthens a claim presented
               in the first paragraph.
        (E)   It presents an alternative approach to understanding the
               historical trends discussed in the first paragraph.

133.   Which of the following best describes the organization of the
        first paragraph of the passage?

        (A)   A viewpoint is introduced, and its historical evolution is
               outlined.
        (B)   Opposing viewpoints are discussed, and evidence is
               provided that supports one of the viewpoints.
        (C)   A hypothesis is described and then refuted.
        (D)   An alternative viewpoint is presented, and evidence is
               provided to question it.
        (E)   An outline is presented, and then the main point of the
               outline is shown to be false.

Questions 134-135 refer to the following passage:

Since the early 1990s, cancer researchers have recognized the role of heat shock proteins (HSPs) in "chaperoning" peptides and assisting the immune system in its constant effort to recognize and destroy diseased cells. Unlike the many illnesses that take advantage of weakened immune systems, cancerous tumors can "trick" an immune system because their cells are derived from normal cells and thus do not elicit a response. It is the task of researchers, then, to identify and isolate unique cancer cell antigens that are more likely to stimulate immune systems to take action. It turns out that members of the HSP60, HSP70, and HSP90 families carry peptides generated within cells; when those HSPs are taken from infected cells, the peptides they carry have similar properties and can spur an immune system into action.

In contrast to the cancer vaccines that rely on antigen-presenting peptides in HSPs, viral vector vaccines are manufactured in the laboratory. Such a vaccine involves manipulating a gene similar to the targeted tumor and injecting it into the patient in an attempt to trigger the immune system to attack not only the [manufactured cells], but also the cancerous cells already present in the body. Both approaches rest on the assumption that each patient's tumor is unique and that the vaccine must be created specifically to induce an immune system response. While the first method is better established, the second may turn out be both more cost-effective and easier to use in treating large numbers of patients.

134. Which of the following best describes the overall content of the second paragraph of the passage?

(A) It describes a type of treatment and compares it to another treatment detailed in the first paragraph.

(B) It describes a method of vaccine production and explains how it is inferior to the method presented in the first paragraph.

(C) It offers a potential solution to a problem inherent in vaccine distribution.

(D) It provides further explanation of the mechanics of a vaccine described in the first paragraph.

(E) It describes the similarities between two types of treatments and explains why one is preferable to the other.

135.   Which of the following best describes the function of the first
       paragraph of the passage?

       (A)   It presents two opposing views that will be reconciled
             in the second paragraph.
       (B)   It attempts to explain the importance of an approach that
             is to superior to the one presented in the second
             paragraph.
       (C)   It describes a method that utilizes a contrasting
             approach to the method explained in the second
             paragraph.
       (D)   It provides details of one approach that has been
             superseded by the approach described in the second
             paragraph.
       (E)   It suggests that a technique has the potential to save lives,
             something also true of the technique mentioned in the
             second paragraph.

44 RC: Strategies For Speed

Many GMAT students have a difficult time handling Reading Comprehension passages in a reasonable amount of time. By my standard, you should be reading passages in 3-4 minutes, which doesn't include the time it takes to answer the associated questions. Most passages aren't very long and should be manageable in that amount of time, but the problem remains.

Many people with this issue ask me how to skim passages. I don't think that skimming (or worse, skipping parts) is the answer, but you can read more efficiently. Often, the biggest problem is having to repeatedly re-read the passage. If you only read the passage once, carefully, the time limitations should be easy to meet.

That said, some parts of a GMAT RC passage are more important than others. While you should read every word, certain sentences are worthy of more attention.

What follows is a short-hand way of looking at this subject. Many GMAT passages are structured in one of a small number of ways. Many contain exactly three paragraphs–an introduction, followed by two supporting points, or two different positions, or an exposition of a topic.

Obviously not every sentence is of equal importance. Let's say that typical three-paragraph passage has four sentences per paragraph. I'll denote the most important sentences with an "A," sentences of moderate importance with a "B," and those of the least importance with a "C."

P1: Sentence 1: A
P1: Sentence 2: B
P1: Sentence 3: B
P1: Sentence 4: A

P2: Sentence 1: A
P2: Sentence 2: C
P2: Sentence 3: C
P2: Sentence 4: B

P3: Sentence 1: A
P3: Sentence 2: C
P3: Sentence 3: C
P3: Sentence 4: B

As you can probably tell from the ratings, the most important sentences are at the beginning and end of each paragraph. Often, you can determine the structure of a passage simply by reading the first sentence of each paragraph. That's a great start, but the final sentence sometimes contains stronger hints regarding the author's position, and that's something the GMAT loves to test.

Once again, you shouldn't skip the "C"-rated sentences, but you shouldn't spend much time on them, either. Especially on topics that are opaque to you (such as science passages), it's easy to get bogged down in the details–but it isn't worth the time to make the effort to fully understand them.

Not every passage has three paragraphs of four sentences each! For instance, some GMAT RC passages have just one long paragraph. Here are some general rules:
1.   The first sentence is always very important.
2.   The first sentence of each paragraph is also key, especially for understanding structure.
3.   The last sentence of each paragraph–especially the first–is crucial, especially for understanding the author's viewpoint.
4.   No matter what the structure, there will always be examples and minor details. They are more likely to come near the end of the passage, and they are always rated "C."

Like all Reading Comprehension techniques, this takes some time to incorporate into your plan of attack. It may slow you down when you first try it, but that isn't a reason to discard it immediately. Once you've used it on 10-12 passages, you should find that it gives you the confidence you need to read through the passage without spending too much time on the details that aren't worth the effort.

Prioritizing RC Questions

I hope that the previous section will save you a great deal of time, and that you can use the time saved to carefully answer every question. Sometimes, though, that simply isn't possible. The following few paragraphs outline a method you can use if you are truly pressed for time. There's no magic bullet that will allow you get every question right in half the time, but you can follow these steps and identify what questions you *can* handle even in a rush.

This strategy should help you get through an entire passage and set of questions in as little as two or three minutes. Again, don't use it if you don't have to.

Passage: Scan it, focusing on structure, topic sentences, and the author's opinion. Don't bother with details. Focus on the "A" sentences identified above, with a bit of attention to "B" sentences. This should take no more than two minutes. You may be able to accomplish it in 60-90 seconds.
Scope-based questions ("global" or "main topic"): Answer it. A skilful skim of the passage should have given you enough information.
Detail-based questions: Try to answer it. Your skim should be enough to go back to the passage and look for the detail.

110

Inference-based questions: Unless you have a reasonably good idea about how to answer this question, guess and move on. Even on Verbal questions, guessing is ok.

Structure-based questions: Same as scope-based. If you did a good job skimming, you should have a good chance of getting this right.

45   RC: Common Wrong Answer Choices

If you've been reading the explanations to the practice questions in this book, you've seen the same phrases come up again and again when I explain why answer choices are incorrect. That's the purpose of this section and the next one–to share those categories, and explain a little bit more about them. This chapter discusses three common types of wrong answer choices, and the next chapter covers two trickier types.

Some of these are the same as the common wrong answer choices discussed in the Critical Reasoning section–the wrong answer choices have even more in common than the question types do!

Off-Topic

Plenty of wrong answer choices, especially on scope- and inference-based questions, are outside the scope of the passage. This, again, is why it's so important to understand the scope of the passage–even without having a good idea of the correct answer to a question, you can often eliminate a choice or two. If a scope-based question asks for the primary purpose of a passage about the positions held by post-Keynesians, you can confidently eliminate a choice that refers only to neoclassical economists.

You'll also see plenty of wrong answer choices that refer to the wrong part of the passage. This is particularly common on inference questions, on which you may not be able to locate the answer in one specific sentence. In this case, it isn't just the scope that can help you, it's a good grasp of the outline of the passage. In a competing theories passage, two consecutive paragraphs can present very different answers to the same question through the competing perspectives they describe. If you're researching in the wrong place, you can end up with a very wrong answer. The GMAT knows this, and that answer choice is waiting for you.

Irrelevant Comparisons

This type of wrong answer choice is just as common in Reading Comprehension as it is in Critical Reasoning. Like off-topic choices, it appears most frequently in scope- and inference-based questions. Many of those questions are themselves about comparisons–they contrast competing theories, or the author's position with the one she attacks.

An irrelevant comparison is usually half-right: It compares one thing that is within the scope of the passage to another thing that isn't. Or, the other half of the comparison is within the scope of the passage, but the two things being compared never appear in the same place. Consider the post-Keynesian passage you've now seen a few times. In those two paragraphs, there are references to neoclassical economists, traditional Keynesians, post-Keynesians, and the classical theory of unemployment. There are a lot of ways an answer choice can pair two of those and create an answer choice, but not all of them were compared to one another in the passage itself.

Misplaced Detail

In the chapter on detail-based questions, I pointed out that many correct answers will be very similar to a relevant phrase in the passage. If you find something like that, it's a good sign that you've identified the correct answer. However, the GMAT knows you're looking for a detail, and it provides answer choices that are very similar to parts of the passage that aren't what you're looking for.

If you return to the practice section a few chapters back and look at any of the detail questions, you'll probably find two–sometimes three or four–wrong answer choices that are very close to a phrase in the passage. If you understand the relevant details, you will never fall for those choices. But as I discussed in the science passages chapter, there will almost certainly be occasions when you don't understand the relevant details. In those cases, take some extra time to identify exactly which detail the question is concerned with. Odds are many similar details are represented among the wrong answer choices.

46 RC: Mixed Review 1

Questions 141-145 refer to the following passage:

The best-known method of classifying living things, Linnaean taxonomy, denotes species using a hierarchical structure, starting at the general level of kingdom, then phyla, order, family, genus, and, finally, species. Remarkably, Linnaeus's system has proven robust, despite the fact that he devised it in the mid-1700s, long before Charles Darwin's theory of evolution drastically altered our understanding of the natural world. That doesn't mean, however, that Linnaean taxonomy has gone unchanged in the subsequent 250 years. Most oddly, Linnaeus began with three kingdoms, one each for plants, animals, and minerals. Not only has the mineral grouping been eliminated, but several new kingdoms— for bacteria, protozoans, and fungi—have been added. More seriously, the taxonomy has required vast numbers of additional levels of classification, especially in species-rich fields such as entomology. Even in zoology, the categories of "subspecies" and "morph" further delineate subgroups of individual species, and cladistics—the classification of species based on evolutionary ancestry—has brought about a parallel hierarchy that sometimes, but certainly not always, overlaps with the traditional Linnaean divisions. As scientists in these fields understand finer-grained distinctions between groups of living things, this 250-year-old methodology is likely to be stretched even further.

141.   The primary purpose of the passage is to

(A)   describe a scientific model and the ways it has
        accommodated advances in its field
(B)   discuss ways of updating a classification structure
        that has remained in use for too long
(C)   explain the process by which a taxonomy is expanded
        to reflect new scientific discoveries
(D)   detail the adjustments made to a traditional hierarchy
(E)   report the current state of a taxonomy commonly used
        in the fields of entomology and zoology

142. According to the passage, cladistics differs from Linnaean taxonomy in that cladistics

    (A) allows for more subtle distinctions between categories of beings
    (B) rarely classifies species in the same hierarchies that Linnaean taxonomy does
    (C) does not distinguish between the levels of "subspecies" and "morph"
    (D) includes several new kingdoms classifying life that Linnaeus was not aware of
    (E) represents hierarchies based on evolutionary relationships

143. It can be inferred that the author describes Linnaean taxonomy as "robust" in order to emphasize which of the following?

    (A) The number of levels Linnaeus included in his initial classification system
    (B) The mistake Linnaeus made in considering minerals one of his three kingdoms
    (C) The difference in scientific understanding of species relationships before and after the discovery of the theory of evolution
    (D) The small number of scientific claims made in the mid-1700s that are still in use today
    (E) The many ways in which the classification system has had to be altered to accommodate scientific discoveries in the 250 years since

144. The passage suggests which of the following about entomology?

    (A) Since the Linnaean kingdoms do not include "insect life," entomologists must classify species using a parallel system.
    (B) It caused the addition of the category of "subspecies" to the Linnaean system.
    (C) 250 years ago, it was not even considered by Linnaeus when he devised his initial taxonomy.
    (D) It is a field that is better understood by relying on cladistics-based taxonomies.
    (E) The demands of classifying living beings within the field have placed particular stress on the Linnaean system.

145.   Which of the following best describes the organization of
       the passage?

       (A)   A method is described, challenges to that method are
             detailed, and an alternative is offered.
       (B)   Competing methods are presented, and challenges are
             offered that suggest the need for a third method.
       (C)   A traditional approach is described, supported with
             specific evidence, and then reaffirmed.
       (D)   Evidence is offered to support the position that a
             centuries-old method ought to be replaced.
       (E)   After alternative approaches are described, a
             reconciliation is attempted but not successful.

47 RC: Difficult Wrong Answer Choices

Once you've eliminated the wrong answer choices in the categories described in the previous chapter, you'll often be left with two choices. We all know the feeling: You can defend both of the two choices, and you can't figure out how either one of them could possibly be wrong.

On RC questions, the second- or third-best answer choice is often partially right. However, half-right (or even three-quarters right) isn't good enough for GMAT Reading Comprehension. If there is anything wrong in an answer choice, eliminate that choice. Here are two ways to categorize partially right answers.

Strong Language

By this point in the book, I hope you've noticed some patterns in the tone of GMAT RC and CR passages. With only a handful of Critical Reasoning exceptions, these passages are not worded very strongly. Sure, an argument can be strident now and then, but usually, claims are riddled with words like "may," "might," and "often." In short, there aren't many absolutes in these passages.

If an answer choice contains an absolute, then, it's probably wrong. For instance, here's choice (B) from question #123:
> To a post-Keynesian, it solves all of the problems associated with inefficiencies in the labor market.

You shouldn't have to re-read the passage, or even check the exact question, to suspect that this one is wrong. The key word is "all"–there's nothing in any of these passages that "solves all of the problems" in a field. Words like "every," "none," "always," and "never" should trigger the same response.

Half-and-half

On scope- and structure-based questions, many choices have two parts. One of the many examples you've seen already is choice (A) from question #141:
> describe a scientific model and the ways it has accommodated advances in its field

If this choice is to be correct (which, as it turns out, it is), two things must be true. The passage must (1) "describe a scientific model," and (2) describe "the ways it has accommodated advances in its field." Frequently, a scope-based question will have five similarly-structured choices, all of which with an "and" in the middle. When presented with that set of choices, expect that most of the answers will have at least one correct half. Instead of looking for reasons to select a choice as your answer, hunt for problems that will give you cause to eliminate the choice.

If you spend enough time analyzing explanations, whether in this book or in The Official Guide, you'll probably identify more patterns of your own. As you've worked through the Reading Comprehension section of this book, you've learned that the content of the passages, the structure of the passages, and the types of questions are all carefully patterned. There's no reason to treat the answer choices any differently.

48 RC: Mixed Review 2

Questions 151-155 refer to the following passage:

Although Chinese foreign trade under the Ming Dynasty in the 16th century reflected a policy of openness that exceeded any previous dynasty, the relationship between the Chinese and the visiting Portuguese was a fractious one for nearly fifty years after Rafael Perestrello completed the first successful European trading voyage to China. It is a testament to how highly the Portuguese valued the commercial potential of China that they persisted for so long: The members of one early expedition were never permitted to reach the court of the emperor and died in a Chinese jail; the antics of the Portuguese ambassador's brother fed rumors that the Portuguese were kidnapping and eating Chinese children. Given the contemporary Chinese experience of Japanese piracy in coastal areas, it is no surprise that authorities were skeptical of foreigners, even those who made elaborate formal efforts to open trade through official channels.

The Portuguese established a foothold by providing silver after trade with Japan was halted, but relatively soon afterwards, most imported silver came from Spain's colonies in the Americas. Ultimately, this reliance on foreign silver contributed to the demise of the Ming Dynasty, as one source after another was affected by skirmishes between Protestant European nations such as England and the Catholic empires of Spain and Portugal. Protestant raids even shut down traffic in the Japanese silver that was brokered to China through European powers as Japan drastically cut its own foreign trade. The resulting inflation in silver values, combined with the environmental effects of what is now known as the "Little Ice Age," led to economic disaster for rural Chinese, and opened the door for the Manchus to topple the Ming Dynasty in the early 17th century.

151. With which of the following generalization regarding the Ming Dynasty would the author most probably agree?

(A) It was the dynasty most open to foreign trade in Chinese history.

(B) The trade with European powers that it ultimately accepted had an unexpected effect on its fate.

(C) It could not survive without some form of interaction with Japan.

(D) Protestant nations did more good for the long-term security of the Ming than did Catholic powers.

(E) Its treatment of foreign visitors was frequently harsh and often excessive in severity.

152.   The passage suggests that Ming-Japanese interaction differed
        from Ming-Portuguese interaction in that

        (A)   The initial welcome the Ming granted the Japanese was
                warmer than the welcome extended to the Portuguese.
        (B)   The Portuguese traded goods harvested and manufactured
                in its colonies while the Japanese brokered goods from
                other sources.
        (C)   Japanese traders were often jailed, while Portuguese
                visitors were accepted as visitors of the court.
        (D)   The Portuguese traded in child slaves, while the Japanese
                mainly limited themselves to luxury goods.
        (E)   Japanese traders were considered illegal and unwelcome,
                while the Portuguese were eventually accepted as part of
                China's economy.

153.   The passage is primarily concerned with

        (A)   arguing that the Ming created the state of affairs that
                led to its own demise by opening up trade with the
                Portuguese
        (B)   explaining that religious conflicts in Europe had a major
                impact in China
        (C)   suggesting that only European traders are important to
                the economic history of the Ming Dynasty
        (D)   explaining that the Ming was reluctant to open trade with
                Europeans, and that the decision to do so contributed to
                their downfall
        (E)   emphasizing that the traditional Chinese isolationism has
                not always been the case, and that China was better off
                in the eras defined by more openness.

154. According to the passage, the Chinese were reluctant to trade with the Portuguese because

   (A)   their attempts to make official contact with the Ming court were thought to be insincere
   (B)   the climate effects of the Little Ice Age limited the goods they could offer in trade
   (C)   the visitors were rumored to be abducting Chinese children
   (D)   bad experiences from coastal raids conducted by the Japanese affected their views of all non-Chinese
   (E)   the Chinese traditionally avoided contact with outsiders, and the strong economy in the early Ming years provided no incentive to do otherwise

155. Which of the following, if true, would seriously undermine the conclusion that inflation in silver values contributed to economic disaster for rural Chinese?

   (A)   The rural economy rebounded relatively soon after the Manchus conquered China.
   (B)   The environmental effects of the Little Ice Age meant that the supply of necessities, such as food, was extremely scarce at any price.
   (C)   Most rural Chiense in the Ming era did not use hard currency, instead operating a highly advanced barter economy.
   (D)   The famine brought about by the Little Ice Age caused many rural Chinese to relocate to urban areas.
   (E)   Economic problems in Europe at this time were completely unrelated to the price or availability of silver.

49 Introduction to Sentence Correction

Unlike GMAT Critical Reasoning and Reading Comprehension, which are familiar question types on many standardized tests, GMAT Sentence Correction is fairly unique. Instead of focusing on your understanding of content, it tests your ability to identify clear, grammatically-written sentences.

In large part, GMAT Sentence Correction is a grammar test. There are no items that explicitly ask about the names of verb tenses, and you're not required to diagram sentences, but those skills–if you have them already–will come in handy.

To get a feel for what you're up against, here's an example question:

> It is not known whether paper made from rocks will emerge as the leading type of ecologically-friendly paper, or <u>if, as scientists continue to look for alternatives, another solution will become the standard.</u>

The five answer choices offer different ways of replacing the underlined portion of the sentence. Choice (A) is always exactly the same; it is the answer that says, "The sentence is correct as written."

Usually, there are patterns in the choices. In this example, (A) and (B) retain the word "if" at the beginning of the underlined portion, while (D), and (E) replace it with "whether." Similarly, some of the choices keep the word "continue," while others switch to "continued."

One of the key strategies that will help you move through Sentence Correction questions more efficiently is to identify those patterns. Not only do they help you eliminate more than one answer quickly, but they also can help you identify mistakes in the first place, by seeing how groups of choices differ from each other.

The Grammar

There are several grammatical areas that come up frequently on Sentence Correction items:

      verb tenses
      subject/verb agreement
      modifiers
      comparisons and parallelism
      pronoun usage
      idioms
      clarity

(You might note that many of those categories match the title of the chapters in the remainder of this section.)

The last two aren't really rules, and they can be the most complicated. For that reason, they should be among your last priorities. You will never learn all the idioms that the GMAT could test, and you'll probably never agree 100% with how the GMAT test-makers define clarity, so better to focus on the large chunk of Sentence Correction that is more straightforward. This concept is a tricky one, and I'll cover it at more length in the chapter below called "The Hierarchy of Errors."

Especially if English is not your first language, idioms can be the most difficult part of Sentence Correction. As noted, you won't learn them all. It isn't even worth your time to try.

However, that doesn't mean you shouldn't learn any. As you go through practice questions, note those idioms that arise. A couple dozen that particularly common. Some of the most important ones are highlighted in the Idioms chapter later in this book. If you learn those, you'll be able to handle most of the idioms you'll see on test day, and you won't have spent countless hours mastering obscure verb/preposition combinations that you are unlikely to see on the GMAT.

Like every type of GMAT question, there are easy items and more difficult items. If you're aiming for a higher-than-average score on the Verbal section, you'll need to be prepared for the trickier flavors of Sentence Correction questions. There are a few ways that SC items get harder:

Sentences get longer.

The underlined portion gets longer (sometimes including the
    entire sentence).

The correct answer is less appealing.

Length is a challenge, especially since it makes patterns more difficult to spot. But with focus, longer sentences can usually be reduced to familiar problems.

The toughest problems are those where all five choices don't sound very good. While on some items, "clarity of expression" is the difference between a right answer and a wrong answer, there are others where none of the choices would pass the "clarity of expression" test. There are many subtle errors included in this catch-all category of "clarity of expression," or the similar category of "rhetorical construction," and many of those are addressed in the last Sentence Correction chapter, "Other Errors."

On these questions, four of the questions will have unambiguous grammatical mistakes, and the fifth will not. Even if that fifth choice is wordy, or somewhat confusingly worded, it must be right: a grammatically incorrect sentence will always be wrong.

Don't worry too much about difficult problems at the outset: there are plenty of fundamentals to learn, and you can get a long way toward your goal score by mastering the basics of GMAT Sentence Correction.

How This Section Works

The answer choices are more important in SC than in CR or RC, so we'll start by focusing on the strategies you can use to take advantage of them. After that, we'll turn to a discussion of what errors matter more than others, followed by an overview of the parts of speech. The remaining chapters each cover one category of grammatical mistake that the GMAT tests, presenting grammar rules, common errors, and strategies for recognizing and resolving those errors.

50 SC: Answer Choices

In the majority of GMAT Sentence Correction questions, the entire sentence is not underlined. Sometimes the underlined section is just a word or two, while in other items the underlined section can be multiple lines long. Any time the underlined section is about three words or longer, but does not include the entire sentence, there are two parts of the underlined section that are more important than the rest.

The two crucial elements of the underlined portion are the beginning and the end. Errors can turn up anywhere, but they are most likely to show up in those two locations. There are a couple of structural reasons why that is.

Remember that SC questions were written by a person, and that person is trying to write **standardized** test questions. Much as SC questions may appear bewildering, they follow predictable patterns. Pick any question out of the Official Guide or the practice sections of this book, and look at the beginning and end of all five answer choices. It is extremely rare that all of the beginnings or all of the ends are the same.

If the beginnings or ends were all the same, why would they underline that part of the sentence? They're giving you a portion to analyze, and if all five choices are the same, there's nothing to analyze there. This isn't a guarantee that the beginning or end is a mistake (obviously, the correct answer could be (A)), but they are two places that you almost always have to consider.

Another reason why the errors tend to show up at the beginning and the end is that Sentence Correction forces you to read fragments out of context. When you read the initial sentence, you can generally follow along. Even a very poorly constructed sentence can be understood. But when you read through the answer choices, you are reading only a part of a sentence. To pick an example at random:

> due to their enhancement of reproduction
> or survival, but that they are

Do you have any idea whether "due to" is correct, or whether "but that they are" needs to be changed? Of course, it's a little easier when you've just read the sentence, but no matter how fresh that sentence is in your mind, you've also got several other answer choices competing for attention.

In other words, the testmaker can insert a glaring error at the beginning or end of a choice (particularly at the end) and many GMAT test-takers will miss it.

One solution to that problem is to read through the sentence five times, once with each of the answer choices. That is probably overkill–there are typically a couple of choices you can eliminate without that much effort. However, if you eliminate all but two or three choices, it is usually worth your while to read through the entire sentence to check on the beginning and end.

Looking for Patterns

As I've noted, many of the differences in the choices appear at the beginning and end of the fragments. In addition, because of the way the choices are lined up for you, you can use the choices to determine what the mistakes might be. This is true whether the mistake is at the beginning, at the end, or in the middle of the choices.

As SC items get more difficult, it is tougher to tell from the initial sentence what the mistake is. (Or if there is a mistake at all.) Many test-takers redouble their efforts on the sentence, reading it three or four times in search of an error.

But because of the structure of the questions, remember that every possible mistake is right in front of you. If there is a way the GMAT wants you to improve the sentence, it's in one of the answer choices. Take advantage of this!

Let's look at an example. Here are the answer choices from one practice question:

> (A) had expected it to and its business will improve
> (B) had expected and that its business would improve
> (C) expected it would and that it will improve its business
> (D) expected them to and its business would improve
> (E) expected and that it will have improved its business

The answers–even out of the context of the sentence itself–give you plenty to work with. Here are just some of the issues:

"had expected" or "expected?" Should the verb be past or
    past perfect?
"it" or "them?"
"will improve" or "would improve?" (Or "will have improved?")
"and" or "and that?"
"expected" or "expected...to?"

As is common on GMAT Sentence Correction questions, there are multiple errors in every wrong answer choice. You don't need to recognize every single one of them. In fact, as it turns out on this question, "had expected" and "and that" are both correct, making (B) the only possible answer. There are a lot of other ways to eliminate choices, so you don't need to puzzle out every grammatical possibility.

To be clear: I certainly don't mean to suggest you need to thoroughly analyze the choices in every SC question, or that you should look at the choices before the sentence. There are plenty of questions on which you'll recognize the error(s) on the first read-through, and there's no reason to change your strategy.

Analyzing the choices, whether all five or just a couple of remaining choices, is a good backup strategy. Practice it, and take the pressure off of your careful reading of the sentence.

Choice (A)

There are a lot of myths and rumors circulating about the GMAT. One particularly persistent one is that certain answer choices occur more than others. This is not true, and it's particularly important to realize in Sentence Correction.

The five answer choices are equally distributed in the question pool. Put another way, there are just as many (A)'s as (B)'s, (D)'s as (E)'s, etc.

That doesn't mean you should count your answers as you go through the test–not only would it be silly, but it would miss the point. There's no guarantee that your 78 GMAT questions will consist of 15 or 16 of each of the five choices. But there are some useful SC tips that you can take away.

I've never studied it, but I suspect that if we were to track GMAT students as they progressed from novice status to test day, we could watch them choose more and more (A)'s in Sentence Correction. Here's why.

Early on, you get in the habit of looking for mistakes. That's the right way to go about a SC question. Really, it's one of the only ways. But it has its dangers. If you're looking for errors, you may find them even if they aren't there.

Thus, when you are committed to finding an error, you'll find one whether its in the original sentence or not, and you'll eliminate (A) without thinking too much about it. Then, if all of the other choices are bad, you'll choose the least offense of the remaining four answers. In the process, you'll never pick (A).

Eventually, you see the pattern. (A) comes up just as often as any other choice, but that doesn't mean it's only correct when the sentence glistens with perfection and efficiency.

For most students, the toughest SC questions are those where all of the choices are inefficient, or just clunky. The same reading skills that make you better at Reading Comprehension and Critical Reasoning can be harmful on SC because you are that much more ready to eliminate a choice just because it's not well written.

You must realize, though, that when all of the choices are undesirable, (A) is just as likely as the other choices to be correct. In fact, it seems to me that it's a little more likely than the others in those cases. Maybe that's just mental–an overcorrection for throwing (A) out in the first place–but it may be a useful way for to keep (A) in mind even when it isn't particularly well-phrased.

As you might have noticed, there's a little more strategy involved in Sentence Correction than in the other parts of the GMAT Verbal Section. In a sense, SC is more like the GMAT Quantitative section than the other Verbal question types are. The questions are shorter, the patterns are more obvious, and you can spend a little more time with every little detail.

51 SC: The Hierarchy of Errors

Most Sentence Correction questions are fairly clear cut. You'll identify an error or two in the original sentence (or you'll find one by analyzing the differences in the answer choices), and you'll be able to eliminate four choices, leaving you with one grammatically correct choice.

However, you will occasionally come to a SC question where all of the choices look wrong. No matter how much you practice and study grammar rules, you will find yourself in this situation. When that happens, turn your focus away from clarity and efficiency. Hone in on more technical grammatical rules, such as verb tense and parallelism. If one choice has an incorrect verb tense and another is inefficient, the first will never be correct, while the second could be.

In a sense, there is a **hierarchy of errors**. The hard-and-fast grammar rules, like verbs and modifiers and some idioms, automatically eliminate a choice. Other problems are more ambiguous. Excessive wordiness and inefficient expression sometimes differentiate between two decent choices. In other cases, there's only one choice left standing after you eliminate all of the technically wrong choices.

Fortunately for you, the hierarchy isn't very complicated. You don't need to memorize a ranking of dozens of different error types. In fact, there are exactly three categories you need to worry about.

Category 1: Technical grammar rules

These include most of what the following chapters discuss: incorrect verb tense, subject/verb disagreement, misplaced modifiers, lists that don't use parallel construction, comparisons that don't compare like things, and incorrect pronoun usage. These are the sorts of things that show up in grammar books.

When you find an error that falls into one of these categories, it is wrong. There's no ambiguity–a choice that breaks one of these fundamental grammar rules will never be right.

Category 2: Idioms and Mood

Part of the problem with idioms, as I alluded to in the previous chapter, is that there is almost an infinite number of idioms in English. Some of them, such as the rule that determines using "less" and "fewer," are unambiguous. Many more of them, like the hundreds of guidelines that pair verbs and prepositions ("concerned with," "concerned for," "concerned about") are not nearly as clear. In the Idioms chapter below, you'll find the unambiguous ones. Those generally belong in Category 1. However, everything else belongs here. If you think you've found an obscure idiom problem, you might be right...or the test might be using another obscure idiom that you aren't familiar with.

The other issue in this category is the passive mood, or as it is more commonly known, "passive voice." In general terms, a sentence uses passive voice when the object precedes the subject. ("John was complimented by Kim" is passive, while "Kim complimented John" is active.) The GMAT prefers active voice. That said, long sentences can be passive without the mood causing many problems, and some sentences are active but are still awkward. Passive voice just isn't as clear-cut as the technical rules in Category 1.

When you identify an error in Category 2, you can probably eliminate the choice, but be careful. A choice with a Category 2 error will, in rare cases, be correct. Such a choice is correct if and only if all four of the other choices have Category 1 errors.

Category 3: Clarity (and everything else)

If you read through the explanations in The Official Guide to GMAT Review, you'll find frustratingly vague descriptions of grammatical errors. Terms like "clarity of expression," "elegance of expression," and "rhetorical construction" appear again and again. Sometimes, even I don't know what they mean, and I've been studying those examples for years.

In general, those terms refer to the efficiency with which a sentence is written. All else equal, a short sentence is better than a long one. Active voice is one way to achieve that, but sometimes it's just a matter of rearranging phrases. The GMAT would prefer that no sentence ever be awkward, redundant, inelegant, or unnecessarily long.

However, lots of correct SC answers have some of those characteristics. This occurs more often on harder questions and on items where the entire sentence is underlined. When you encounter these Category 3 errors, be very careful: Lots of choices with Category 3 errors end up being correct.

As with choices that contain Category 2 errors, choices with Category 3 errors could be right or wrong. It depends on the other answers. A Category 3 choice will probably be wrong more often than it is right, but it can be right–if and only if the other four choices have Category 1 and/or Category 2 errors.

Tracking the Categories

This idea–that some answers are more wrong than others–may call to mind one of the first chapters in this book. When I discussed scratchwork, especially for Critical Reasoning and Reading Comprehension, I noted the value of a consistent system to track answer choices with.

Using these category distinctions, you'll look at each choice in two ways. First, you'll see whether it must be wrong. Second, you'll see whether it could be wrong. To keep track, jot down "A B C D E" on your scratch paper for each SC question. If a choice is clearly wrong, put an "X" through that choice. If a choice might be wrong, put a "?" next to it.

Thus, at a glance, even if you think all five choices could be wrong, you can look back only at those choices that earned question marks (Category 2 and 3 errors). It saves time, and keeps you focused on the choices that matter.

52 SC: Parts of Speech

You don't need to know anything about grammar or the parts of speech to answer Sentence Correction questions. A little knowledge does help, though. Many of the following chapters, which focus on the various common errors found in SC questions, use some grammar terminology. In this chapter, I'll introduce you to some of the most common terms.

Nouns. A noun is a person, place, or thing. "Tom Hanks" is a noun, as is "window." Nouns that are capitalized (such as the names of people or locations on a map) are referred to as "proper nouns."

The most important noun-related issue on the GMAT is the distinction between plural nouns and singular nouns. Both of the examples I gave in the previous sentence are singular nouns–each refers to one thing. However, the word "examples" is a plural noun. It refers to three things. Generally, plural nouns end in "s" and singular nouns do not, but not all nouns that end in "s" are plural (such as "Tom Hanks," which is singular), and not all plural nouns end in "s."

Pronouns. A pronoun is a word that stands in for a noun, such as "he," "it," or "they." When a pronoun is used, it should be clear what it refers to. For instance, in "The economy is strong, but it is expected to weaken," the pronoun "it" refers to "the economy."

Adjectives. An adjective is a word that modifies, or describes, a noun. "Handsome," "speedy," and "thorough" are all adjectives. They almost always appear just before a noun, as in "The handsome man," "a speedy runner," or "thorough due diligence." In general terms, good writing does not rely too heavily on adjectives, and you won't see a lot of them in GMAT sentences.

Verbs. A verb is an action word, such as "jump," "examined," or "writing." Technically, a verb can contain multiple words: "have been playing" is a verb, as is "will pack." Verbs in English are complicated, and there are several important GMAT-related verb issues. In fact, the entire next chapter is devoted to verbs.

Adverbs. Adjectives describe nouns, and adverbs describe (or modify) verbs. Often adverbs end in "ly" or "ily," as in "beautifully" or "completely." An adverb can appear right before or right after a verb, as in "That was phrased beautifully," or "I'm completely finished."

Prepositions. Prepositions are words that indicate relationships between things. In the sentence "She leaned against the wall," the preposition is "against." Some other prepositions are "above," "among," "before," "from," "into," "past," "toward," and "with." Note that many of these indicate physical relationships (where one thing is located compared to another), but prepositions can also link things in time, as in "I went to bed **before** nine o'clock."

Prepositions aren't tested explicitly on the GMAT, but they are important. Instead of trying to memorize every possible permutation in which a preposition might appear in a sentence, focus on the precise meaning of these words. For instance, "before" will always be used when comparing times. "Toward" appears when one thing is moving in the direction of another. Many questions are mistakenly considered idioms when you could answer them with a better knowledge of exactly what the prepositions mean.

This isn't a complete list of the parts of speech, but it does cover all of those that will arise frequently in GMAT Sentence Correction.

53 SC: Verbs

One of the Sentence Correction themes that I briefly brought up in the previous chapter (and will mention again!) is precision of meaning. When you're confronted with a difficult or complicated sentence, focus on exactly what the words mean, and whether the sentence structure makes sense.

Generally, when we read a newspaper or memo, we give the author the benefit of the doubt–it's in our best interest to figure out what the author meant to say, not precisely what the author did say. There is often a difference. In a Sentence Correction question, it's reversed: We don't want to give the sentence the benefit of the doubt. Just as we prod Critical Reasoning arguments for loopholes and unstated assumptions, so we should look for imprecision and nonsensical phrasings in SC.

This idea, of demanding precision, applies to nearly every sub-category of Sentence Correction questions. Within the category of verbs, it is particularly pertinent when discussing verb tenses.

You are probably familiar with the simple past, present, and future tenses:
"He wrote an essay."
"He writes an essay."
"He will write an essay."

There are two other types of tenses that are important: the progressive tenses and the perfect tenses.

The progressive tenses describe actions that are not complete, often using verbs that end in "ing."
"He was writing an essay."
"He is writing an essay."
"He will be writing an essay."

The perfect tenses describe an action that happened before the corresponding simple tense. For instance, if you want to describe something that happened before another event in the past tense, you should use the past perfect tense.
"Before the economy's recent recovery, it had had made investors nervous."
"The economy is recovering, but it has made investors nervous."
"By the time the economy recovers, it will have made investors nervous."

There is also a perfect progressive tense ("had been," "has been," "will have been"), but you don't need to be as concerned with that as the progressive and the perfect. There are a few general rules regarding verb tenses:

134

1.   Verb tenses must make logical sense. If the meaning of the sentence indicates the order in which two events occur, the earlier event must be described using an earlier tense than the later event.

2.   Progressive tenses are generally not desirable. Use of a progressive tense is definitely a Category 3 error; you will see correct answers using progressive tenses. However, just about any "ing" verbs can be improved, and often the GMAT gives you a better option.

3.   In general, perfect tenses cannot be used unless the corresponding simple tense is also present in the sentence. For instance, it wouldn't be grammatically correct to say, "The economy had been slumping." The past perfect tense implies that it had been slumping before some other event occurred. To be correct, the sentence needs to include something in the past tense. For example, "The economy had been slumping before legislators passed a comprehensive aid package." The event described using past perfect precedes the event described using simple past.

4.   The one exception to the previous rule is present perfect. It is acceptable to use the present perfect without also describing an event using simple present. For instance, "The economy has been slumping" could be correct.

Subject/Verb Agreement

Grammatically speaking, a "subject" is often a noun, but it sometimes encompasses more words. For example, "the office" could be a subject, or "the people who work for Citibank," or "the citizens of Bulgaria." The exact scope of the subject depends on context.

In addition to a subject, every sentence must have a verb. For instance:
"The office needs to be cleaned."
"The people who work for Citibank put in long hours."
"The citizens of Bulgaria are looking forward to the next election."

In each of those sentences, the verb ("needs," "put," and "are looking") depends on whether the subject is singular or plural. "The office" is straightforward: There's only one office.   "The people who work for Citibank" is plural–there is more than one person. "The citizens of Bulgaria" is also plural, as there is more than one citizen.

The important thing to recognize here is that the verb doesn't depend on the number (singular or plural) of the nearest noun. "Are looking" is plural because "citizens" is plural, not because of "Bulgaria," which is singular. The GMAT constructs sentences that move the subject and verb very far away from each other.   Consider this example, which you'll get to try in the following practice section:

The list of countries <u>that qualifies for an investment-grade</u>
<u>(i.e., AAA, AA, or A) rating by the credit agency has been</u>
<u>reduced to eliminate</u> several countries seriously affected by
the recent economic downturn.

You may be able to tell that the sentence is wrong, but what are the subject and verb? The subject is "The list," though the sentence tells you a lot more about that list. The verb doesn't appear until nearly twenty words later: "has been reduced." It can be difficult to determine exactly what the subject is, and what determines whether the verb should be plural or singular. One way to check is to keep shortening the subject until it stops making sense:

The list of countries that qualifies for an investment-grade
     rating...has been reduced.
The list of countries that qualifies...has been reduced.
The list of countries...has been reduced.
The list...has been reduced.

If the meaning of the sentence is still reflected (albeit in abbreviated form), that final, shortest version of the sentence tells you what the subject is. Similarly, you could determine the proper verb by shortening "the citizens of Bulgaria" to "the citizens" and "the people who work for Citibank" to "the people."

The Subjunctive Mood

There are many aspects of the subjunctive mood in English, but there are only two that will concern us here.

First, if a sentence expresses a hypothetical, use the verb "were" instead of "was." For instance, this is correct:
     If I were to apply to an MBA program, I might be accepted.

The key word is "if," which signals the hypothetical.

The other important aspect of the subjunctive is technically known as the "mandative subjunctive," which is the proper grammatical construction when various forms of commands are described. It addresses verbs such as "request," "demand," and "command."

In common usage, speakers and writers avoid the subjunctive by avoiding those verbs altogether. Instead, they might write something like this:
     "You should finish your work."
     "I think you need to decide."

In those cases, the meaning isn't very different from "request" or "demand." However, they can be reworded:

"I request that you finish your work."
"He demanded that the decision be made."

There are several details to note. First, the mandative subjunctive applies to any tense. ("Request" is present, while "demanded" is past.) Second, the words "should" and "need" are gone altogether. Requesting and demanding imply that the work should be done and that the decision be made. Finally, note in the second sentence the use of the word "be." It might feel more natural to write, "He demanded that the decision should be made," but as I've pointed out, the word "demanded" implies that it "should" be made. The word "should," then, is redundant.

54 SC: Verbs: Practice

201. Less than 15 years after the patent of the direct current
system of electricity distribution by Thomas Edison, its
main competition, the alternating current method devised
by Nikola Tesla, had been adopted as the method of
sending electricity from Niagara Falls to Buffalo, New York.

    (A)   Less than 15 years after the patent of the direct current
system of electricity distribution by Thomas Edison

    (B)   In less than 15 years since patenting the direct current
system of electricity distribution by Thomas Edison

    (C)   In less than the 15 years since the direct current system
of electricity had been patented by Thomas Edison

    (D)   It took less than 15 years from the patent of the direct
current system of electricity by Thomas Edison

    (E)   It took less than the 15 years beyond when the direct
current system of electricity was patented by Thomas
Edison, and then

202. The list of countries that qualifies for an investment-grade
(i.e., AAA, AA, or A) rating by the credit agency has been
reduced to eliminate several countries seriously affected by
the recent economic downturn.

    (A)   that qualifies for an investment-grade (i.e., AAA, AA,
or A) rating by the credit agency has been reduced to
eliminate

    (B)   that qualifies for the investment-grade (i.e., AAA, AA,
or A) ratings by the credit agency has been reduced
and eliminates

    (C)   that qualifies by an investment-grade (i.e., AAA, AA,
or A) rating for the credit agency has been reduced to
eliminate

    (D)   that qualify for an investment-grade (i.e., AAA, AA, or
A) rating by the credit agency has been reduced to
eliminate

    (E)   that qualify for earning the investment-grade (i.e., AAA,
AA, or A) ratings by the credit agency has been reduced
and eliminates

203. The company's chief executive, whose technological expertise, views on the future of the industry, and decision-making style <u>were impressive to the managers who worked with her, was also acknowledged as a leading strategist by many people outside her firm, including executives at rival companies, whose approaches often differed substantially from</u> her own.

   (A) were impressive to the managers who worked with her, was also acknowledged as a leading strategist by many people outside her firm, including executives at rival companies, whose approaches often differed substantially from

   (B) impressed the managers who worked with her, also was acknowledged as a leading strategist by many people outside her firm, including executives at rival companies, whose approaches often differed substantially from

   (C) was impressive to the managers who worked with her, was also acknowledged as a leading strategist by many people outside her firm, that included executives at rival companies, whose approaches were different substantially in comparison to

   (D) was impressive to the managers who worked with her, also acknowledged as a leading strategist by many people outside her firm, who included executives at rival companies, the approaches of whom differed substantially when compared to

   (E) were an impression to the managers who worked with her, also was acknowledged as a leading strategist by many people outside her firm, including executives at rival companies, whose approaches were often substantially different from that of

204. The study showed that carbon dioxide emissions increased much less in the last year than analysts <u>had expected them to and general pollution levels will flatten</u> out this year.

   (A) had expected them to and general pollution levels will flatten

   (B) had expected and that general pollution levels would flatten

   (C) expected they would and that general pollution levels will be flattening

   (D) expected it to and general pollution levels would flatten

   (E) expected and that general pollution levels will have flattened

205.   Often incorrectly referred to as cross-cultural psychology,
        cultural psychology, practitioners of which <u>collect data through
        ethnographic and experimental approaches, is</u> a field of
        psychology which assumes the idea that culture and mind are
        inseparable.

        (A)   collect data through ethnographic and experimental
               approaches, is
        (B)   collect data by ethnographic means and experimental
               approaches to them, is
        (C)   use ethnographic and experimental approaches to
               collect data, are
        (D)   approach data ethnographically and experimentally, is
        (E)   approach data ethnographically and experimentally
               collect it, are

206.   Horace Mann's leadership methods and his areas of reform—
        the separation into classes by age, the reduction of flogging,
        the establishment of state-wide school systems instead of local
        districts—<u>was as radical in his own time as it is</u> standard for ours.

        (A)   was as radical in his own time as it is
        (B)   were as radical in his own time as they are
        (C)   has been as radical to his own time as they are
        (D)   had been as radical to his own time as it was
        (E)   have been as radical in his own time as

55 SC: Lists

The entire content of this chapter can be summed up in four words:
Lists must be parallel.

Let's look at an example. Here's a fairly straightforward sentence containing a list:
I went to the store, stopped at the bank, and drove home.

If you really wanted to, you could break that sentence up into three shorter sentences:
I went to the store.
I stopped at the bank.
I drove home.

Those three sentences use the same verb form, just as the three items in the initial list do. A list is essentially an abbreviation of a set of sentences like these three.

When you encounter a list in a GMAT Sentence Correction question, the odds are very high that at least some of the choices test your awareness of parallelism. For instance, a choice might read:
I went to the store, stop at the bank, and I drove home.

There are actually two different kinds of errors in that alteration. First, "stop" is not the same tense as "went" and "drove." Almost always, the items in a list all have a verb of some kind, so you should always check to make sure the verbs use the same tense.

Second, the last item in the list restates the word "I." The structure of the sentence (at least that of the first two items in the list) implies that "I" precedes each item, though it is unstated for the last two. When I broke up the initial sentence into three shorter sentences, I included that first "I" as the beginning of each sentence. However, consider what results if we do the same with the altered sentence:
I went to the store.
I stop at the bank.
I I drove home.

Clearly the third sentence is wrong! As parallelism questions get harder, this kind of error is more common that the verb tense issue.

To check for this kind of error, identify the point at which the sentence "branches off." In the case of the initial sentence, it branches off after the word "I." From there, it goes in three different directions, but all three directions start with the word "I." Once you've identified that point, check and make sure that every branch makes sense. The creation of three short sentences may have seemed like an academic exercise, but it is an useful strategy to use on this sort of question. On each of the questions in the following practice section, give it a try.

56 SC: Lists: Practice

211.　　The researcher, presenting his recent research that addressed the topic of dexterousness in nonhuman primates, demonstrated that he was challenging established opinion concerning captive animals, <u>comparing "termite-fishing" to nut-cracking, and he combed</u> the published data on tool use in the wild.

(A)　comparing "termite-fishing" to nut-cracking, and he combed

(B)　comparing "termite-fishing" to nut-cracking, and combing

(C)　was comparing "termite-fishing" to nut-cracking, while he combed

(D)　he compared "termite-fishing" to nut-cracking and combed

(E)　he was comparing "termite-fishing" to nut-cracking, and combing

212.　<u>Translating the recently discovered Levantine tablet fragments will increase our understanding of Imperial Aramaic, shed</u> light on dialect differences in the fourth-century BCE, and aid research into proto-Pahlavi writing systems.

(A)　Translating the recently discovered Levantine tablet fragments will increase our understanding of Imperial Aramaic, shed

(B)　To translate the recently discovered Levantine tablet fragments will increase our understanding of Imperial Aramaic, and shed

(C)　Having translated the recently discovered Levantine tablet fragments will, in increasing our understanding of Imperial Aramaic, shed

(D)　To translate the recently discovered Levantine tablet fragments would increase our understanding of Imperial Aramaic, shedding

(E)　Translating the recently discovered Levantine tablet fragments, increasing our understanding of Imperial Aramaic, would be shedding

213. In its heyday, Hull House's founding of a public kitchen, a sociological institution, and the schools for adults and young children indicating Jane Addams's desire to benefit society in a variety of ways, expanding women's rights foremost among them.

(A) the schools for adults and young children indicating
(B) founding schools for adults and young children, indicates
(C) it founded schools for adults and young children, which indicates
(D) schools for adults and young children indicates
(E) schools that it founded for adults and young children, indicating

214. While they protect employees from financial ruin, give customers peace of mind, and encourage safety, corporate liability insurance policies also provide cost certainty for companies that purchase it, and, as an increasingly well-publicized perk, that make it easier for firms to recruit top personnel.

(A) purchase it, and, as an increasingly well-publicized perk, that make
(B) purchase it, and an increasingly well-publicized perk, are makers of
(C) purchase it and, as an increasingly well-publicized perk that are making
(D) purchase it and an increasingly well-publicized perk, for making
(E) purchase it and, as an increasingly well-publicized perk, make

215.   Salicylate drugs such as aspirin have numerous side effects,
        weakening the body's resistance to ulcers, but they are widely
        used either to prevent heart attacks and blood clot formation,
        to aid recovery after a heart attack, or also for relieving pain
        and reducing fever.

    (A)   either to prevent heart attacks and blood clot formation,
           to aid recovery after a heart attack, or also for relieving
           pain and reducing fever
    (B)   either for preventing heart attacks and blood clot
           formation, aid recovery after a heart attack, or for pain
           relief and fever reduction
    (C)   to prevent heart attacks and blood clot formation, for
           recovery after a heart attack, or relieving pain and
           reducing fever
    (D)   for preventing heart attacks and blood clot formation,
           to aid recovery after a heart attack, or also pain relief
           and fever reduction
    (E)   to prevent heart attacks and blood clot formation, aid
           recovery after a heart attack, or relieve pain and reduce
           fever

216.   Double-blind experiments at the Sudbury Neutrino Observatory,
        a center where physicists study subatomic particles that travel
        close to the speed of light, is designed toward controlling
        scientists' preexisting expectations and toward the elimination
        of "observer bias."

    (A)   is designed toward controlling scientists' preexisting
           expectations and toward the elimination of
    (B)   is designed to control the preexisting expectations of
           scientists and to eliminate
    (C)   are designed to control scientists' preexisting
           expectations and the elimination of
    (D)   are designed toward the control of scientists'
           preexisting expectations and toward eliminating
    (E)   are designed toward controlling the preexisting
           expectations of scientists and eliminating

57 SC: Comparisons

Comparisons are much like lists. When two items are compared, they must be grammatically similar. I won't spend any more time rehashing that, since grammatically similar lists are the entire subject of the previous chapter.

What makes comparisons different is what, precisely, is being compared. This is an area where you need to focus on exactly what the sentence is saying– as I've pointed out in earlier chapters, the more you can zero in on the precise meaning of each phrase, the more easily you'll find the correct answer.

Consider the following comparison:
> "Kubla Khan," one of Coleridge's most famous works, is superior
> to William Wordsworth.

It doesn't take much to figure out what the writer of this sentence is trying to say. But is it correct? The sentence compares two things: "Kubla Khan" and "William Wordsworth." One is a poem, the other is a poet. Technically speaking, they cannot be compared. To fix it, we can compare poems to poems, or poets to poets:
> "Kubla Khan," one of Coleridge's most famous works, is superior
> to the poetry of William Wordsworth.
> Coleridge, the author of "Kubla Khan," should be considered
> superior to William Wordsworth.
> Coleridge, the author of "Kubla Khan," wrote poetry superior to
> that of William Wordsworth.

In each of those three examples, the sentence compared two like things. In the first case, it was poetry and poetry. Second, a poet and a poet. Third, poetry and poetry. That third case is the most interesting: Often, to create a grammatically correct comparison, the phrase "that of" comes in handy. In this case, it stands in for "the poetry of," but since it is being compared to "poetry," there is no need to state the word again.

Identifying Comparisons

As is the case with lists, when a comparison appears in a Sentence Correction question, at least some of the answer choices will hinge on your awareness of that comparison. There are several words and phrases that signal a comparison:
> like / unlike
> in contrast to / compared to
> whereas

Of course, a comparison can be present without one of those words. The example discussed above doesn't have one; the only way to recognize the comparison is by understanding the meaning through words like "superior."

58 SC: Comparisons: Practice

221. Juan Trippe, the founder of Pan American Airways, because he planned to expand his airline's service to include intercontinental routes, he acquired several Central and South American airlines in order to win government contracts delivering mail to the region.

   (A) Juan Trippe, the founder of Pan American Airways, because he planned to expand his airline's service to include intercontinental routes, he
   (B) The expansion of his airline's service to include intercontinental routes was planned by Juan Trippe, the founder of Pan American Airways, and so he
   (C) Planning to expand his airline's service to include intercontinental routes, Juan Trippe, the founder of Pan American Airways,
   (D) Juan Trippe, the founder of Pan American Airways, planning to expand his airline's service to include intercontinental routes and
   (E) The founder of Pan American airways, planning to expand his airline's service to include intercontinental routes, Juan Trippe

222. In contrast to rising unemployment rates in the United States and Canada, the Chinese unemployment rate fell by more than ten percent due to increasing demand abroad for Chinese goods.

(A) In contrast to rising unemployment rates in the United States and Canada, the Chinese unemployment rate fell by more than ten percent due to increasing demand abroad for Chinese goods.

(B) In contrast to rising unemployment rates in the United States and Canada, China cut its unemployment rate, falling by more than ten percent due to increasing demand abroad for Chinese goods.

(C) When compared with rising unemployment rates in the United States and Canada, China cut its unemployment rate by more than ten percent due to demand abroad for Chinese goods that had increased.

(D) Compared with rising unemployment rates in the United States and Canada, China cut its unemployment rate by more than ten percent due to increasing demand abroad for Chinese goods.

(E) Compared to rising unemployment rates in the United States and Canada, increasing demand abroad for Chinese goods caused China's unemployment rate to fall by more than ten percent.

223. Unlike many collective bargaining agreements, which insist on treating broad classes of workers as equals, employees at the aluminum plant are compensated based on a wide range of criteria even if they have less than six months on the job.

(A) broad classes of workers as equals, employees at the aluminum plant are compensated based on a wide range of criteria

(B) broad classes of workers as equal to each other, employees are compensated in the plant's agreement based on a wide range of criteria

(C) workers as classes of equals, the aluminum plant's agreement compensates its employees based on a wide range of criteria

(D) broad classes of workers as equal to one another, the aluminum plant's agreement establishes that employees are compensated based on a wide range of criteria

(E) broad classes of workers as equals, the aluminum plant's agreement establishes that employees are compensated based on a wide range of criteria

224. <u>Bald eagles having straighter-edged ones, golden eagles possess wings that are slightly raised.</u>

    (A)   Bald eagles having straighter-edged ones, golden eagles possess wings that are slightly raised.

    (B)   With bald eagles having straighter-edged ones, golden eagles possess wings that are slightly raised.

    (C)   Whereas bald eagles have straighter-edged ones, with golden eagles possessing wings that are slightly raised.

    (D)   Golden eagles possess wings that are slightly raised, whereas bald eagles have straighter-edged ones.

    (E)   Golden eagles possessing wings slightly more raised, bald eagles have straighter-edged ones.

225. In his photographic motion studies, Thomas Eakins used a single negative for several exposures, <u>an approach which favorably contrasted with that of his contemporary Eadweard Muybridge, but did not earn</u> him as much acclaim in his lifetime, though opinions of his work have shifted dramatically since then.

    (A)   an approach which favorably contrasted with that of his contemporary Eadweard Muybridge, but did not earn

    (B)   an approach that favorably contrasted with his contemporary Eadweard Muybridge, but that did not earn

    (C)   an approach that favorably contrasted with that of his contemporary Eadweard Muybridge, but did not earn

    (D)   an approach which favorably contrasted with that of his contemporary Eadweard Muybridge, but did not earn

    (E)   an approach which favorably contrasted to that of his contemporary Eadweard Muybridge, but did not earn for

226.   Like the telephone, the internet represented a so-called
        "disruptive technology" and ultimately changed the way humans
        interact with one another.

        (A)   Like the telephone, the internet represented
        (B)   Like the telephone, the internet's representation was
        (C)   As the telephone, the internet represented
        (D)   As did the telephone, the internet's representation was
        (E)   The internet represented, as the telephone,

59 SC: Modifiers

A modifier is a part of a sentence like a subject or verb phrase. It can be as short as one word–an adjective is a kind of modifier, as is an adverb–but more commonly on the GMAT, a modifier is several words long.

As you might guess from the name, a modifier tells you something about (that is, "modifies") some other part of the sentence. Such a phrase can come before or after what it is modifying:

Before: "An early programming language adopted by artificial intelligence researchers, Lisp is still in use today."
After: "Lisp, an early programming language adopted by artificial intelligence researchers, is still in use today."

Both are correct. If the sentence were longer, one might be preferable for style reasons, but as the sentences stand now, they are interchangeable.

The important thing to note about those two forms of the sentence is that, in both cases, the modifier ("an early programming language adopted by artificial intelligence researchers") is immediately adjacent to what is being modified. If you moved the modifier to the end of the sentence, it would no longer be grammatically correct:
Lisp is still in use today, an early programming language adopted
    by artificial intelligence researchers.

That construction makes it sound like the modifier is referring to "today," while the meaning makes it clear that the phrase is meant to modify the name of the language, Lisp.

One more note before moving on. When a modifier is separated from the rest of the sentence by a pair of commas, the sentence needs to be grammatically correct with and without that modifier. For instance, this sentence:
"Lisp, an early programming language adopted by artificial
    intelligence researchers, is still in use today."

also needs to be grammatically correct in this form:
"Lisp is still in use today."

In some questions, the modifier won't even be underlined, meaning that you can ignore it altogether. Certainly the abbreviated sentence is easier to work with. If you know the modifier is correct, you can limit yourself to the shorter phrase.

"That" and "Which"

Many modifiers are connected to the rest of the sentence using the words "that" and "which." The difference between them is something that confuses more test-takers than any other grammatical issue. Here are a couple of examples of the words in action:

> "Lisp, the programming language that was adopted by early
> artificial intelligence researchers..."
> "Lisp, which was an early programming language, was adopted
> by artificial intelligence researchers..."

The biggest superficial difference between the two is the use of the comma. Most of the time, "which" is preceded by a comma, while "that" is not.

Technically, there is a more important distinction. "That" is restrictive, while "which" is non-restrictive. In layman's terms, "that" is an integral part of defining a subject, while "which" is providing some extra information. Consider the examples above.

That: "...the programming language that was adopted..."
In this case, "the programming language" isn't very specific. It isn't accurate to say that Lisp is "the programming language"–there are many programming languages, and Lisp is just one of them. However, "that" further defines the term. "...the programming language that was adopted..." tells us exactly what programming language we're talking about.

Which: "Lisp, which was an ..., was..."
Here, we can eliminate the entire phrase starting with "which" without losing much. Sure, the phrase provides some information that might be useful, but it doesn't affect the meaning of "Lisp," nor is it grammatically necessary.

Usually, checking for the comma is sufficient, but on more difficult problems, the more sophisticated understanding of "that" and "which" usage is necessary.

Be Careful With "Only"

One of the most misused words in the English language is "only"–and most of the time, it's a modifier. Place it next to a subject, and you know more about that subject. For instance, instead of saying, "I have seven questions remaining," you might say, "I have only seven questions remaining." By modifying "seven" with "only," you're adding meaning.

Note that "only" comes after the verb ("have") and before the subject ("seven questions"). Now consider an alternative: "I only have seven questions remaining." That probably sounds acceptable, since placing "only" before the verb is the most common mistake related to this word.

We've grown to accept the misuse of "only," so we've forgotten what it means to place "only" before the verb. This is a little difficult to explain, so you may need to re-read the following a couple of times.

When we modify a subject with "only," we're saying that that subject is "all there is." Let's reconsider the above two examples and try to translate them.

I have only seven questions remaining (correct)
Modification: "Only" modifies "seven questions."
Translation: All that's remaining is seven questions. There isn't an eighth question or a twentieth question.

I only have seven questions remaining (incorrect)
Modification: "Only" modifies "have."
Translation: All there is is "having" the seven questions; I won't eat the questions or cherish the questions or [any other verb] the questions.

The second example is tough to understand because it doesn't mean anything that we might want to express. In rare cases, we may want to place "only" before a verb. For instance, if you're not hungry, you might say, "I'm only drinking tonight" to indicate that you are not eating as well.

At a bare minimum, pay close attention to the word "only" when it appears in Sentence Correction questions and answers. With practice, you'll learn to parse the (sometimes senseless) meaning no matter where "only" is placed.

60   SC: Modifiers: Practice

231.   Based on extant archeological evidence, each hunting season women and men collaborated in pursuit of game animals that would feed the tribe and that, contrary to textbook histories, women hunting alone were not uncommon.

  (A)   Based on extant archeological evidence, each hunting season women and men collaborated in pursuit of game animals that would feed

  (B)   Based on extant archeological evidence, each hunting season women and men had collaborated in pursuit of game animals which would feed

  (C)   According to extant archeological evidence, each hunting season women and men collaborated in pursuit of game animals that would feed

  (D)   Extant archeological evidence indicates that each hunting season women and men collaborated in pursuit of game animals with which they fed

  (E)   Extant archeological evidence indicates each hunting season women and men had collaborated in pursuit of game animals for feeding

232.   The typical military coup fails relatively bloodlessly, amassing little support, collapsing within hours of its first public claim to power, but, having usually gotten the full attention of a country's leaders, eventually, once an initial retaliation period ends, the ideology behind the coup makes subtle inroads in the nation's government.

  (A)   support, collapsing within hours of its first public claim to power, but, having usually gotten the full attention of a country's leaders,

  (B)   support, collapses within hours of its first public claim to power, but with the usual full attention of a country's leaders gotten,

  (C)   support and collapsing within hours of its first public claim to power, but it usually gets the full attention of a country's leaders, and

  (D)   support and collapsing within hours of its first public claim to power, but with the usual full attention of a country's leaders, and

  (E)   support, collapses within hours of its first making a public claim to power, but with the usual full attention of a country's leaders, and

233. The gypsy moth, although it is eradicated in the northwestern United States, it has established itself throughout the continent and is able to defoliate over one million acres of forest each year.

    (A)   The gypsy moth, although it is eradicated in the northwestern United States, it has established itself throughout the continent and is able to

    (B)   The gypsy moth, although eradicated in the northwestern United States, it has still established itself throughout the continent and can

    (C)   Although still established throughout the continent, the gypsy moth has been eradicated in the northwestern United States and can

    (D)   Although having been eradicated in the northwestern United States, the gypsy moth has still established itself throughout the continent and has the potential to

    (E)   Although eradicated in the northwestern United States, the gypsy moth has established itself throughout the continent and can

234. Displayed one hundred years to the day after the signing of the Declaration of Independence on July 4, 1876, residents of San Francisco witnessed electric light for the first time.

    (A)   Displayed one hundred years to the day after the signing of the Declaration of Independence on July 4, 1876, residents of San Francisco witnessed electric light for the first time.

    (B)   Displayed on July 4, 1876, one hundred years to the day after the signing of the Declaration of Independence, electric light was witnessed by residents of San Francisco for the first time.

    (C)   Displayed on July 4, 1876, one hundred years to the day after the signing of the Declaration of Independence, residents of San Francisco witnessed electric light for the first time.

    (D)   Witnessing electric light for the first time, the display for residents of San Francisco on July 4, 1876 one hundred years to the day after the signing of the Declaration of Independence.

    (E)   Witnessing electric light for the first time, one hundred years to the day after the signing of the Declaration of Independence, on July 4, 1876, the display for residents of San Francisco took place.

235. Nearly 20 genera of electric fish are classified in the
Mormyridae taxon, which includes 203 different species,
more than all the other taxons of electric fish combined.

(A)   Nearly 20 genera of electric fish are classified in the
       Mormyridae taxon, which includes 203 different species,
       more than all the other taxons of electric fish combined.
(B)   With 203 different species, that is more than all the other
       taxons of electric fish combined, the Mormyridae taxon
       has nearly 20 genera of electric fish that are classified
       in it.
(C)   The Mormyridae taxon, with nearly 20 genera of electric
       fish are classified in it, it includes more different species
       than all the other taxons of electric fish combined, 203.
(D)   While nearly 20 genera of electric fish are classified in
       it, the Mormyridae taxon includes 203 different species,
       which is more than all the other taxons of electric fish
       combined.
(E)   More than all the other taxons of electric fish combined,
       the Mormyridae taxon, with nearly 20 genera of electric
       fish classified in it, includes 203 different species.

61   SC: Pronouns

As discussed in the "parts of speech" chapter above, pronouns are words that stand in for nouns. Pronouns include "it," "he," and "they," among others.

There are two basic rules that govern pronoun usage on the GMAT. The first is relatively straightforward: the pronoun used must be correct in type and in number.

Type: A human being is a "he" or "she," and things belonging to a human belong to "him" or "her." An animal or inanimate object, however, is always an "it."

Number: This is the same idea as subject/verb agreement. If a pronoun is standing in for a singular noun, use a singular pronoun, such as "it" and "she." If it is standing in for a plural noun, use a plural pronoun, such as "they" or "their."

Because these first rules are so straightforward, make it a habit to check every time you see a pronoun. The GMAT uses the same kind of tricks to disguise plural and singular nouns when testing pronouns as it does when testing subject/verb agreement.

Clarity of Reference

When a sentence uses a pronoun, it must refer to something. It wouldn't be correct to write, "She is driving across town," unless we knew who "she" was.

Similarly, it must be clear what, exactly, the pronoun refers to. Consider this sentence:
"Janelle and Kiva are roommates, and she is driving across town."

In this case, "she" could refer to either of two people, but the sentence gives us no way to know which. That isn't correct either. It's usually easy to spot that error when there are multiple people named, but when the word "it" is used, it can be much more difficult to spot the various singular nouns "it" could refer to.

None of these rules are particularly tricky, especially when compared to the various verb tenses and some of the modifier rules presented in the previous chapter. For some students, that's what causes the problem. Pronoun guidelines are easy to understand, but the key on the GMAT isn't just to know the rules, it's to spot those occasions when they must be applied. Whenever you see a pronoun, check for the following:

1. Is its type correct?
2. Is its number correct?
3. Does it refer to something?
4. Is there only one thing it could refer to?

If the answer to any of those questions is "no," hunt for a better choice!

62   SC: Pronouns: Practice

241.   To protect the depleting supply of migratory bird resting and nesting areas, state agencies are using water resources twice as fast as <u>their natural rate, consulting with experts</u> prior to the construction of new dams, and studying the effects of pollution on migratory patterns.

   (A)   their natural rate, consulting with experts
   (B)   their natural rate, experts consulted with
   (C)   naturally using them, consulting with experts
   (D)   the previous rate, consulting with experts
   (E)   the previous rate, a result of experts consulted with

242.   The Navajo people adapted to life in captivity in New Mexico in the second half of the nineteenth century, bringing <u>a distinctive weaving style with them, through which was maintained both a livelihood and</u> a way of preserving their traditional culture.

   (A)   a distinctive weaving style with them, through which was maintained both a livelihood and
   (B)   a distinctive weaving style with them, and through which maintaining both a livelihood and
   (C)   with them a distinctive weaving style, through which they maintained both a livelihood and
   (D)   with them a distinctive weaving style, through which maintains both a livelihood and
   (E)   with them a distinctive weaving style, and maintaining through it both a livelihood and

243. When the company released its flagship product in 1988,
      <u>they had already built a worldwide distribution system
      comprising six geographical regions based on customer
      demand for</u> its existing catalogue.

      (A) they had already built a worldwide distribution system
           comprising six geographical regions based on customer
           demand for
      (B) they already had built a worldwide distribution system
           comprising six geographical regions that was based
           on customer demand made of
      (C) they already had built a worldwide distribution system
           that comprised six geographical regions based on
           demand by customers for
      (D) it had already built a worldwide distribution system
           that comprised six geographical regions based on
           customer demand for
      (E) it already had built a worldwide distribution system
           comprising six geographical regions being based on
           customer demand it had for

244. According to project managers, the recent decrease in Project
      Phoenix funding <u>so that it was the lowest in a decade</u> signals that
      public interest in identifying sources of extraterrestrial intelligence
      is waning.

      (A) so that it was the lowest in a decade
      (B) so that it was the lowest decade-long level
      (C) to what would be the lowest in a decade
      (D) to a decade-long low level
      (E) to the lowest level in a decade

160

245. <u>With a recognition that there are challenges associated with adopting new curriculum and securing additional funding,</u> local school boards handling teacher requests typically encourage creative solutions that utilize existing resources.

- (A) With a recognition that there are challenges associated with adopting new curriculum and securing additional funding
- (B) Because adopting new curriculum and securing additional funding have challenges they recognize
- (C) Because of a recognition that adopting new curriculum and securing additional funding having challenges
- (D) Recognizing the challenges associated with adopting new curriculum and securing additional funding
- (E) Since adopting new curriculum and securing additional funding have challenges associated with them and they recognize it

246. Tsunami-related property damage rose 3.1 percent in the 12 months that ended in March, considerably <u>more than it did</u> in the previous year.

- (A) more than it did
- (B) more than they did
- (C) more than it was
- (D) greater than
- (E) greater than it was

63 SC: Idioms

Idioms are one of the most problematic areas of study for GMAT test-takers, especially those for whom English is not a first language. There are literally thousands, even tens of thousands, of English idioms, and there is simply no way to learn them all.

Thankfully, you have two things working in your favor. First, there are a small number of idioms that are tested much more frequently than the rest. I'll discuss those in this chapter. Second, most Sentence Correction sentences and choices have more than one error. If you don't know an idiom, a question might be harder than if you did, but you may still have a chance to answer it correctly without guessing.

Before we get to the list, one more note. In addition to catalogues like the one in this chapter, the best way to learn idioms is to do practice questions and study explanations. There are over 100 Sentence Correction practice questions in each of The Official Guide for GMAT Review and The Official Guide for GMAT Verbal Review, and each one of those practice questions has an explanation written by the makers of the test. Not every one includes an idiom, but if you learn all of the idioms tested in those practice questions, you'll know nearly all of those that might arise on test day. Beyond that, your time is better spent studying other parts of the exam than looking for a still longer list of idioms to master.

Without further ado, on to the list.

Comparisons

Most of the common idioms on the GMAT have to do with comparisons.

Less and fewer. When items can be counted (such as apples or raindrops), use "fewer." When they cannot be counted (such as courage or sand), use "less." For example, "I have less money than you do." (Money cannot be counted, though dollars can be.) By contrast, "I have more coins in my pocket than you do."

Many and much. Like less and fewer, "many" refers to things that can be counted: "I don't have many vacation days remaining." "Much" is used when they can't be counted: "I don't have much time left." (Note, again, time cannot be counted, though days, minutes, or hours could be.)

Like and as. "Like" compares things, while "as" compares actions. For instance, "I have a car just like yours," and "I'm driving to school tomorrow, just as you are."

162

Like and such as. "Such as" indicates an example, while "like" indicates something similar. "This year's team has played many important games, such as the one last Saturday." Or: "This year's team, like last year's team, has played many important games."

Either...or. Whenever the word "either" signals a comparison, the word "or" will separate them. "They will either sell their shares this afternoon or wait until tomorrow morning."

Neither...nor. Whenever the word "neither" signals a comparison of things, the word "nor" will separate them. "I neither agree with his politics nor do I appreciate his tone."

Both...and. When a pair of items is introduced with the word "both," the word "and" will separate them. "I cheer for both the Athletics and the Raiders."

Less/more...than. When a comparison is introduced using either "less" or "more," the second item being compared is preceded with "than." An example: "I've spent less time in Southeast Asia than I have in Europe."

As...as. When starting a comparison with "as," the second term must be introduced with "as" as well. For instance, "Few poems are as powerful as Whitman's."

Not only...but also. When the first part of a comparison is introduced with "not only," the second must start with "but." The word "also" has to be part of the second term as well. For instance, "They not only passed the bill, but they also did so without caving to the opposition."

Whether and if. When there are two possibilities, "whether" is appropriate. If there is one event that might or might not happen, use "if." For instance, "I'll attend the party whether she is there or not." Or: "If she'll be there, I'll attend the party."

A Couple of Others

Between and among. Use "between" when describing a choice of two items, and "among" for more than two items. "It was difficult to choose between the two candidates." Or: "I had a hard time selecting a sweater from among the many styles on sale."

Each, both, and all. "Each" is a singular subject: "Each of the members of the legislature is an elected official." "Both" and "all" create plural subjects: "Both [or "All"] of the candidates are campaigning on domestic issues."

This is Important

I've said it before, but it's worth repeating. The list here is not meant to be exhaustive, or anything close. You can't learn every idiom you might see on the test, and you shouldn't try. It is better to assume that you'll miss a question or two on your GMAT because of some obscure idiom than to spend a disproportionate amount of your study time memorizing hundreds of idioms in the hope of getting those one or two questions right. This list is important, but if you go very far beyond it, the law of diminishing returns will severely affect your time spent learning idioms.

64 SC: Idioms: Practice

251.   Founded in 1963 at the Lincolnshire apiary of Terence Theaker, the Bee Breeder's Association uses DNA analysis of native strains of honeybees along with morphometric methods <u>for establishing lineage of as many as, or of</u> more than 100 bee species, including 35 subspecies of the Dark European Honeybee.

(A)   for establishing lineage of as many as, or of
(B)   to establish lineages of as many, or
(C)   to establish the lineage of
(D)   that establishes the lineages of
(E)   that establishes the lineage of as many as, or

252.   Having finally mollified the opposition leadership by granting it a seat in the new government, <u>it must now be ascertained by the president's advisors how the country can both expand foreign trade and work effectively toward peace in the region, which they were unable to do in the past.</u>

(A)   it must now be ascertained by the president's advisors how the country can both expand foreign trade and work effectively toward peace in the region, which they were unable to do in the past

(B)   it must now be ascertained by the president's advisors how the country can both expand foreign trade and must work effectively toward peace, which they were unable to do in the past in the region

(C)   the president's advisors must now ascertain both how the country can expand foreign trade and work effectively toward peace in the region, which they were unable to do in the past

(D)   the president's advisors must now ascertain how the country can both expand foreign trade and work effectively toward peace in the region, which they were unable to do in the past

(E)   the president's advisors must now ascertain how the country can both expand foreign trade and also how to make it work more effectively than in the past toward peace in the region

253. Rejecting the limitations of the acoustic instruments used in traditional bluegrass music, upright bass player Ebo Walker and his band decided <u>of including electronic instruments in bluegrass so that it could continue to expand</u> its boundaries to accommodate "fusion" styles influenced by genres such as jazz and rock.

  (A) of including electronic instruments in bluegrass so that it could continue to expand
  (B) that electronic instruments should be included in bluegrass, and that it expanded
  (C) about the importance of electronic instruments included in bluegrass while expanding
  (D) that electronic instruments could be included in bluegrass, which has continued to expand
  (E) of the inclusion of electronic instruments being in bluegrass and expand

254. The personal reminiscences of many personal acquaintances and business associates support the notion <u>of there being many women who were significant figures</u> in Andrew Carnegie's formative years.

  (A) of there being many women who were significant figures
  (B) of there being many women who significantly figured
  (C) of many women who significantly figured
  (D) that there were many women who significantly figured
  (E) that there were many women of figurative significance

255. A recent biography suggests that until Tolstoy published *War and Peace*, he did not have, <u>or</u> seem likely to develop, a reputation as an important novelist.

  (A) or
  (B) nor
  (C) or did
  (D) nor did he
  (E) nor did he not

65 SC: Other Errors

Many of the errors that fall into this final chapter were briefly discussed in the chapter above that discussed the hierarchy of errors. These remaining topics are all Category 2 and Category 3 errors–that is, they don't automatically disqualify an answer choice. Instead, they are "tie-breakers" of sorts, ways to choose between a pair of possible answers when neither of them is very attractive.

Passive Voice

Every sentence has a subject, and most sentences have an object as well. An object is a second noun (or phrase, like "the citizens of Bulgaria") that the subject acts on. In the sentence, "The citizens of Bulgaria will vote in the election," the subject is "The citizens of Bulgaria" and the object is "the election."

That example is structured in "active voice" because the subject comes first. The subject acts on the object, rather than the other way around. The term "passive voice" refers to sentence structures in which the object in presented first, such as, "The election will be voted in by the citizens of Bulgaria."

Usually, sentences using passive voice require a few extra words, and they don't sound as forceful. For this reason, the GMAT prefers active voice.

Punctuation

I have never seen a GMAT Sentence Correction question that hinges entirely on punctuation usage, but there are occasional questions with punctuation mistakes. In those cases, there are other grammatical errors that help you identify the correct answer, but if you know some basic punctuation rules, you will have an edge. The following two rules are, by far, the most common on the GMAT:

1. ", and." If two phrases are separated by the word "and," and the word "and" is preceded by a comma, the two phrases must both be complete sentences. For instance, "He is awake, and he is ready to go," is correct, but "He is awake, and ready to go" is incorrect. The latter example would only be correct if the comma were removed. The same rule applies to the word "but" instead of "and."

2. Semi-colon usage. There are two forms of acceptable semi-colon usage. If a list contains an item that includes a comma, the items in the list should be separated by semi-colons. For instance, "He traveled with three pieces of luggage: a garment bag; a small duffel; and a briefcase, in which he kept his important papers." The semi-colon usage is only correct because the third item in that list includes a comma. Otherwise, the list items should be separated with commas.

The other acceptable form is to separate two phrases that are complete sentences. This is rare, but I have seen it on the occasional GMAT practice question. An example of proper usage would be, "He is awake; he's ready to go." As long as what precedes the semi-colon and what follows the semi-colon are both complete sentences, it is correct.

Everything Else

As I mentioned in the chapter above on the hierarchy of errors, the GMAT likes efficiency. All else equal, it prefers brevity. If you have eliminated all but two choices and have absolutely no idea how to eliminate one more, it's generally a good bet to select the shorter of the two answers.

Ultimately, there are no hard and fast rules when it comes to style issues like awkwardness, sentence construction, and efficiency. The best way to understand what the GMAT is looking for is to examine a lot of realistic practice questions. As I noted in the idioms chapter, the makers of the GMAT have published hundreds of Sentence Correction questions, all of which went through the same editors who determine what you will see on your exam. Take advantage of those questions.

There is a distinct tone to GMAT Sentence Correction questions, and it is one that many test-prep providers have not succeeded in capturing. It is vastly better to spend your time with SC questions from The Official Guide than SC practice questions from a Kaplan or Manhattan GMAT book. The general grammar issues will be correct no matter which resources you use, but only in retired GMAT questions will you be constantly exposed to the tone of the "real thing."

Analyze as many realistic practice questions as you can, and carefully read the explanations, as well. By the time you take your GMAT, many of the rules in the preceding chapters will be internalized, so you won't have to consciously go through my four-point pronoun checklist, or think about Category 1, 2, and 3 errors. You'll probably never correctly answer every SC question you see, but with the skills and strategies discussed in this section, you can get close.

66   SC: Other: Practice

261.   Artificial Intelligence researchers have designed interactive "bots" that emulate <u>human conversation, and task management has been automated as well, whether it be for technology professionals or</u> also for computer users with no knowledge of the field.

(A)   human conversation, and task management has been automated as well, whether it be for technology professionals or

(B)   human conversation, automating task management as well, both for technology professionals but

(C)   human conversation and also automating task management, for technology professionals and

(D)   human conversation and they automate task management, whether it be for technology professionals or

(E)   human conversation and automate task management, not only for technology professionals but

262.   Trade analysts are devising a number of models that can isolate causes of <u>economic inefficiency, to which they will then generate solutions; their aim is mainly creating</u> a system that will encourage unrestricted international trade.

(A)   economic inefficiency, to which they will then generate solutions; their aim is mainly creating

(B)   economic inefficiency, then generating solutions to them; mainly to create

(C)   economic inefficiency and then generate solutions to them; the analysts' main aim is to create

(D)   economic inefficiency as well as generating solutions to them; their main aim is creation of

(E)   economic inefficiency and generating solutions to them; mainly, the analysts' aim is creating

263.   Even though the poetry of Gerard Manley Hopkins is best
        known for its confluence of religious and erotic imagery,
        some critics say that it is most remarkable for its extensive
        use of rhetorical devices such as alliteration, assonance,
        onomatopoeia and internal rhyme that <u>pointed the way for
        free verse, even</u> apparently dissimilar poets such as Jack
        Kerouac.

        (A)   pointed the way for free verse, even
        (B)   pointed the way to free verse, even by
        (C)   points to free verse, so even by
        (D)   pointed the way to free verse, even the work of
        (E)   points for free verse, even the work of

264.   Although concerned with the number of venomous copperhead
        snakes he encountered on his trek, the traveler recognized
        <u>dangers posed by this sort of snake as far less than they
        typically are for more mundane matters, such as hydration.</u>

        (A)   dangers posed by this sort of snake as far less than
               they typically are for more mundane matters, such as
               hydration
        (B)   dangers posed by this sort of snake as being far less
               than what the dangers typically are for more mundane
               matters, such as those like hydration
        (C)   dangers typically being posed by this sort of snake to
               be far less as they typically are for more mundane
               matters, like hydration
        (D)   that the dangers posed by this sort of snake were far
               less than the dangers typically posed by more mundane
               matters, such as hydration, are
        (E)   that the dangers posed by this sort of snake were far less
               than those associated with more mundane matters, such
               as hydration

170

265.   When testing the inactivated poliovirus vaccine that was
        licensed for a mass vaccination campaign in the United
        States in 1955, combined in it by the vaccine's creator,
        Jonas Salk, were three wild, virulent reference strains.

   (A)   When testing the inactivated poliovirus vaccine that
         was licensed for a mass vaccination campaign in the
         United States in 1955, combined in it by the vaccine's
         creator, Jonas Salk, were three wild, virulent reference
         strains.
   (B)   Combining three wild, virulent reference strains, a test of
         the inactivated poliovirus vaccine that was licensed for a
         mass vaccination campaign in the United States in 1955
         that Jonas Salk created.
   (C)   When the inactivated poliovirus vaccine created by Jonas
         Salk was licensed for a mass vaccination campaign in the
         United States in 1955, three wild, virulent reference strains
         had been combined in it.
   (D)   Three wild, virulent reference strains, combined in Jonas
         Salk's test of the inactivated poliovirus vaccine in 1955,
         that was licensed for a mass vaccination campaign.
   (E)   When Jonas Salk tested the inactivated poliovirus vaccine
         that was licensed for a mass vaccination campaign in the
         United States in 1955, he combined in it three wild,
         virulent reference strains.

266.   Three newly-formed democracies received diplomatic
        recognition from Great Britain this year, bringing to 11 the
        number of countries so recognized since the current
        administration came to power.

   (A)   bringing
   (B)   and brings
   (C)   and it brings
   (D)   and it brought
   (E)   and brought

67   Further Resources

The GMAC, the organization that administers the GMAT, has done you a favor. Two books–The Official Guide for GMAT Review, and The Official Guide for GMAT Verbal Review–contain hundreds of practice verbal questions, written by the makers of the test. There are dozens, maybe even hundreds of other sources for practice material, but there's no need to use anything other than these two.

Between these two books, you have over 600 practice verbal questions (along with explanations, also written by the makers of the test) at your disposal. The most successful GMAT students take full advantage of those, both studying the details in the explanations and absorbing the unique tone of the questions. They won't show you every possible permutation of a test item you might encounter on the GMAT itself, but they'll get close.

If you find that additional practice would be useful, the best resource is my book, GMAT Verbal Challenge, which is scheduled to be published in Summer 2011. It contains 600 practice GMAT Verbal questions, and will be available at gmathacks.com, Amazon.com and other retailers.

68 Additional Practice: Critical Reasoning

301. Containers formed from plastic and bound together by biodegradable cornstarch form a vacuum that is highly useful for keeping food fresh, but unfortunately leave behind ecological waste when they decompose. No other containers can keep food fresh for as long a time. Fully biodegradable containers, on the other hand, although not as effective, can be changed regularly while food is stored. Clearly, therefore, using containers that create ecological waste can play no part in long-term food storage.

The argument is most vulnerable to the objection that it fails to

(A) consider that there might be technology available to mitigate the ecological impact of plastic containers

(B) identify any type of container for food storage that could be used instead of the container it rejects

(C) distinguish among the various kinds of fully biodegradable containers

(D) allow for the possibility that some circumstances necessitate the use of containers that create ecological waste

(E) allow for the possibility that containers that create ecological waste may be useful in storing non-food items

302. Which of the following most logically completes the argument given below?

Members of a vegan commune tend to live a largely cooperative life-style, and they rarely take jobs in the outside world. Few of them enter into disputes, and the disputes that do occur rarely require legal intervention, as is common in the rest of society. Such members often do become embroiled in lawsuits when they leave the commune and take mainstream jobs. Though suggestive, these factors do not establish jobs as the reason for the increase in their involvement in lawsuits, however, because _____.

(A) once a member has left the commune, he or she must find a job or will have a difficult time surviving in the outside world

(B) leaving the commune entails many other sorts of lifestyle changes beyond that of employment

(C) it is possible to maintain gainful employment without developing any kind of legal trouble

(D) people who spend their entire adult lives working in the corporate world generally find themselves named in a lawsuit at least once in their careers

(E) vegan communes require that their members submit problems to community mediation before seeking legal recourse

303. When people who have been deprived of water are shown pictures of liquids and asked whether they are thirsty, they respond, "No." Some scientists try to reconcile this response by suggesting that the human mind has evolved a psychological defense against severe thirst, and that the people convince themselves that they are hydrated when in fact they have drunk nothing for hours.

Which of the following challenges indicates the most serious weakness in the attempted explanation described above?

(A) Why do dehydrated people all respond the same way in the situation described?

(B) How many hours of liquid deprivation are necessary before a person demonstrates this response?

(C) How would the response differ if a dehydrated person were shown a glass of water instead of pictures?

(D) Why is the response is need of any special explanation?

(E) What is the evolutionary advantage of falsely believing one is hydrated?

304.   English teachers have modified their curriculums, increasing the curriculums' relevance to students' lives. Teachers who taught the student-centered curriculum last school year spent saw higher levels of student engagement and their students still passed state-mandated standardized tests at rates comparable to those achieved using the old curriculum. Teaching the old curriculum, however, requires a considerably more regimented approach, and what these teachers gained in terms of student engagement was balanced by a decline in classroom behavior. Therefore, for most teachers, switching to a more student-centered curriculum would be unlikely to improve students' overall learning experience.

Which of the following would it be most useful to know in order to evaluate the argument?

(A)   Whether, for students who must take state-mandated standardized tests, the results of the tests reflect what they have learned during the past year

(B)   Whether the quality of the students' learning experience is related to the level of classroom behavior

(C)   Whether the modified English curriculums are comparable to modified curriculums in other subject areas

(D)   Whether the state-mandated standardized tests have changed in the past few years

(E)   Whether, after teachers return to the old curriculum, the behavior of their students will improve

305.   Because few scientists want to be associated with controversial findings in the eyes of an supervisor, information about climate change is progressively warped and twisted as it goes up each rung on the academic ladder. The lab director is, therefore, less knowledgeable about current climate change research than are post-doctoral fellows or research assistants.

The conclusion drawn above is based on the assumption that

(A)   some scientists are more concerned about experimental validity than about their hopes of future promotion

(B)   lab directors know nothing about current climate change research beyond what their subordinates tell them

(C)   climate change is a more controversial topic among young research assistants than among older lab directors

(D)   scientists should be rewarded for innovation, not for skill in office politics

(E)   on the most important issues, lab directors rarely agree with post-doctoral fellows and research assistants

306.   Since name-brand products are generally considered superior to
        their generic counterparts, customers are willing to pay more for
        name-brand products. Thus, firms that manufacture name-brand
        products should earn higher profits per unit sold than do firms that
        manufacture comparable generic products.

        Which of the following, if true about firms that manufacture
        name-brand products, casts the most serious doubt on the
        conclusion drawn above?

        (A)   Firms that manufacture name-brand products generally
               own the patents to their products, while their generic
               counterparts often must license production methods.
        (B)   Firms that manufacture generic products are usually
               subsidiaries of retailers, and the low prices of their
               products serve as advertisements for their parent
               companies.
        (C)   The rate of defective products that reach store shelves is
               no higher for generic products than it is for name-brand
               products.
        (D)   Name-brand products are supported by costly media
               advertising campaigns, which generic products usually are
               not.
        (E)   Most manufacturing companies are publicly owned, so any
               profits end up in the hands of shareholders.

307.   In Arcadia, of residents who installed new smoke alarm systems in
        their homes, the fraction who purchased their equipment from Fire-
        Away Home Protection Systems has declined by ten percent over
        the last five years. Since the company is one of the biggest
        employers in Arcadia, this drop is expected to result in numerous
        job losses and therefore damage the city's overall reputation.

        Which of the following, if true, most seriously weakens the
        argument given?

        (A)   The percentage of homes in Arcadia with smoke alarm
               systems installed is one of the highest in the nation.
        (B)   A company that gained market share in the last five years,
               Smoke-Off Inc., does not employ any Arcadia residents.
        (C)   The majority of Fire-Away's annual revenue comes from
               maintaining existing smoke alarm systems.
        (D)   In the last five years, thirty percent of Arcadia residents
               have purchased new carbon monoxide alarms, which
               Fire-Away does not sell.
        (E)   Since Fire-Away relocated to Arcadia, the amount of fire-
               related damage to property in Arcadia has decreased by
               two-thirds.

308.   In the northern regions of Brazil, the rise in pressure from
        environmental groups has led to a drop in the deforestation process
        by the agricultural industry, where protected acreage is up 60%
        when compared to seven years ago. Farmers in these regions
        have discovered, however, that the amount of soybeans that were
        harvested decreased substantially in the first three years after
        protection began, but has risen to pre-protection levels in the last
        four years.

        Which of the following, if true, most helps to explain the change
        between the first three years and the following years in the soybean
        harvest?

        (A)   The harvests of other staple crops in northern Brazil, such
               as maize, did not rise to their pre-protection levels until
               at least one year after the soybean harvest did.

        (B)   Soybean farmers have attempted to cultivate land where
               deforestation has taken place, but with little success to
               date.

        (C)   A severe drought affected many crops in these regions over
               the first three years in which the protection was in effect.

        (D)   The increase in protected acreage was mostly seen in the
               first and last years of the seven-year period.

        (E)   The size of the labor pool available to soybean farmers
               increased as protection spread due to the lessened demand
               for workers in the lumber industry.

309.   Hot Coals Paving Co. has recently shifted at least partly from traditional asphalt formulas that include high levels of petrochemicals to environmentally safer ones based on biodegradable products. The question has been raised whether it can be determined that **for a given paved surface Hot Coals now causes fewer petrochemicals to be introduced into the environment than were introduced previously.** The response, undoubtedly, is yes, since the amount of biodegradable sealant needed to create a smooth roadway surface is equal to the amount of petrochemical-based sealant, provided that all other conditions are equal.

In the argument given, the two boldfaced portions play which of the following roles?

(A)   Each provides support for the conclusion of the argument.

(B)   The first provides support for the conclusion of the argument; the second calls that conclusion into question.

(C)   The first states the conclusion of the argument; the second calls that conclusion into question.

(D)   The first provides support for the conclusion of the argument; the second identifies the content of that conclusion.

(E)   The first identifies the content of the conclusion of the argument; the second provides support for that conclusion.

310.   Importer: Murano glass, currently sold in stores all over the world, was first produced in Venice in the late thirteenth century. Artisans claim that the glass produced today is as similar to the original glass as in possible in modern workshops. Although pieces such as lampshades are clearly only useful for modern customers, the glass from which those pieces are made is produced using largely the same techniques that would have been employed more than seven hundred years ago.

The considerations given best serve as part of an argument that

(A)   the artisans that design Murano's products must have based their lampshades on similar artifacts from late thirteenth-century Venice

(B)   the presence of lampshades among Murano's offerings does not serve as evidence against the artisans' claim

(C)   in Italy the training of glassmakers is based on the same underlying principles that guided the training of glassmakers in Italy for the last seven hundred years

(D)   while lamps did not exist in thirteenth-century Venice, similarly-

shaped items served other purposes

(E)   glass made by the same process as was used in the thirteenth century is much more fragile than most glass manufactured today

311.   Last year many high-calorie foods forbidden to members of the Weight-Off weight loss program were consumed in secret. This practice had the result that many members failed to lose weight. In order to increase the amount of weight that Weight-Off members lose to 25 percent over last year's levels, Weight-Off has refined its weight loss regimen. This year nutritionists will monitor members' food diaries to limit the number of cheating dieters to two-thirds of last year's number.

Which of the following is required for the retooled Weight-Off program to achieve its goal?

(A)   The total number of Weight-Off members will be no higher this year than it was last year.

(B)   The food diaries kept by Weight-Off members will accurately reflect the foods they consume.

(C)   The Weight-Off program will allow its members a small amount of high-calorie food to help control cravings.

(D)   The distribution and monitoring of food diaries for each member will not be financially prohibitive for the program.

(E)   This year, no high-calorie foods will be consumed by Weight-Off members.

312. The most advanced version of high-speed train manufactured in Colbyville has traditionally been considerably faster than that manufactured in nearby Harpertown. Since Harpertown lifted its embargo on Colbyville's trains last year, the number of passengers traveling by high-speed train in Harpertown has remained stable. Nevertheless, recent statistics show an increase in the number of high-speed trains manufactured in Colbyville and purchased by Harpertown. Consequently, revised passenger statistics will most likely show that the number of passengers riding high-speed trains in Harpertown has risen.

Which of the following is an assumption on which the argument depends?

(A)   There is a relationship between the number of trains manufactured in Colbyville and the number of trains manufactured in Harpertown.

(B)   There is a relationship between import levels and public transit usage in Harpertown.

(C)   There is a relationship between the speed of trains in service and the number of passengers riding those trains.

(D)   Trains manufactured in Colbyville have safety features that trains manufactured in Harpertown do not.

(E)   Train riders in Colbyville place a higher value on speed than do train riders in Harpertown.

313. Spectrum Labs runs hundreds of experiments daily with electron microscopes, which feature magnification capacities of up to 200,000 times. Spectrum Labs depends for its research on detailed and high-definition images and therefore is planning to upgrade its current electron microscopes to Cray electron microscopes, whose exceptional magnification capacities lead to increased discoveries and fewer disputes over conflicting analyses of specimens.

Which of the following, if true, could present the most serious disadvantage for Spectrum Labs in replacing their existing electron microscopes with Cray microscopes?

(A) At magnification levels beyond 100,000 times, Cray microscopes do not produce high-definition images.

(B) None of Spectrum Labs' competitors that use electron microscopes use Cray microscopes.

(C) Higher magnification levels are likely to reduce the need for some human analysis, which may lead to layoffs among researchers at Spectrum Labs.

(D) It is commonly believed in the industry that, each year, electron microscopes become both more powerful and more inexpensive.

(E) The Cray microscopes would allow Spectrum Labs to market to clients who currently require services beyond Spectrum's ability to deliver.

314.   Regietheater is the practice of reinterpreting from a traditional staging an opera or a play that previous directors have attempted to stage in a traditional manner. Since a theater's ultimate goal is to attract the largest possible audience to the art of theater, any play or opera that can be staged in an avant-garde manner while drawing larger audiences than would be drawn by a traditional production should be encouraged.

Which of the following, if true, most seriously weakens the argument?

(A)   One of the main reasons audiences are drawn to reinterpretations is the common avant-garde practice of involving audience members in each night's performance.

(B)   In order to stage a convincing performance of a traditional play in an avant-garde manner, the director must be an expert in both the context of the original work and the aesthetics of the avant-garde.

(C)   The works of certain playwrights, such as Shakespeare, are commonly reinterpreted, while others, such as Marlowe, are rarely presented in an avant-garde manner.

(D)   Avant-garde productions often succeed in drawing audiences but fail in pleasing those audiences, making it less likely that theatergoers will attend other productions of the same work.

(E)   The freedom of reinterpreting a traditional work generally gives the director many more choices in casting, staging, and framing a piece.

315.　According to a prediction made about the early twenty-first century published in 1960, the process of freeze-drying would revolutionize ice cream production. A partial vacuum would force out water, and the dehydration process would prevent melting and increase shelf life.

Which of the following, if true, most strongly indicates that the logic of the prediction above is flawed?

(A)　Buyers generally prefer ice cream at a temperature higher than that at which ice cream freezes.

(B)　Since ice is merely a different form of water, any process that removes water would also remove ice, a critical component in ice cream.

(C)　It cannot be taken for granted that an increase in shelf life is always beneficial.

(D)　If the proposed plan for freeze-drying ice cream were implemented, distributors would be under less pressure to deliver ice cream quickly.

(E)　In order for production-line workers to avoid the danger inherent in working near such a powerful vacuum, the entire process could be automated.

316.　Which of the following best completes the passage below?

People buy moral superiority when they buy organic products. They want to be associated with something healthy. Bulk availability and generic brands should not be made available at natural grocery stores because _____.

(A)　there is no reason that purchases made in bulk cannot result in healthier diets

(B)　an ever-smaller percentage of purchasers respond to the appeal of moral superiority

(C)　generic versions of non-organic products are often healthier than non-generic versions.

(D)　customers consider generic brands "average," which is not notably healthy

(E)　purchasers of organic products value price as well as health

317.   Plan: Concerned about the health of its Amazon Parrot population, ornithologists at the Milltown zoo decided four years ago to increase the number of zoo-provided vitamin tablets given to all Amazon Parrots in the aviary.

Result: Many of the Milltown zoo's Amazon Parrots have no higher vitamin levels than they had before the increase.

Further information: The annual illness rate of Amazon Parrots since the vitamin increase has been below 3 percent, and the increased number of vitamin tablets has been duly received by all the aviary's birds.

In light of the further information, which of the following, if true, does most to explain the result that followed implementation of the plan?

(A)   The vitamins in the tablets provided to the Amazon Parrots are most effective at preventing, not curing, illness.

(B)   The annual illness rate of birds other than Amazon Parrots in the aviary has also been below 3 percent.

(C)   When Amazon Parrots are provided vitamin tablets, they are less likely to eat foods containing those vitamins.

(D)   While visitors to the zoo are discouraged from feeding the birds, Amazon Parrots occasionally receive food from sources other than the zoo's ornithologists.

(E)   The connection between vitamin levels and illness rate in Amazon Parrots has not been conclusively established.

318.   The ecological innovation of car manufacturers is a reflection of the kinds of criteria they are trying to meet. The only car buyers genuinely unconcerned with a car's effects on the environment and willing to pay the price are luxury car collectors. Therefore, minimum fuel efficiency standards for car technology are determined by what average buyers will accept as necessary for purposes of clean air.

Which of the following is an assumption made in the drawing the conclusion above?

(A)   Luxury car collectors are unconcerned with fuel efficiency even when purchasing non-luxury cars for everyday use.

(B)   The demand for luxury cars will not increase unless luxury cars meet the same fuel efficiency standards that other cars do.

(C)   Average car buyers consider fuel efficiency to be one of the most important criteria when purchasing a new car.

(D)   Minimum fuel efficiency standards are established with minimal concern for the desires of luxury car collectors.

(E)   Car manufacturers aim for high fuel efficiency so that their product meets the legal standard in every major national market.

319.   Which of the following most logically completes the argument:

Legionnaire's Disease, an illness that sometimes affects hotel guests, is acquired by these guests through air-conditioning systems. Even though office workers are often exposed to the same type of air-conditioning systems identified as the source of Legionnaire's Disease in hotel guests, Legionnaire's Disease is rarely seen in office workers. This fact, however, does not demonstrate that most office workers are resistant to the bacterium that causes Legionnaire's Disease, since

_ _ _ _ _ _ _ _ _ _ .

(A)   office workers spend more time in their office than hotel guests spend in their hotel

(B)   the type of air-conditioning system that facilitates the spread of Legionnaire's Disease is not used solely in offices and hotels

(C)   Legionnaire's Disease can be contracted by people not exposed to the illness via air-conditioning systems

(D)   hotel guests who work in offices are more likely than other hotel guests to contract the illness.

(E)   the fatigue that commonly afflicts travelers results in weakened immune systems and an increased likelihood of illness for hotel guests

185

320. In the last five years, there has been a significant drop in the amount of time children spend watching television. During the same period, there have been numerous studies about the adverse impact of cartoon viewing on childrens' IQ. Therefore, the decrease in children's television watching must have been caused by parents' awareness of the harmful effects of non-educational programming.

Which of the following, if true, most seriously calls into question the explanation above?

(A) Sales of televisions to families with children has steadily increased over the last five years.

(B) No study conclusively established that cartoons were specifically to blame for differences in IQ; it may be that educational programming is little better.

(C) On average, children spend twice as much time playing games and watching non-educational programming on the internet than did children of the same age five years ago.

(D) On average, children watch 20 percent more educational programming than did children of the same ago five years ago.

(E) Children accustomed to watching non-educational programming often find educational programming boring and confusing.

321.   Contrary to anthropologists' predictions, the size of remaining
        hunter-gatherer societies has not decreased in recent decades.
        Yet even though deforestation and the disappearance of traditional
        food sources have continued, the size of hunter-gatherer societies
        over the last ten years has increased by more than 5 percent over
        the previous ten years' levels.

        Any of the following statements, if true about the last ten years,
        helps to explain the increase in the size of hunter-gatherer
        societies EXCEPT:

        (A)   The anthropologists' predictions are now known to have
               ignored several environmental factors that affect the
               survival of these societies.

        (B)   Many traditionally violent hunter-gatherer societies have
               been unusually peaceful, losing few men in battle with
               other tribes.

        (C)   State financial support, designed to allow hunter-gatherer
               societies to survive in their present form, increased by 20
               percent.

        (D)   Wildlife conservation programs around the world have
               made it easier for these societies to successfully hunt big
               game.

        (E)   Droughts, which typically strike many of the regions where
               hunter-gatherer societies live every three to five years,
               have been mild.

322.   Ecologist: The prairie vole, a small North American grassland rodent, burrows underground and feeds on the roots of grasses and other plants. The runways they create and the damage to lawns and crops they cause has lead to voles being treated by farmers as pests in many areas. One of the methods used to eliminate prairie voles is the laying of poisoned oats or corn. Although this method is effective in the short term, it is not recommended because the poisons ingested by the voles can also harm any predators that feed on them.

Which of the following, if true, most seriously undermines the conclusion of the argument?

(A)   No other method of eliminating prairie voles is as effective as poisoning oats or corn.

(B)   The pesticides that are used to poison oats and corn are proven to be harmless for human consumption.

(C)   When a significant number of prairie voles have been eliminated, the population of the vole's predators also dwindles.

(D)   Prairie voles represent a bigger problem in harsher, northern climates than in milder southern climates.

(E)   Most of the prairie vole's predators are also considered by farmers to be pests.

323.   Anti-Pollution Poster:

Scientists report that floating seaweed farms reduce carbon dioxide emissions by fifty percent more than any other non-industrial means. This shows that floating seaweed farms are the most effective tool for reducing carbon dioxide emissions.

Which of the following, if true, most seriously weakens the argument on the poster?

(A)   The need for floating seaweed farms would be greatly reduced if first-world citizens changed their lifestyles to reduce the overall levels of carbon dioxide emissions.

(B)   Technological advances that curtail the carbon dioxide emissions of large factories have a much larger effect on emissions than do floating seaweed farms.

(C)   The cost of floating seaweed farms makes it difficult to build them in many parts of the world.

(D)   Scientists are often criticized for focusing on non-industrial emissions reductions rather than industrial emissions reductions.

(E)   Many strategies that are less effective than floating seaweed farms are in widespread use.

324.   Finding of a poll of international business owners: Ninety percent of requests for solar panels for companies trying to improve their energy efficiency came from United States business owners.

Findings of a poll of international solar-power companies: Seventy percent of requests for solar panels for companies trying to improve their energy efficiency came from United States business owners.

Which of the following would best explain the discrepancy between the two findings?

(A)   Solar panels are less likely to increase the energy efficiency of United States businesses than businesses in other countries.

(B)   The poll of international solar-power companies did not distinguish between companies registered in the United States and companies headquartered in the United States.

(C)   In the United States and Europe, many businesses publicize their efforts to become more energy efficient in an effort to win customers.

(D)   Solar power companies are not the other enterprises that provide solar panels to United States business owners.

(E)   The poll of international business owners did not survey an adequate number of United States business owners.

325.   Workplace safety guidelines for the retail industry recommend
        that workers at the checkout counter stand on anti-fatigue mats,
        use a footrest, and have at least four inches of space beneath the
        counter in which to place their feet. This allows them to stand
        closer to the counter to avoid reaching, and alleviates the fatigue
        that can result from standing for long periods. Insurance companies
        also encourage these practices, as they reduce the number of
        claims filed for work-related health issues.

        Which of the following most logically follows from the statements
        above?

        (A)   Since these techniques for employee comfort are only
               guidelines, many companies do not provide workers with
               anti-fatigue mats and footrests.
        (B)   Workplace safety guidelines are designed in large part of
               prevent fatigue on the part of retail workers.
        (C)   Companies that rigorously enforce these safety guidelines
               may be able to take advantage of lower insurance costs.
        (D)   Standing for long periods of time is considered to be more
               likely to induce injury than sitting for the same lengths of
               time.
        (E)   Insurance companies are more concerned with the number
               of claims filed than with the underlying health of the
               workers they insure.

326. According to a national wildlife conservation organization, a program consisting of raising grouse in captivity to later be released into the wild would increase a dwindling grouse population dramatically. The organization suggests that the program may be financed over the next five years by raising the fees on fox hunting licenses. Although the proposed program is indeed needed to ensure the future of grouse hunting in the state, the organization's plan for securing the necessary funds should be rejected because it would unfairly force fox hunters to absorb the entire cost of something from which they receive no benefit.

Which of the following, if true, would cast the most doubt on the effectiveness of the organization's plan to fund the grouse-raising project by raising the fees on fox hunting licenses?

(A) The last time fox hunting licenses increased in cost, many fox hunters chose instead to purchase licenses to hunt other animals.

(B) The president of the conservation organization does not hold a fox hunting license, but does hold a grouse hunting license.

(C) The last time the legislature voted to increase the cost of hunting licenses, many legislators lost when they next ran for re-election.

(D) Whenever fox hunting license costs are increased, a large number of forms must be reprinted, incurring a substantial cost.

(E) In order to ensure long-term success, the grouse-raising program must be maintained for at least ten years.

327.   A cable network's two channels performed with remarkable
       consistency over the past three years; in each of those years, a
       channel focused on science documentary programming has
       accounted for roughly 20 percent of advertising sales and 40
       percent of profits, and a channel that provides science programs
       for children for the balance.

       Which of the following can properly be inferred regarding the last
       three years from the statement above?

       (A)   The channel focused on science documentary programming
              has realized higher profits per dollar of advertising sales
              than has the channel that provides science programs for
              children.
       (B)   The programming on each of the cable network's channels
              has remained the same.
       (C)   The cost of producing science programs for children is
              considerably higher than the cost of producing science
              programs for adults.
       (D)   Advertising rates for the channel focused on science
              documentary programming are, on average, higher than
              rates for the channel that provides science programs for
              children.
       (E)   When the same show is aired on both of the channels, it is
              more profitable when aired on the channel focused on
              science documentary programming.

328. Since Mrs. Deval opened her daycare center three months ago, waiting lists at other Redlands daycare centers have decreased ten percent. During the same period, there has been an equivalent increase in the number of mothers reentering the workforce in the Redlands area. Clearly, the opening of Mrs. Deval's daycare has made it possible for many mothers to enroll their children in daycare and return to the workforce.

Which of the following, if true, casts the most serious doubt on the conclusion drawn above?

(A) Many of the mothers who enrolled their children in Mrs. Deval's daycare center did not reenter the workforce.

(B) Before opening her daycare center, Mrs. Deval was a respected pre-school teacher at a Redlands-area elementary school.

(C) Mrs. Deval's daycare center charges rates that are 20 percent higher than that of the average daycare center in the Redlands area.

(D) Three months ago, a factory in the Redlands area laid off several hundred employees, most of whom were fathers of single-income families.

(E) Surveys indicate that Redlands area women are no less concerned about the dangers of daycare programs than they were three months ago.

329. Which of the following best completes the passage below?

During a recent meeting of gauge manufacturers, most participating companies favored restrictions on the size of gauges, whether or not resulting products could be of use to all buyers. What must, of course, be shown, in order to prevent an excessively narrow range of sizes, is that _____.

(A) the manufacturers supporting restrictions currently manufacture a wide range of sizes

(B) gauge wholesalers support the narrower range of sizes

(C) all manufacturers present agree to the restriction for a period of at least two years

(D) existing gauge manufacturing plants are able to produce all sizes within the proposed range

(E) currently profitable gauge sizes are not eliminated

330.   Since the ban on rejecting individuals with pre-existing conditions was enacted, health insurance premiums in Williston have increased by 20%. To eliminate this issue, more of the full and almost-full coverage plans offered to consumers must be eliminated in favor of plans with more limited levels of coverage.

Which of the following, if true, casts the most doubt on the effectiveness of the solution proposed above?

(A)   Before the ban was enacted, individuals with pre-existing conditions were able to purchase limited levels of coverage through a state-funded insurance scheme.

(B)   After the ban was enacted, two major insurance companies stopped offering new policies to Williston residents.

(C)   The goal of the ban was to allow individuals with pre-existing conditions access to plans offering full or almost-full coverage.

(D)   Since the ban was enacted, the number of individuals insured in Williston has increased by more than 20%.

(E)   The last time Williston changed its health insurance law, insurance rates increased, only to fall a short time thereafter.

331.   At a hydroponic vegetable factory in Illinois, purchase of spinach plants is severely restricted: grocery stores in Illinois are each limited to a fixed number that they may buy. But the plant also sells to grocery stores in Wisconsin. Clearly, therefore, if the factory were to stop selling to grocery stores in Wisconsin, more spinach plants would be available in Illinois grocery stores.

Which of the following, if true, most seriously weakens the argument?

(A)   The demand for spinach plants in Illinois far outstrips the volume supplied by the hydroponic vegetable factory.

(B)   There are more hydroponic vegetable factories producing spinach plants in Wisconsin than there are in Illinois.

(C)   The restriction on purchases within the state of Illinois is meant to ensure that the supply of spinach plants is consistent throughout the year.

(D)   State price ceilings limit the profit that the factory can earn on sales within Illinois to the extent that the factory loses money on in-state transactions.

(E)   The factory works with a single wholesaler who resells spinach plants to Wisconsin grocery stores, which simplifies the logistics of selling across state lines.

332. Iron Man insurance company offers its clients a free trial of the home security system manufactured by Hytek Security. These clients are then given the chance to sign a five-year contract that provides them Hytek's system and maintenance at a discounted rate.

Which of the following, if true, is the most appropriate reason for homeowners <u>not</u> to accept Iron Man's offer?

(A) Hytek's security systems are are considered to be among the most reliable in the industry.

(B) Many homeowners sell their homes and relocate at least once every five years.

(C) Iron Man insurance receives a commission on every contract signed by one of its clients as a result of the free trial.

(D) Studies show that consumers who accept a free trial of a product are less likely to make an educated decision regarding the merits of the product when they choose whether to make a purchase.

(E) Iron Man clients are eligible for a discount in their insurance premiums if they use a security system provided one of a list of companies, which does not include Hytek.

69 Additional Practice: Reading Comprehension

Questions 333-335 refer to the following passage:

Although theoretical considerations are significant in determining the relationship between the urban and rural labor markets in developing countries, one commonly observed fact is that urban wages exceed rural wages; an urban steel worker in Ivory Coast earns 8.8 times the wage of a rural counterpart. Many studies of developing countries' economies show that government intervention in the form of minimum wage laws is a common feature of these urban labor markets. This is one of many factors that guarantee that urban wages increase and remain above the equilibrium level to a point where employers demand less labor, a situation that creates an excess supply of workers. This makes the **workers' fate** ironic: the incentive to stay in an urban area may allow the worker to improve his prospect of high wage employment but increases his risk of unemployment.

Theoretical models acknowledge none of these factors, but maintain that equilibrium wages are determined solely by the supply of and demand for urban and rural workers. Analysis of these rather simplistic models suggests that, contrary to the actual results observed in the real world, rural wages will equal urban wages, since workers will move between the two markets until a single equilibrium wage is reached.

333. According to the passage, theoretical models and real-world results agree in that both

(A) attribute the higher wage levels in urban areas to external forces

(B) emphasize the danger of government manipulation in labor markets

(C) argue that rural workers do not face the same risk of unemployment that urban workers do

(D) suggest that when wage levels in urban areas are high, workers have incentives to work in urban areas

(E) suggest that the equilibrium wage should be the same in urban and rural areas

196

334.   Which of the following can be inferred regarding the "workers' fate" mentioned in the highlighted text?

(A)   Many workers elect to move back to rural areas after failing to secure employment in urban areas.

(B)   Some workers are paid more than the rural average in urban areas, while others are paid less.

(C)   Some workers are rewarded for relocation to urban areas, while others suffer for it.

(D)   Many workers would earn less in urban areas if the government did not enact minimum wage laws.

(E)   Many workers frequently change employers in order to stay in urban areas.

335.   The author of the passage is primarily concerned with

(A) presenting two views
(B) reconciling two antithetical claims
(C) assessing conflicting evidence
(D) weakening a generally accepted argument
(E) tracing the development of an ideology

Questions 336-338 refer to the following passage:

Tornadoes arise from either cell storms, which are relatively small, or line storms, which may stretch for hundreds of miles. Of the nearly 4,000 tornadoes characterized from 1998 to 2000, about 80% originated in cell storms. Thus, most tornado prevention research has focused on characterizing meteorological aspects of cell storms. Moreover, cell storm-derived tornadoes are by far the most common kind to occur in "tornado alley," a region covering parts of Texas, Oklahoma and Kansas.

Research has recently focused more on line storm-derived tornadoes. While these are less common overall, they form a significant portion of the total number of tornadoes in certain regions of the country. For example, nearly half of the tornadoes formed in Indiana originate from line storms. While cell storms most often form in the spring during the afternoon, line storms tend to form late at night between October and March. These differences have important implications in the timing of the issuing of tornado warnings; most tornado warnings are based on data from cell storms and are issued late at night; but the line storms that may also cause tornadoes don't even begin forming until then. When considering the safety of U.S. residents who live outside of tornado alley, there is substantial incentive for additional research into the nature of line storm-based tornadoes.

336.   In the passage, the author is primarily concerned with

(A)   describing the common characteristics of cell storm-based tornadoes

(B)   proposing alternatives to current methods of predicting tornadoes

(C)   emphasizing the importance of research into tornadoes that originate in line storms

(D)   explaining how line storm- and cell storm-based tornadoes differ

(E)   criticizing the usual method of issuing tornado warnings in the U.S.

337.   The author cites which of the following as a characteristic of cell storm-based tornadoes?

(A)   They are less dangerous than line storm-based tornadoes.

(B)   They are more common outside of tornado alley than line storm-based tornadoes.

(C)   They begin forming late at night.

(D)   They are small in size, compared to line storm-based tornadoes.

(E)   They are more common in tornado alley than they are outside of tornado alley.

338.   The passage suggests that research regarding line storm-based tornadoes is important because they

(A)   last longer and cause more damage than cell storm-based tornadoes

(B)   are most common between the months of October and March

(C)   would pose less danger to humans if they could be accurately predicted earlier

(D)   can stretch for hundreds of miles

(E)   are a particular threat to U.S. residents of tornado alley

Questions 339-341 refer to the following passage:

Dark matter and dark energy have both been postulated by astrophysicists to fill a gap in the fabric of the cosmos which is known as the puzzle of the missing mass. In doing so, astrophysicists sought to bring the characteristics of the universe better in line with Einstein's Theory of Relativity, which predicts that the density of the universe is about 25 times greater than has been heretofore observed. Only 4% of the universe is thought to be composed of conventional matter and energy; about 22% is thought to be composed of dark matter and the remaining 74% is thought to be dark energy. Dark matter does not interact with conventional matter or energy by electromagnetic forces and thus its presence cannot be detected directly. The presence of dark matter must be inferred through its indirect manifestations: anomalous gravitational effects, the rotational velocity data of stars in spiral galaxies and the unusual distribution of mass in a star system known as the Bullet Cluster. Although dark matter was conclusively detected through its gravitational lensing effect in August 2006, many aspects of dark matter remain speculative. It has been noted that the terms "dark matter" and "dark energy" serve mainly as expressions of human ignorance, much like the marking of early maps with "terra incognita."

339.　Which of the following best expresses the central idea of the passage?

(A)　Dark matter and dark energy can be directly identified.

(B)　Astrophysicists are ignorant of many important details of the universe's composition.

(C)　Although not well understood, dark matter and dark energy help reconcile theory with observation.

(D)　Despite a recent observation, the existence of dark matter and dark energy is still debated in the scientific community.

(E)　Dark matter and dark energy were suggested by Einstein's Theory of Relativity.

340.　According to the passage, each of the following is true of dark matter or dark energy EXCEPT:

(A)　They explain why the universe may be 25 times denser than has been observed.

(B)　They are thought to account for 96% of the universe.

(C)　They are not well understood by physicists.

(D)　Their existence can be deduced from observations such as unexpected mass distributions.

(E)　They may solve the puzzle of the missing mass.

341. The passage suggests which of the following about anomalous gravitational effects?

    (A)   The Theory of Relativity does not adequately account for them.

    (B)   Their appearance is not understood by physicists.

    (C)   They may explain the puzzle of the missing mass.

    (D)   Without the existence of dark matter, they cannot be satisfactorily explained.

    (E)   They are related to the distribution of mass in the Bullet Cluster.

Questions 342-344 refer to the following passage:

The nineteenth century American woman was expected to find her strength and meaning of self in her submissive state and in her dedication to her family. During the early 1800s, Americans believed that there was a clear difference between the sexes—man was active, assertive and dominant while woman was modest, passive, submissive and domestic. Consequently, the 1800s cannot be characterized as a period of radical feminism.

The 19th-century "ideal of true womanhood" certainly slowed the advance of women's rights. However, as a result of industrialization, modernization and the accompanying changes in society, women became increasingly, though gradually, more independent and empowered. A primary example of this was in the area of education. Several female academies and seminaries opened during the early 1800s, primarily in the East. Many of the curricula stressed practical, utilitarian education, rather than purely academic training. However, courses in arithmetic, astronomy, chemistry, history, philosophy and other scholastic subjects were also available. These educational opportunities were paramount in making American women a more visible segment of society, no longer considered a mere adornment for males or solely relegated to the kitchens and parlors of their homes.

342. The primary purpose of the passage is to

    (A)   evaluate the choices made by leading American women in the 19th century

    (B)   describe the difficulties of making general claims about a large segment of society

    (C)   examine the relationship between educational opportunities and radical feminism

    (D)   discuss the origin of "the ideal of true womanhood"

    (E)   discuss the roles available to women in nineteenth-century America

343.   According to the passage, which of the following is true of education in the early 1800s?

    (A)   It taught that there was a definite distinction between the sexes.

    (B)   It was closely affiliated with the leading religions of the time.

    (C)   It provided women an opportunity to accomplish things outside of their own homes.

    (D)   It was largely limited to the East.

    (E)   It primarily offered instruction in practical subjects.

344.   Which of the following can be inferred from the passage about common expectations regarding women in 19th-century America?

    (A)   They changed slowly as women became visible outside of the domestic sphere.

    (B)   They were in stark contrast to "the ideal of pure womanhood."

    (C)   They were different in various parts of the country.

    (D)   They changed based on the curricula in female academies and seminaries.

    (E)   They were dependent on an individual woman's family and educational background.

Questions 345-348 refer to the following passage:

Union membership, as a percentage of the private sector workforce, has been in unrelenting decline for nearly half a century. Journalist Michael Wachter has claimed that there is a single cause for this decline: the United States' change from a corporatist-regulated economy to an economy based on free competition. Unions are central to a corporatist regime and are peripheral in a liberal pluralist regime. He also points out that unions may still continue to prosper as a niche movement in the government sector, which is the sole remaining noncompetitive sector, and in sectors where individual firms or industries take advantage of either uninformed or immobile workers to enforce below-competitive pay packages.

Other scholars also ascribe a role to the changing conditions of the 1980s and 1990s in the decline of union influence and power. Though the decline was already underway, management, feeling the heat of foreign and domestic competition, was less inclined to accede to union demands for higher wages and benefits. Management also became more aggressive in fighting union attempts to organize workers. Strikes were infrequent in the 1980s and 1990s, as employers became more willing to hire strikebreakers and keep them on the job after the strike's end. They were emboldened in this stance when President Ronald Reagan in 1981 fired illegally striking air traffic controllers employed by the Federal Aviation Administration.

345. The passage mentions each of the following as a factor in the decline of union membership EXCEPT

   (A)   the centrality of unions in corporatist economies
   (B)   increasing foreign and domestic competition for corporations
   (C)   Ronald Reagan's decision to fire striking federal employees
   (D)   the increasing size of the government as a percentage of the workforce
   (E)   a shift from a corporatist-regulated economy to a more free economy

346. The passage suggests which of the following about corporate conditions in the 1980s and 1990s?

   (A)   They allowed companies to enforce pay packages lower than they could in a more free economy.
   (B)   They caused an increasing number of strikes among organized workers.
   (C)   They allowed U.S. companies to grow without heated competition from foreign entities.
   (D)   They gave rise to a liberal pluralist regime in government.
   (E)   They led companies to more readily employ strikebreakers.

347.   Which of the following best describes the content of the passage?

    (A)   A chronology of trends in union membership in the last half-century

    (B)   A discussion of how government can affect the strategies of corporate leaders

    (C)   An argument concerning the importance of employee organization in large companies

    (D)   An argument concerning the causes of a shift in corporate America

    (E)   A proposal for returning union membership to its previous levels

348.   The passage provides information in support of which of the following assertions?

    (A)   Foreign competition poses a threat to union membership in the U.S. in large part because foreign workers are not themselves unionized.

    (B)   Strikebreakers are more properly employed in sectors where strikes are not legally permitted, as was the case with air traffic controllers.

    (C)   A rise in worker mobility may be sufficient to destroy remaining unions, even in noncompetitive sectors.

    (D)   In a liberal pluralist regime, unions are more likely to be successful in noncompetitive sectors than competitive sectors.

    (E)   Ronald Reagan's actions related to unions are best described as supportive of a corporatist-regulated economy.

Questions 349-351 refer to the following passage:

The Iroquois confederacy was a union of five tribes under one government, based on equality, with each tribe remaining independent in matters of local governance. Often, the Iroquois confederacy and its constitution have been credited as a major influence on The Articles of Confederation and the U.S. Constitution. In 2004, the U.S. government acknowledged the influence of the Iroquois Constitution on the framers of the U.S. Constitution. It is a historical fact that prominent Founding Fathers, such as Thomas Jefferson and Benjamin Franklin, held many meetings with Iroquois leaders.

The sentimentalized concept that the Iroquois Constitution and government had a significant influence on the genesis of early U.S. government has been questioned by many scholars. Historian Jack Rakove notes that the voluminous records still remaining from the constitutional debates of the late 1780s contain no significant references to the Iroquois. Moreover, researcher Brian Cook points out that while the Iroquois probably held some sway over the thinking of the framers of the U.S. Constitution, that influence was not as great as some historians would like it to be; the major influences were European and classical in nature. Clinging to the notion that the Iroquois Constitution played a vital role in the shaping of the U.S. Constitution ignores the inclusion of women in the former, a practice the framers of the U.S. Constitution did not see fit to follow.

349. According to the passage, each of the following is true of the constitution of the Iroquois confederacy EXCEPT:

(A) It granted each of its member tribes autonomy over internal matters

(B) It has been recognized by the U.S. government as an influence on the U.S. Constitution.

(C) It substantially affected the nature of the U.S. Constitution.

(D) It united five tribes as equal members of the confederacy.

(E) It treats women differently than does the U.S. Constitution.

350. Information in the passage suggests that the author would be most likely to agree with which of the following statements concerning the influence of the Iroquois constitution on the Founders?

    (A) The U.S. Constitution developed independently of the Iroquois constitution.

    (B) The Iroquois constitution was incompatible with the existence of a U.S. Constitution that was to govern much of the same territory.

    (C) The Iroquois constitution was familiar to the Founders, but it was not among the most important influences on the U.S. Constitution.

    (D) The original motivations behind the framing of the U.S. Constitution may have been inspired by the existence of the Iroquois constitution.

    (E) Several later amendments to the U.S. Bill of Rights are ultimately attributable to the Iroquois constitution.

351. Which of the following best summarizes the main point of the passage?

    (A) The Articles of Confederation may owe much to the Iroquois constitution, but the U.S. Constitution clearly does not.

    (B) The Founders carefully considered the content of the Iroquois constitution but ultimately rejected it when writing their own.

    (C) The Iroquois constitution did not reflect contemporary views on women, but it nevertheless represented an important source for the framers of the U.S. constitution.

    (D) The United States is correct to recognize the influence of the Iroquois constitution on their own, but the relationship between the documents should not be overstated.

    (E) The U.S. Constitution is a flawed document, but those flaws should not be attributed to the influence of the Iroquois constitution.

Questions 352-355 refer to the following passage:

Research has established that large bureaucratic firms are less innovative than other firms. This reduced innovativeness is likely to be exacerbated when large firms engage in market control. In cultural industries, the effects can be especially pernicious, resulting in the failure to provide audiences with artistic quality or product diversity. The recent success and increased market penetration of small, independent film producers is a consequence of these effects. Increased concentration among generalists has had a positive effect on **foundings of specialist producers and specialist distributors**, and the specialists have been more active in the creation of new film genres.

As organizational size, formalization and complexity are obstacles to innovation, the presence of smaller, less structured and relatively specialized firms may be crucial to the ability of an industry to generate needed innovations. This is not a new phenomenon. While the increased visibility and success of smaller, more specialized film producers would seem to indicate that they are something new or different, in reality, they have existed alongside the more generalist, large Hollywood producers ever since the dawn of the American film industry. Then, as now, the specialists were more innovative than the generalists, but relatively few samples of their product have survived to the present day. It is estimated that over half of the films produced prior to 1950 no longer exist.

352.   The primary purpose of the passage is to

    (A)   explain and critique the methods used by generalist firms
    (B)   compare and contrast a historical situation with a
            current-day one
    (C)   describe and explain a pattern in the marketplace
    (D)   discuss historical opposition to small, innovative firms
    (E)   trace the origin of a contemporary industry

353.   Each of the following disadvantages of generalist firms is mentioned in the passage EXCEPT their

    (A)   bureaucratic structure
    (B)   lack of innovation
    (C)   inability to generate quality products
    (D)   increased market penetration
    (E)   lack of specialization

354.   The passage suggests which of the following about the "foundings
       of specialist producers and specialist distributors" mentioned in the
       highlighted text?

    (A)   They provided supply-line support to the increasingly
       concentrated generalist firms.

    (B)   They responded to a need in the marketplace brought about
       by the practices of generalist firms.

    (C)   They had a crushing effect on the quality and diversity of
       firm offerings.

    (D)   They arose because an earlier generation of specialist firms
       had gone out of business.

    (E)   They offer little reason to expect that more than half of the
       firms they produce will survive the next half-century.

355.   The author suggests which of the following about films produced by
       specialists before 1950?

    (A)   They represented a diversity of styles that is not reflected
       in contemporary films produced by generalists.

    (B)   They have failed to survive because of consistently low
       quality.

    (C)   Their makers went on to more successful careers working
       for generalist producers.

    (D)   Their artistic quality reached levels that films produced by
       generalists could not match.

    (E)   They were more formal and complex than films produced
       by generalists.

Questions 356-358 refer to the following passage:

Scientists have found that because the duck-billed hadrosaur, Hypacrosaurus, became fully grown faster than did its predators, it was able to partially overcome its intrinsic vulnerability to those predators. Hypacrosaurus, which lived from 67-80 million years ago, was one of three common prey for tyrannosaurs and velociraptors, and was the most vulnerable, possessing long limbs and a soft body; it is sometimes described as the **"Thomson's gazelle"** of the late cretaceous era. The duck billed hadrosaur grew at a two- to five-fold faster rate than any potential predators that lived alongside of it. Research suggests that it took 10 to 12 years for Hypacrosaurus to become fully grown while tyrannosaurs, by contrast, reached adulthood after 20 to 30 years. By the time the hadrosaur was fully grown, the tyrannosaurs were only half grown—a huge survival edge for Hypacrosaurus. These conclusions were reached partially through observation and analysis of thin sections of fossil leg bones. Key to the analysis was the counting and measurement of growth rings in the bone, each of which represent one year of life. At least one study suggests that a similar survival strategy is employed by some living animals, including the killifish, a freshwater fish found mainly in the Americas, which matures faster when predators lurk. Researchers also see signs of this phenomenon in butterflies, toads, salamanders, guppies and some birds. Lisa Cooper notes that throughout history, this evolutionary strategy seems to be prevalent.

356.   The primary purpose of the passage is to

(A)   identify the threats to survival facing a certain species
(B)   discuss the implications of a commonly-used strategy
(C)   present examples of an evolutionary strategy
(D)   defend a controversial assertion against a variety of counterarguments
(E)   explain under what circumstances a well-known phenomenon occurs

357.   The passage suggests that if hadrosaurs matured at the same rate as tyrannosaurs, which of the following would be likely?

(A)   The hypacrosaurus population would have rapidly dwindled and soon become extinct.
(B)   Fossil leg bones of hadrosaurs would not have been available for study by present-day archaeologists.
(C)   Hadrosaurs would have evolved to develop either shorter limbs or a sturdier body.
(D)   The vulnerability of Hypacrosaurus would be heightened.
(E)   Velociraptors would struggle to compete with tyrannosaurs for food.

358. The passage suggests which of the following about the "Thomson's gazelle" mentioned in the highlighted text?

    (A) It would have fit more logically into the ecosystem of the cretaceous era than it does in today's.

    (B) Its most distinctive feature is its long legs.

    (C) It matures much more rapidly than do its predators, most notably the cheetah.

    (D) Its physical characteristics leave it particularly susceptible to predators.

    (E) Its small size would not have prevented it from joining tyrannosaurs and velociraptors as threats to hadrosaurs.

Questions 359-361 refer to the following passage:

When historians discuss labor activism, they are usually referring to workers' collective efforts to wrest control over their working conditions from owners and managers. However, African- Americans living in Detroit during the 1920s and 1930s would not have agreed with this. Most would have viewed labor activism as referring to access to jobs, one of the most important labor issues that they confronted. They would also have seen occupational segregation and discrimination as labor concerns. African-American union activists consistently articulated the belief that they could only share the benefits of unionization if they remained diligent about ensuring that their needs were heard, understood, and incorporated into demands formulated by white activists.

When World War II arrived, it was a watershed for black employment. Activism alone did not open workplaces to blacks. Corporate leaders, facing a desperate shortage of workers because of wartime mobilization and the draft, opened their doors to black workers for the first time, particularly in the automobile industry. Because auto industry jobs were unionized and relatively well-paying, black autoworkers became an African-American labor "aristocracy." Work in auto plants was a major step up for African-Americans. This relatively prosperous period for African-Americans proved to be short lived. In the immediate post World War II years, automation and decentralization in the auto industry eliminated many of these new African-American jobs.

359.   According to the passage, the arrival of World War II had which of
        the following effects?

(A)   A shortage of workers in Detroit resulted in a number of
        jobs becoming available to African-Americans.
(B)   African-African labor activists became less important in
        comparison to white activists.
(C)   It provided the conditions that allowed auto industry plants
        to unionize.
(D)   Discrimination in the workplace sharply decreased as the
        nation saw whites and African-Americans serving together
        in the military.
(E)   The number of jobs available to African-Americans declined
        due to automation and decentralization.

360.   According to the passage, which of the following describes a way in
        which African-American activists differed from white activists in
        Detroit?

(A)   White activists did not want to see the evolution of an
        autoworker "aristocracy."
(B)   African-American activists welcomed the arrival of World
        War II because of the employment opportunities it
        generated.
(C)   African-American activists were more concerned with
        access to jobs than unionization.
(D)   White activists wanted to share the benefits of unionization
        with African-American workers.
(E)   African-American activists viewed discrimination as a greater
        problem than occupational segregation.

361.   The author of the passage is primarily concerned with

(A)   identifying similarities in two different theories
(B)   evaluating the effectiveness of a strategy of social change
(C)   describing the effects of a brief success
(D)   debunking a revisionist interpretation of World War II
(E)   exploring the relationship between labor activism and
        corporate priorities

70 Additional Practice: Sentence Correction

362. Proton-induced X-ray emission's original function was as a
pollution detector, a means of improving air quality; instead, it
is something else entirely different, a means of chemical
analysis in a wide variety of situations.

(A) Proton-induced X-ray emission's original function was as
a pollution detector, a means of improving air quality;
instead, it is

(B) Proton-induced X-ray emission was originally intended to
function as a pollution detector, a means of improving air
quality, but which is

(C) Proton-induced X-ray emission was originally intended to
function as a pollution detector, a means of improving air
quality; instead, it has become

(D) Proton-induced X-ray emission was originally intended to
be a pollution detector, a means of improving air quality,
which has become

(E) Proton-induced X-ray emission was originally intended to
be a pollution detector, a means of improving air quality,
other than what it is,

363. As bee populations started to decline in the United States
around the turn of the twenty-first century, some leading
entomologists dropped their research to collaborate with other
scientists whose knowledge of bees was more extensive.

(A) whose knowledge of bees was more extensive

(B) where there was access to knowledge about bees that was
more extensive

(C) where they had more extensive bee knowledge

(D) with more extensiveness on bee knowledge

(E) having more extensiveness to bee knowledge

364. Named as one of the universe's best-known stars, Polaris has
guided generations of sailors; its name–also known as the
North Star–is invoked more frequently than any visible
star to navigators.

(A) than any

(B) than any other

(C) than are any

(D) than that of any other

(E) as are that of any

365. One of the major differences <u>between Schoenberg's career with</u>
<u>that of Bartok may not be founded so much in any specific</u>
<u>promotional ability but</u> in Bartok's capacity to persuade
disciples he met in one place to follow him to another.

    (A)   between Schoenberg's career with that of Bartok may not
be founded so much in any specific promotional ability
but

    (B)   between Schoenberg's career with that of Bartok may not
be found so much in any specific promotional ability
but

    (C)   between Schoenberg's career and that of Bartok may not
be found so much in any specific promotional ability
as

    (D)   between the career that Schoenberg had and that of Bartok
may not be found so much in any promotional ability
specifics as

    (E)   of Schoenberg's career to that of Bartok may not be
found so much in any promotional ability quality but

366. The cooling system in most homes is not centralized air
conditioning, in which a mechanism extracts heat from all areas
<u>simultaneously; rather</u> a type of individual machine that uses
electricity to create ventilation.

    (A)   simultaneously; rather
    (B)   simultaneously, but rather
    (C)   simultaneously, but rather that of
    (D)   simultaneously, but that of
    (E)   simultaneously; it is that of

367.   Ambleside, which is a rural English village and tourist
        attraction, includes a number of features both central to the
        English tradition of quaint churches and landscaped gardens,
        yet in many ways its industrial past sets it apart from other
        similar towns.

   (A)   Ambleside, which is a rural English village and tourist
          attraction, includes a number of features both central
          to
   (B)   Ambleside, which is a rural English village and a
          tourist attraction, includes a number of features that
          were central to both
   (C)   Ambleside, a rural English village and tourist
          attraction, includes a number of features that
          centralize
   (D)   Ambleside, which is a rural English village and tourist
          attraction, includes a number of features central to
   (E)   Ambleside, a rural English village and a tourist
          attraction, includes a number of features centralizing
          both

368.   Frequently overshadowed by ancient Egypt, the lost civilization
        of Mohenjo Daro was discovered in the twentieth century
        by Rakhaldas Bandyopadhyay, an Indian historian, was led to
        the site by a Buddhist monk.

   (A)   Mohenjo Daro was discovered in the twentieth century by
   (B)   Mohenjo Daro was discovered in the twentieth century
          when
   (C)   Mohenjo Daro was discovered in the twentieth century
          and when
   (D)   Mohenjo Daro, discovered in the twentieth century when
   (E)   Mohenjo Daro, discovered in the twentieth century by

213

369.   An announcement by the American Medical Association has confirmed that <u>much of the intensely painful stomach ulcers from which Americans are suffering result</u> from bacteria in the stomach.

   (A)   much of the intensely painful stomach ulcers from which Americans are suffering result
   (B)   much of the intensely painful stomach ulcers that Americans are suffering from result
   (C)   much of the stomach ulcers that are intensely painful and that Americans are suffering from result
   (D)   many of the stomach ulcers that are intensely painful and Americans are suffering from result
   (E)   many of the intensely painful stomach ulcers from which Americans are suffering result

370.   The only way for paleontologists to preserve exposed dinosaur fossils is <u>to cover them rapidly with a tarp before they are ruined when bad weather descends.</u>

   (A)   to cover them rapidly with a tarp before they are ruined when bad weather descends
   (B)   if they are covered rapidly with a tarp before bad weather descends to ruin them
   (C)   for them to be covered rapidly with a tarp before the bones ruined when bad weather descends
   (D)   if they are covered rapidly with a tarp before bad weather descends to ruin them
   (E)   to have them covered rapidly with a tarp before bad weather descends and the bones are ruined

371. Including 36 locks and an elevation differential of 565 feet, the Erie canal seems ideal for transporting any ware that manufacturers could think to ship, but its relatively rapid decline in importance during the twentieth century shows that a failure to compete with certain technology improvements led to its obsolescence.

   (A) seems ideal for transporting any ware that manufacturers could think to ship, but
   (B) seems to have been ideal for transporting any ware that manufacturers could think to ship but
   (C) seems as ideal for transporting any ware that industrial-era manufacturers could think to ship, but
   (D) seemed as ideal for transporting any ware that industrial-era manufacturers could think to ship, but
   (E) seemed to have been ideal to transport any ware that industrial-era manufacturers could think to ship, but

372. Once he had observed ice-polished rocks far from present-day glaciers, Louis Agassiz could not deny whether the age when they were produced was one that had contained great ice sheets.

   (A) could not deny whether the age when they were produced was
   (B) could have no denial whether the age when they were produced was
   (C) had not denied that the age when they were produced was
   (D) had no denial whether the age when they were produced was
   (E) could not deny that the age when they were produced was

373.   The 375 languages that comprise the Afro-Asiatic family are
        distantly linked to many ancient dialects and in fact
        <u>include a branch known as Semitic, which was found to be
        thousands of years old and is</u> characterized by its guttural
        sounds.

(A)   include a branch known as Semitic, which was found to
       be thousands of years old and is

(B)   include a branch known as Semitic, found to be
       thousands of years old and is

(C)   include a branch known as Semitic, finding to be
       thousands of years old and being

(D)   includes a branch known as Semitic, which was found to
       be thousands of years old and is

(E)   includes a branch known as Semitic, which was found to
       be thousands of years old and it is

374.   When traffic jams multiply, some frustrated politicians in
        urban areas will try <u>and set limits for the number of
        areas automobiles are to be allowed to enter and to impose</u>
        higher tolls on heavily used bridges citywide.

(A)   and set limits for the number of areas automobiles are
       to be allowed to enter and to impose

(B)   and set limits for the number of areas able to be
       allowed to enter by automobiles and to imposing

(C)   setting limits for the number of areas automobiles are
       allowed to enter and to impose

(D)   to set limits on the number of areas automobiles
       allowing to be entered by automobiles and imposing

(E)   to set limits on the number of areas that automobiles
       are allowed to enter and to impose

375. Environmental regulations help restrict toxic chemicals in the rural areas of the American states in that a rigid ban is effected during all of the year's times.

(A) states in that a rigid ban is effected during all of the year's times

(B) states, effecting a rigid ban during all of the year's times

(C) states when they effect a rigid ban during all of the times of the year

(D) states, for a rigid ban is effected during all times of the year

(E) states by effecting a rigid by during all times of the year

376. The rental agreement stated that the management company should repaint peeling walls, new flooring should be laid down, and install window guards on all windows.

(A) should repaint peeling walls, new flooring should be laid down, and install window guards on all windows

(B) will repaint peeling walls, new flooring should be laid down, and window guards should be installed on all windows

(C) should repaint peeling walls, new flooring should be laid down, and install window guards should be installed on all windows

(D) will repaint peeling walls, new flooring would be laid down, and window guards on all windows installed

(E) should repaint peeling walls, lay down new flooring, and install window guards on all windows

377.   A 1994 biography reveals that the early years of Josephine
       Baker's life were so miserable they created the desire of
       the singer for fleeing her Missouri home and family, the result
       was, to become a star of the jazz age.

    (A)   they created the desire of the singer for fleeing her
             Missouri home and family and, the result was, to become

    (B)   that they created the singer's desire to flee her
             Missouri home and family and, as a result, to become

    (C)   that they created the singer's desire to flee her
             Missouri home and family and, the result of this, she
             became

    (D)   that they created the desire of the singer to flee her
             Missouri home and family, and resulted in becoming

    (E)   as to create the desire of the singer for fleeing her
             Missouri home and family, resulting in her becoming

378.   Alexander Pope began his translations of The Illiad in 1713,
       increasing to five the number of English versions fully
       rendered since George Champman began translating Homer from
       Greek in 1603.

    (A)   increasing
    (B)   and increases
    (C)   and he increases
    (D)   and he increased
    (E)   and increased

379.   Investigations of galaxy formation often focus on the resemblance between quasars, the furthest observable objects in the universe, and their smaller and similar cousins, microquasars, when astrophysicists find themselves interested in fundamental questions about entities whose distance from earth has suggested their potential to answer questions about the universe's beginnings.

    (A)   resemblance between quasars, the furthest observable objects in the universe, with their smaller and similar cousins, microquasars, when

    (B)   resembled quasar, the furthest observable objects in the universe, to their smaller and similar cousins, microquasars, while

    (C)   resemblance that is observed between quasars, the furthest observable objects in the universe, and their smaller and similar cousins, microquasars, when

    (D)   observable resemblance between quasars, the furthest observable objects in the universe, with their smaller and similar cousins, microquasars, when

    (E)   the furthest observable objects in the universe, quasars, and their resemblance with their smaller and similar cousins, microquasars, as

380.   Dr. Patrick Steptoe was elected a fellow of the Royal Society for showing how female fertility could be easily enhanced to create a virtual endless number of potential "test-tube" babies, each intended specifically for growth in the body of the mother or a surrogate.

    (A)   virtual endless number of potential "test-tube" babies, each intended specifically for

    (B)   virtual endless number of potential "test-tube" babies, each intended specifically in

    (C)   virtual endless number of potential "test-tube" babies, all specifically intended to

    (D)   virtually endless number of potential "test-tube" babies, all of them intended specifically in

    (E)   virtually endless number of potential "test-tube" babies, each specifically intended for

381. Known as a cercaria in its infective stages and populating open bodies of water, the schistosoma parasite, the organism responsible for causing people to develop Bilharzia, causes its sufferers chills and enlargement of organs in several places in the body, is moved into the lungs, and is treated with Praziquantel because it has been demonstrated to cure symptoms.

    (A) body, is moved into the lungs, and is treated with Praziquantel because it has been demonstrated

    (B) body, is moved into the lungs, while being treated with Praziquantel because it has been demonstrated

    (C) body and is moved into the lungs, and treated with Praziquantel because it has been demonstrated

    (D) body, moves into the lungs, and is treated with Praziquantel because it has been demonstrated

    (E) body, having been moved into the lungs and treated with Praziquantel, having been demonstrated

382. Because a downturn in the economy has sent museum attendance plummeting, the director has proposed that the museum will cut operating costs by reducing its hours three days per week.

    (A) Because a downturn in the economy has sent museum attendance plummeting, the

    (B) Because of plummeting attendance to the museum, which is due to a downturn in the economy, the

    (C) Because museum attendance has been sent plummeting, which resulted from a downturn in the economy, the

    (D) Due to plummeting attendance rates from a downturn in the economy, its

    (E) Due to a downturn in the economy, with the result that museum attendance has been plummeting the

383. Learning from farmers who came before them in Europe, livestock breeders created their own prize-stock animals, judged on exhibiting such characteristics like structural and muscular correctness, the performance of athletic feats, and demonstrating other physical and mental traits.

    (A) judged on exhibiting such characteristics like structural and muscular correctness, the performance of athletic feats, and demonstrating other physical and mental traits

    (B) judged on such characteristics as the presence of structural and muscular correctness, the performance of athletic feats, and the demonstration of other physical and mental traits

    (C) and judging it on the exhibition of characteristics like structural and muscular correctness, performing athletic feats, and the demonstrating of other physical and mental traits

    (D) and they base it on structural and muscular correctness, the performance of athletic feats, and demonstrating other physical and mental traits

    (E) and they based in on their exhibiting such characteristics like structural and muscular correctness, their performance of athletic feats, and they demonstrated other physical and mental traits

384. In essentially every kind of narrative in every literary genre, good authors engage the attention of critics, who are the writers' attempting to attract, or sell books to, the readers that are dedicated to them.

    (A) attempting to attract, or sell books to, the readers that are dedicated to them

    (B) attempting that it attract, or sell books to, the readers that are dedicated to them

    (C) instrument to try to attract, or sell books to, such a dedicated audience

    (D) instrument to try and attract, or sell books to, the readers that are dedicated to them

    (E) instrument to attract, or sell books to, their dedicated readers

385.   As contrasted with the heart, the liver can be removed
       partially without severe consequences and contains certain
       cells that can cause significant regeneration.

       (A)   As contrasted with the heart, the
       (B)   In contrast to the heart's, the
       (C)   Unlike the removal of the heart, the
       (D)   Unlike that of the heart, the
       (E)   Unlike the heart, the

386.   Corn production increased 15 percent in 2007, spurring
       predictions that crop yield in the fall harvesting season
       significantly surpassed that of the 10 percent increase rate
       in crop yield for the previous season.

       (A)   that crop yield in the fall harvesting season
             significantly surpassed that of
       (B)   that crop yield in the fall harvesting season would
             significantly surpass
       (C)   of crop yield in the fall harvesting season, that it
             significantly surpassed
       (D)   of crop yield in the fall harvesting season
             significantly surpassing that of
       (E)   of crop yield in the fall harvesting season, that it
             would significantly surpass that of

387.   A decrease in new dark spots and a drop in solar
       prominences signal that the sun might not have as much
       electromagnetic activity as some astronomers previously
       believed.

       (A)   prominences signal that the sun might not have as much
             electromagnetic activity as some astronomers previously
             believed
       (B)   prominences signals that the sun might not have as much
             electromagnetic activity as some astronomers have
             previously believed
       (C)   prominences signal that the sun might not have as much
             electromagnetic activity as have previously been
             thought by some astronomers
       (D)   prominences, signaling that the sun might not have as
             much electromagnetic activity as previously thought by
             some astronomers
       (E)   prominences, signaling the sun might not be as
             electromagnetically active as previously thought to be
             by some astronomers

388. Certain structures can withstand what would typically be destructive levels of wind because they have a reinforced metal framework which prevented the foundation from becoming too battered.

   (A) which prevented
   (B) that prevents
   (C) which has prevented
   (D) that has been preventing
   (E) having prevented

389. As its rate of major breakthroughs has outpaced that of similar institutions, the laboratory has become more likely to fight for the top scientific researchers they would formerly have left to competitors.

   (A) they would formerly have left to competitors
   (B) they would have left previously to their competitors
   (C) that in the past would have been left formerly to competitors
   (D) it formerly would have left to competitors in the past
   (E) it would formerly have left to competitors

390. Of all the several forms of diabetes that have afflicted Americans, perhaps none is more avoidable as the kind that forced 23.6 million people onto low-sugar diets in barely more than twenty years.

   (A) perhaps none is more avoidable as
   (B) it may be that none is more avoidable as
   (C) perhaps it is none that is more avoidable than
   (D) maybe it is none that was more avoidable than
   (E) perhaps none is more avoidable than

391. According to the engineers who developed metallic glass, a particular atomic <u>arrangement is responsible for this novel material's combination of strength and flexibility, made by allowing</u> molten metal to cool without crystallizing.

    (A) arrangement is responsible for this novel material's combination of strength and flexibility, made by allowing

    (B) arrangement is responsible for the combination of strength and flexibility of this novel material, being made by allowing

    (C) arrangement is responsible for the combination of strength and flexibility of this novel material, made by allowing

    (D) arrangement, responsible for this novel material's combination of strength and flexibility, made by allowing

    (E) arrangement, which is responsible for the combination of strength and flexibility of this novel material, made by allowing

392. According to analysts, most technology companies <u>are either growth companies, which produce</u> very little profit as their huge initial revenues are funneled into expansion of the business, as opposed to mature companies, which have stable earnings but little to no growth.

    (A) are either growth companies, which produce

    (B) are either growth companies, producing

    (C) are growth companies that produce

    (D) are growth companies, that produce

    (E) are growth companies, which produce

393.   Data from the national housing department shows <u>that
        homeless people are not as likely to remain homeless as they
        thought in previous reports</u>.

        (A)   that homeless people are not as likely to remain
               homeless as they thought in previous reports
        (B)   that homeless people are not as likely to remain
               homeless as they were thought to be in previous reports
        (C)   homeless people to not be as likely to remain homeless
               as it was thought in previous reports
        (D)   the likelihood that homeless people remain homeless is
               not as high as it was thought in previous reports
        (E)   the likelihood that homeless people remain homeless not
               to be as high as they were thought in previous reports

394.   A similar type of construction can be found in every Romance
        language, <u>each with a consistent order of impersonal
        pronoun, indefinite pronoun, and verb</u>.

        (A)   each with a consistent order of impersonal pronoun,
               indefinite pronoun, and verb
        (B)   each with consistent orders of impersonal pronoun,
               indefinite pronoun, and verb
        (C)   each having a consistent order of impersonal pronoun,
               indefinite pronoun, and verb
        (D)   all having a consistent order of impersonal pronoun,
               indefinite pronoun, and verb
        (E)   all with consistent orders of impersonal pronoun,
               indefinite pronoun, and verb

395.   The Middleville town planning commission has proposed the
        building of a new mixed-use apartment complex, in which it will
        offer 20 affordable <u>housing units to be rented to either
        formerly homeless individuals receiving income assistance or</u>
        low-income working families.

        (A)   housing units to be rented to either formerly homeless
               individuals receiving income assistance or
        (B)   housing units to rent them to either formerly homeless
               individuals receiving income assistance or
        (C)   housing units and it will rent them to either formerly
               homeless individuals receiving income assistance or to
        (D)   housing units, and renting them to either formerly
               homeless individuals receiving income assistance or to
        (E)   housing units, and it will rent them either to formerly
               homeless individuals receiving income assistance or

396. In contrast to other developing nations, <u>Country X has a low child mortality rate, which is thus closer to the U.S. than Country Y is</u> in most public health measures, even though it is often thought of as a nation plagued with disease and social turmoil.

   (A) Country X has a low child mortality rate, which is thus closer to the U.S. than Country Y is
   (B) Country X has a low child mortality rate and is thus closer to the U.S. than Country Y is
   (C) Country X's child mortality rate is low and is thus closer to the U.S. than Country Y
   (D) the child mortality rate of Country X is low and thus closer to the U.S. than Country Y
   (E) the child mortality rate of Country X is low, thus closer to the U.S. than Country Y is

397. A major auto maker pointed out as a justification for its shift toward smaller cars and trucks <u>that the large sport-utility vehicles that sold so well in the last decade were becoming</u> less popular as consumers began to favor more streamlined and fuel-efficient vehicles.

   (A) that the large sport-utility vehicles that sold so well in the last decade were becoming
   (B) that the large sport-utility vehicles, selling so well in the last decade, had been becoming
   (C) that there were large sport-utility vehicles selling so well in the last decade, and they were becoming
   (D) the large sport-utility vehicles that sold so well in the last decade and were becoming
   (E) the large sport-utility vehicles selling so well in the last decade and that they became

398. The Galeries Lafayette department stores in Paris, France, were opened in 1838 by the French retailer Th'eophile Bader, <u>by whom they were christened presumably because its</u> earliest building was located on La Fayette Street.

   (A) by whom they were christened presumably because its
   (B) by whom they were christened presumably and their
   (C) christening them presumably since their
   (D) who so christened them presumably because their
   (E) who so christened it since presumably their

399. Because of their increased access to ultrasound and their preference for male children, experts have predicted that there are fewer than 80 girls for every 100 boys born to the wealthier families of India, and that these girls are thus significantly more likely to marry husbands that can provide for them.

   (A) Because of their increased access to ultrasound and their preference for male children, experts have predicted that there are fewer than 80 girls for every 100 boys born to the wealthier families of India, and that these girls are thus significantly more likely to

   (B) Because of their increased access to ultrasound and their preference for male children, there are fewer than 80 girls for every 100 boys born to the wealthier families of India, experts have predicted, and that these girls are thus significantly more likely to

   (C) There are fewer than 80 girls for every 100 boys born to the wealthier families of India, experts have predicted, which makes these girls significantly more likely to

   (D) Experts have predicted that, because of their increasing access to ultrasound and their preference for male children, there are fewer than 80 girls for every 100 boys born to the wealthier families of India, and that these girls are thus significantly more likely to

   (E) Experts have predicted that, because of increased access to ultrasound and a preference for male children, there are fewer than 80 girls for every 100 boys born to the wealthier families of India, and that these girls are thus significantly more likely to

400.   The present cohort of students in Middleville schools participating in sports at the varsity and junior varsity levels has won at least 57 athletic awards and scholarships estimated at a total value of $675,000, the state's largest award amount.

   (A)   students in Middleville schools participating in sports at the varsity and junior varsity levels has won at least 57 athletic awards and scholarships estimated at a total value of $675,000

   (B)   students in Middleville schools participating in sports at the varsity and junior varsity levels has won at least 57 athletic awards and scholarships that are estimated to have a total value of $675,000

   (C)   students in Middleville schools is participating in sports at the varsity and junior varsity levels, having won at least 57 athletic awards and scholarships estimated at a total value of $675,000

   (D)   students in Middleville schools, participating in sports at the varsity and junior varsity levels, and have won at least 57 athletic awards and scholarships estimated at a total value of $675,000

   (E)   students in Middleville schools, participating in sports at the varsity and junior varsity levels, have won at least 57 athletic awards and scholarships they have estimated as having a total value of $675,000

71 Explanations: CR: Assumption

1.   A

In assumption questions, look for terms that change from the evidence to the conclusion. In this passage, we're told that "the number of customers who had FoodCards was about the same," then the passage concludes that "the number of Palmonters taking advantage of special discounts" did not increase. That shift signals what the assumption will probably be: The argument assumes that the number of customers taking advantage of special discounts is directly correlated to the number of customers who had FoodCards.

Of course, the correct choice won't be worded exactly like that. Choice (A) does provide a link between the evidence and conclusion. The change mentioned in the passage is the increased number of locations, but (A) tells us that those additional locations had little effect on the customers who had FoodCards. In other words, there's no reason why more customers could take advantage of the discounts, so this applies to the shift in the argument.

Choice (B) is not relevant, since the passage is about people who do have FoodCards. (C) is also off-topic, as the profit margin of the store isn't the subject to the passage. (D) is similar to (B): we're concerned about the customers who do have FoodCards. (E) addresses the types of discounts, not the number of customers taking advantage of them. (A) is correct.

2.   C

In an assumption question, there is usually some shift from the evidence to the conclusion. In the background information, we know that the large number of policies and large number of those associated with luxury cars, coupled with the luxury car theft rate, means that if no more policies are sold to owners of luxury cars, fewer theft claims will be submitted. This is a fairly typical type of shift: if the argument is true, the situation last year must stay the same. There's no guarantee, however, that that is the case.

Choice (A) reflects something that stays the same from year to year, but it doesn't apply directly to the argument. It doesn't matter which type of car is stolen more frequently, just that the relative number of luxury and non-luxury thefts stay the same. (B), again, is something that stays the same, but it doesn't take into account any possible new policies sold this year.

Choice (C) is better. The high number of claims last year was due to the rate of luxury car theft; without that number, the record would not have been set. If the number of non-luxury thefts does not go up by much, and no more policies are sold to owners of luxury cars, fewer claims will be submitted this year. (D) is irrelevant: we're concerned with theft claims, not recovery. (E) is another off-topic comparison, as we're only concerned with the number of thefts of cars belonging to policyholders. (C) is the best choice.

3.   B

Any argument concluding that profits are increased or decreased hinges on two things: a change (or lack thereof) in revenues and a change (or lack thereof) in costs. This argument provides evidence that more tenants stay, suggesting that revenues are higher for the management company thanks to the new employee. However, there is a shift from the evidence to the conclusion—just because the revenues are up doesn't mean profits are up as well.

Choice (A) may ultimately contribute to higher revenue, but we don't know the connection between tenant satisfaction and revenue. (B) addresses both costs and revenues, by telling us that the increased costs of the new strategy are not as high as the financial benefits that the strategy brings about.

Choice (C) is irrelevant, as it doesn't matter why the employee was hired. (D) suggests that the new employee may have made a difference, but it doesn't address the cost of the employee or other aspects of the strategy. (E) addresses costs and revenue, but not as thoroughly as does (B). (E) doesn't mention the cost of the new employee, or other costs of finding new tenants. Choice (B) is correct.

72   Explanations: CR: Strengthen

11.   B

The phrase "further evidence... achieve its goal," tells us we're looking at a strengthen question. The argument already tells us that MP Tech's strategy costs about the same as its previous approach, so we're looking for further validation.

Choice (A) weakens the argument a bit. Phone support isn't covered in the passage, but it probably isn't a good thing to make providing phone support less economical. If anything, it certainly doesn't strengthen the argument. (B) tells us that relying on customers (rather than shipping customers) keeps machines safe in transit, which is a concern mentioned in the passage. It's on-topic, and it strengthens the argument.

Choice (C) is irrelevant, comparing MP Tech technicians to technicians who might not need special training. (D) is another irrelevant comparison to other brands; the passage compares the previous MP Tech strategy to the current one. (E) seems neutral; if many of the technicians are the same, regardless of location, there is no change in the quality of service. Choice (B) is correct.

12.   A

The phrase "strongest support" signals a strengthen question. The argument explains that taxes will keep companies from growing past a certain size (500 employees), but that the tax will end up having a somewhat paradoxical effect of adding jobs.

Choice (A) explains how that might happen. The tax will lead to money for small companies, which will hire employees, and will do so "at a faster rate than large companies." That would seem to address the paradox. (B) doesn't matter, as it doesn't address job growth. (C)—like most choices that say something will stay the same, or has no effect—is incorrect. We need a reason why something will create job growth to outweigh the loss created by the tax, and something static won't accomplish that.

Choice (D) tells us why some jobs won't be lost, but we need a reason why jobs will be gained in addition to that. (E), like (C), addresses something in the present that sounds consistent. However, we need to find out something that will change, preferably due to the tax that creates this paradox. Choice (A) is correct.

13.   E

In this strengthen question, we need some additional reason why emissions cause more pollution in the river than pesticides do.

Choice (A) compares emissions in the Ellenville River to emissions in other rivers, which isn't the comparison we're concerned with. (B) tells us something about the pesticide pollution, but nothing about emissions. (C) covers emissions, but not pesticide pollution.

Choice (D) gives us a reason we might not be able to draw a conclusion; that certainly doesn't strengthen the argument. (It doesn't really weaken the argument either; it has no effect.) (E), finally, gives us a comparison between the two forms of pollution, and explains why there may be more emissions-related pollution. At the very least, the effects of that pollution are more noticeable. Choice (E) is correct.

14.   C

This strengthen question has a passage with a clear argument based on causality. It claims that the controversial program led to advertisers ending their association with the network. In EXCEPT questions, remember that the correct answer might not be the opposite of a strengthen answer (a "weaken" answer); it might be an answer that has no effect.

Choice (A) strengthens the argument. If the advertisers have strong political opinions, that is one reason they might not want to support a network that broadcasts a controversial political program. (B) also strengthens the argument, as another network saw the same causal effect. Choice (C) does not strengthen the argument; the argument is based on revenue losses due to advertisers leaving, not advertisers reducing how much they advertise.

Choice (D) suggests that if the network hadn't broadcast the controversial program, it wouldn't have lost the revenue, which strengthens the argument. (E) strengthens the argument as well, by eliminating one possible alternative explanation for the loss in the revenue. Choice (C) is correct.

73 Explanations: CR: Weaken

21.   C

The phrase "most threatens" indicates that this is a weaken question. The underlying assumption, much like the assumption in many "plan" questions, is that the plan will have the desired effect: modern gates and reduced rates at Carnigan will bring back more airlines. We're looking for some reason why the improvements at Carnigan won't have that effect.

Choice (A) is possible, though doubtful; leases might keep airlines from moving back, but there is no specific timetable mentioned in the question, and for all we know, those long-term leases may be about to run out. (B) is an irrelevant comparison, between the rates on older and newer gates at Carnigan. (C) looks good: If airline customers don't want to deal with Carnigan, airlines have a good reason not to relocate there, despite the advantages set forth by the planners at Carnigan.

Choice (D) is another irrelevant comparison: It doesn't matter whether airports serve more than one airport. If anything, the fact that each airport flies out of one location makes the plan more likely to succeed, since there are many airlines with no presence at Carnigan. Choice (E) is yet another irrelevant comparison; the size of the airport has no effect (that we know about, anyway) on business moving from one airport to another. Choice (C) is correct.

22.   D

"Strongly argues" makes this sound like a strengthen question, but the word "ineffective" tells you we're looking to weaken the proposal. Since the passage is broken up like this, it's worth trying to paraphrase the "argument." Basically: "The volcano may erupt, which might make tourists skittish, but we want to keep tourists coming, so we should advertise that the area is still safe."

Choice (A) strengthens the argument by providing a solid reason for the advertisements. (B) is irrelevant, as there is no mention on whether tourists visit those areas when volcanoes are likely to erupt, and what prompts them to do so. (C) is also irrelevant, as we don't know whether the safety issues extend to tourists who are not on the mountain itself.

Choice (D) explains why advertising may not be a good idea. If they aren't aware of the safety issues, they won't stay away; if the advertisements make them aware of the safety issues, they may still come, but they certainly wouldn't be more likely to do so. (E) is irrelevant, as the argument has nothing to do with cost. Choice (D) is correct.

23.   C

The phrase "vulnerable to criticism" tells us we're looking at a weaken question. The argument claims that Satellex would make their present subscribers happier, and perhaps keep them for longer periods of time, if they added talk radio stations.

Choice (A) suggests it would be easy to attract talk radio hosts, which isn't really relevant, but might slightly strengthen the argument. (B) is also off-topic; you could make an argument that, because talk radio is usually free, people wouldn't pay for it, but that requires a lot of thinking beyond the scope of the passage. (C) addresses the issue of "profits" by pointing out that adding talk radio stations would increase costs, and perhaps not increase revenues very much.

Choice (D) is an irrelevant comparison; we don't know that it matters how long listeners spend on any given station. (E) suggests that Satellex's music station quality would go down if talk radio were added, but that may not have a direct impact on profits, which is what we're concerned with. Choice (C) is correct.

24.   D

The argument suggests that founders can make poor hiring decisions, while the question wonders why it would be a mistake for those same founders to outsource the same hiring decisions. This is a "flaw" question, which is closely related to a weaken question.

Choice (A) doesn't weaken the argument, it has no effect. (B) simply reiterates some of what is said in the passage—founders aren't necessarily good at making hiring decisions. (C) is an irrelevant comparison. We're concerned with "good matches," not the amount of time it takes to make decisions.

Choice (D) weakens the argument. The assumption underlying the plan is that firms that handle hiring would not have the same problems as founders. (D) suggests that they do. Choice (E), like (C), is irrelevant, as the passage is not concerned with salary, only with the quality of the match. Choice (D) is correct.

74 Explanations: CR: Explanation

31.   D

As with most explanation questions, there is something of a paradox in the passage. The SM Mall of Asia has a negative effect on other super-malls, but a positive effect on small businesses. There must be some difference in the effect it has on these two types of businesses, so look for that sort of thing in the answer choices.

There isn't any distinction in (A): it doesn't tell us what sort of shopping opportunities tourists seek out. (B) would seem to contradict the passage: if locations are chosen to avoid competition, there is less of a reason why the SM Mall of Asia would threaten the viability of other super-malls. (C) tells us something specific about the SM Mall of Asia, but not anything that tells us about other malls or small businesses.

Choice (D) gives us a reason why all businesses might benefit—an increased number of weekend tourists—and a reason why other super-malls might not— that the tourists only visit one super-mall. This would explain the difference. (E) gives us a difference between the SM Mall of Asia and other super-malls, but no hint on the effect the mall might have on small businesses. Choice (D) is correct.

32.   A

The discrepancy is that while first-year employees assigned to rural areas find it harder to reach their sales target (which is one of the factors considered when deciding who gets a raise), these employees are more likely to get raises. Note that the passage mentions "satisfactory reviews" as another factor in the decision; it's no accident that the GMAT includes a phrase like that even if it doesn't factor in the following sentence.

Choice (A) takes the "satisfactory reviews" into account, and explains the discrepancy. If the only factor in deciding who got a raise was whether or not the employee met the sales target, there would be no way to explain the discrepancy, so we need to look to the other factor, which this choice does. (B) is an irrelevant comparison, since this question is about only those employees working for Allied.

Choice (C) doesn't address the comparison between employees assigned to rural regions and non-rural regions. (D) has the same problem; this applies to all first-year employees. (E) addresses the right comparison (rural regions compared to non-rural regions) but doesn't explain how more sales per customer might lead to more raises. Choice (A) is correct.

33.   B

This explanation question doesn't have an obvious discrepancy in the passage (as many do), so it's important to focus on what needs to be differentiated. The weakness of the currency must have a positive effect on firms with more clients outside of Saradia and a different effect on those with fewer.

Choice (A) is irrelevant, and while we're at it, (D) is too. We're concerned only with how the currency affects companies inside Saradia, and neither choice provides any information why that might be so. Choice (B) is much better. We know the Sarade is weak, so this choice is pertinent; it further explains that goods sold by Saradian firms would be inexpensive (i.e., more desirable) to buyers in countries with stronger currencies. That explains why the difference is between companies that do more and less business outside of Saradia.

Choice (C) explains an effect of the currency weakness, but not one that would affect some Saradian firms but not others. Choice (E) doesn't explain anything, except for eliminating the possibility that firms were somehow making decisions because of their inclusion in the study. Choice (B) is correct.

34.   A

The passage and question of this explanation question comprise something of a paradox: SimInc has chosen to make a substantial financial outlay in additional training, yet it will ultimately save money. We need some information regarding how that money will be saved.

Choice (A) explains it. If hiring pre-trained graduates is more expensive than providing training to non-trained graduates, the cost of the training program is made up in the more inexpensive hiring choices. (B) is off-topic, as we're focused on finance graduates. This choice might be more relevant if we knew that all graduates were becoming more difficult to hire, but the choice is not that broad.

Choice (C), if anything, weakens the argument. However, it makes sense—if all the new hires are in training, productivity will go down until their training is completed. It doesn't address the financial aspects, though. (D) also doesn't address how SimInc saves money. (E) covers one way in which the plan would backfire, but it doesn't explain how the plan will save them money, only how the contracts would prevent them from losing more money. Choice (A) is correct.

75 Explanations: CR: Evidence

41. B

This is an evidence question—very similar to a strengthen question. Basically, the correct answer will fill a gap (like an assumption) left by the passage. The plan is that hiring philosophy professors will lead to more students choosing Inagua College because of the demand for philosophy courses.

Choice (A) is off-topic, as it doesn't matter how many students are awarded doctorates. We're concerned with students entering the college, not leaving it. (B) is very relevant. The argument is based on the idea that the plan will affect students' choices, but there is no evidence in the passage that it will do so. (Perhaps students develop an interest in philosophy after arriving.) This addresses the main weakness of the plan.

Choice (C) is too broad: we're focused on philosophy only. (D) is off-topic; the plan isn't concerned with meeting all student needs, it's about attracting more students in the first place. (E) is an irrelevant comparison. The demand described in the passage isn't for philosophy courses taught by highly-rated professors, it is for philosophy courses. Choice (B) is correct.

42. E

This is an evidence question, so we're looking for answer that addresses an unstated assumption in the passage. The argument is that, because airlines are accountable to their customers, they will follow safety procedures comparable to those followed by the government-mandated ones.

Choice (A) is irrelevant: we're concerned with whether the safety procedures would be as thorough, not how much they would cost. (B) is another irrelevant comparison, as we're concerned only with the effect of the shift in Guravia. (C) might sound tempting, but it doesn't matter who does the work, it matters what standards are set by the organization (the government, or the airlines) who are accountable for it.

Choice (D) is somewhat supported by the passage, but this isn't an inference question. We're looking for evidence to close a loophole in the argument. Choice (E) is what we're looking for. The argument claims that customers will hold airlines accountable, but if there is no way to know which airlines are following safety procedures, the argument would fall apart. Choice (E) is correct.

76 Explanations: CR: Inference

51.   D

The phrase "most strongly supports" indicates an inference question. It's not explicitly an explanation or paradox question, but the passage does have a bit of a discrepancy, between the employment figures in the two regions compared to the different population figures in the two regions.

Choice (A) assumes too much—there may well be enough people in the north to staff tourism-related companies. Beyond that, even if it weren't true, there's no reason the outside recruiting would have to take place in the south. (B) is only true if oil and tourism are the only two industries. Just because they are the largest doesn't mean they are the only ones; they could actually represent a small portion of the economy. (C) explains how more people in the south might be related to the oil industry, but there's no support for this. We don't know that refineries (or other oil-related companies) are in the south, or even in Frobnia at all.

Choice (D) is our answer. We know that more than one-third of working Frobnians work in the tourism industry (which is in the north), while less than one-sixth work in the oil fields (in the south). Thus, a higher proportion of Frobnians work for either tourism or oil in the north than for tourism or oil in the south. (E) is a huge leap, and out of the scope of the passage. We have no idea whether tourists also visit the south. The passage is concerned with employment numbers. Choice (D) is correct.

52.   A

We're looking for a logical inference. All of the information given focuses on the sort of business that hires drivers directly instead of contracting transportation to outside firms. The logical conclusion will probably have something to do with that comparison.

Choice (A) is a logical conclusion. The only difference between firms that sell perishable food items and non-perishable food items is that the former must have their items "delivered in a timely manner." If such firms are so much more likely to hire drivers directly, the timeliness required seems to have at least something to do with the decision.

Choice (B) is not based on the information given, since there is nothing in the passage about costs. (C) is irrelevant, as the customers or suppliers of the businesses mentioned do not arise in the discussion. (D) may be tempting, but all we know is that more firms that transport food items opt to hire their own drivers. If 90% of transported goods are food items, a small percentage of that would still be greater than all of the non-food items put together. (E) is much too precise to be supported by a passage with no firm numbers. (A) is correct.

53.   C

The phrase "most strongly supported" indicates that this is an inference question. Note the careful wording in the passage: "may be just as high" and "may be contributing." Given language like that, the wording of the correct answer will probably not be very strong.

Choice (A) is too extreme. We know that the research was done near Tasmania, but not the specific results of that result as regards the species that live there. (B) confuses the issue. It sounds like systematic sampling is how marine species are measured, but we don't know if it applies to non-marine species, as well.

Choice (C) is well supported. The rate of extinction of marine species is disguised by the lack of systematic sampling, so it makes sense that more systematic sampling would provide more evidence of species extinction. (D) is an unsupported comparison, as we aren't given any data comparing Tasmania to other areas. (E) is far outside the scope of the passage. The statements don't provide any information about how the rate of extinction would be slowed, especially relative to that of non-marine species. Choice (C) is correct.

77   Explanations: CR: Fill-In-the-Blank

61.   A

While this isn't an explanation or paradox question, you're looking for a similar kind of answer. The word "nevertheless" tells you that the final sentence represents something that contrasts with the previous sentence. Somehow, a smaller system can result in a higher yield despite its size. One answer will explain how.

Choice (A) seems to do just that. If bacteria can destroy the algae, that's quite the threat; if a greenhouse can prevent that attack, that would seem to result in a higher yield. (Certainly higher than zero!) (B) offers a difference between greenhouse and no-greenhouse, but we don't know whether "frequent genetic mutations" are good or bad for the algae yield. (C) doesn't address the issue at all; it doesn't provide a contrast to the previous sentence.

Choice (D) is an irrelevant comparison; the passage doesn't include a mention of a photobioreactor, and we don't know that preserving threatened types of algae is the same as resulting in a higher yield. (E) is also irrelevant. We don't know whether limiting cultivation to one species results in a higher yield, a lower yield, or has no effect. Choice (A) is correct.

62.   E

If you know the word "silvicultural," you'll find this question easier than if you don't, but the question is designed to be handled by someone who has never seen the word before. The passage sets up a contrast between "silvicultural" and "commercial," so it's a safe bet that "silvicultural" means something like the opposite of commercial. In this context, "for environmental purposes" is a workable definition.

We're looking for the answer choice that gives us a good reason why commercial clearcutting is not as extensive (not "removing nearly every tree") even though silvicultural (say, "environmentally friendly") clearcutting is. (A) doesn't follow through with the contrast between silvicultural and commercial—it makes it sound like commercial clearcutting is another type of environmental approach.

Choice (B) is an irrelevant comparison: The passage focuses on these two methods in a vacuum, not how the methods might work together, with each used in separate locations. (C) has two irrelevant comparisons: the area of the forest and the type of country is completely foreign to the concepts mentioned in the passage.

Choice (D) assumes that commercial clearcutting is not environmentally friendly, and suggests why it doesn't have to be. It doesn't explicitly detail why commercial clearcutting isn't as extensive, though. Instead, it focuses on why environmental concerns might not always be foremost. Choice (E) is, finally, our correct answer. To rephrase, it says, "the goal of commercial clearcutting is different from that of environmentally-friendly methods, which leads to less extensive cutting." In other words, it explains the contrast between the two methods, which is what the sentence naturally led toward.

63.   E

In the passage itself, there is no difference given between the two companies. There must be some difference; for the passage to be logical, that difference must be contained in the correct answer choice.

Choice (A) gives us a difference, but not one that has any discernable impact on business in Volsinia. Without that, the passage doesn't make logical sense. Choice (B) doesn't even give us a difference between the two companies. Choice (C) offers a difference, but it seems to be in favor of Noratech, while the passage says that Cyberdyne is likely to dominate the market.

Choice (D) is another choice without a difference between the companies. (E), finally, is correct. Not only does it give us a difference, but it explains why that difference would be to the advantage of Cyberdyne. That's what we're looking for.

78 Explanations: CR: Boldface

71.   B

Before looking at the choices, try to understand the structure of the passage. The first two sentences describe a problem. The next two describe a solution. The final sentence concludes that the solution will increase profits.

Choice (A) is incorrect, as the second bold sentence is the main conclusion, not evidence for the conclusion. (B) is better: "the judgment" is similar to "conclusion," and it agrees with our prediction that the first bold sentence is part of a description of a problem. (C) is wrong: the first bold sentence could be a position one would seek to establish, but the additional information doesn't support it. It is taken as a given.

Choice (D), like (C), misrepresents the first bold sentence. The argument doesn't follow up on the claim made in the first bold sentence, it simply takes it for granted. (E), as well, misrepresents the first bold sentence. That sentence does not describe something that is "at issue." The second bold sentence, also, is not in support of the conclusion, it is the conclusion. Choice (B) is correct.

72.   C

Try to grasp the structure of the passage before looking to the choices. The first sentence is one approach, along with the reasoning behind those who choose it. The second is a different method that the passage suggests is better.

Choice (A) has the phrase "alternative strategy," to describe the second bold sentence, but the description of the first sentence is wrong. There is nothing in that sentence about why it might be counterproductive. (B) has better reflects the first sentence except that it says the argument recommends the first strategy, which it does not. (C) is better: it characterizes the second sentence as an alternative strategy, and describes the first as the reasoning behind the first strategy, which aptly describes most of that sentence.

Choice (D) is wrong: it suggests that both bold sentences are related to the same course of action, which they are not. (E) has the same problem, characterizing both sentences as describing aspects of the same strategy. Choice (C) is correct.

79 Explanations: RC: Mixed Review 1

81. D

The passage makes clear that business travelers and last-minute purchasers pay more than average (so a last-minute business traveler will definitely pay more than average), but as always, an assumption question is based on a shift in what is being described. In this case, we don't know how Air Macaria's average rates compare to those of their competition. In other words, is an average fare on Air Macaria better than the last-minute business fare offered by the competition? If the argument is valid, that must be the case, but it isn't stated.

Choice (A) specifies something in the passage, but doesn't address the comparison between Air Macaria and its competition's prices. (B) is irrelevant, as the argument is specific to routes served by an airline that does use tiered pricing and one that does not. (C) is off-topic: The passage is about one specific route, not a hybrid one that must be assembled from multiple airlines.

Choice (D) addresses the assumption identified above. If the average prices on the airlines are the same, then it is true that the higher-than-average ticket price on the airline that uses tiered pricing is greater than the average price on Air Macaria. (E) is incorrect, as the number of passengers that use any particular airline or pricing system is outside the scope of this argument. Choice (D) is correct.

82. B

The dispute is over just how much the two populations of wolves have in common. We're looking to strengthen the argument that, because there is no contact and no interbreeding between the two species, the southern population is a distinct species.

Choice (A) could be construed as supporting the argument, but it would be a stretch. This bit of evidence does relate the southern population to the north, and there's also no way of knowing how much data from less than a century ago affects the definition of species. (B) is better. It not only tells us a difference between the two populations, but explains that a less substantial difference has caused two populations to be defined as different species.

Choice (C) is irrelevant, as we're only concerned with this one species, and even though "endangered" is mentioned in the passage, the argument is about whether the southern population is a separate species, not about the definition of endangered species. (D) is off-topic, as it doesn't matter where the person arguing worked, or what he or she did. (E) is off-topic as well; this tells us nothing about the distinction between populations. Choice (B) is correct.

83. B

To logically complete the passage, we need a reason why Kaiba's expansion wouldn't include an increase in their workforce. We know that decreasing market share led to a decrease in the workforce, so there must be some outside factor that is affecting the usual correlation between the size of the company and the number of workers needed.

Choice (A) is incorrect, as it doesn't give us any change at all, let alone any details that apply directly to Kaiba's situation. Choice (B) tells us something new about Kaiba (their reliance on contractors) that suggests they don't need employees of their own. If they can grow without new employees, and it has had a positive effect on their business, it makes sense that they wouldn't hire new employees as they expand. This looks like a solid choice.

Choice (C) is irrelevant, as it doesn't address employment figures at all. (D) is also irrelevant. We aren't concerned with the specific employees that Kaiba laid off in the past; we care about Kaiba's employment numbers. (E) is on the right track, but if the current workforce is only "at least as productive" as it was before, it would seem to need more employees as it grows. If the current workforce were substantially more productive, they might not need more workers, but we don't know if that's the case. (B) is the correct choice.

84.   E

The phrase "most undermine" tells us we're working with a weaken question. The customers have concluded that Primatech is snubbing them in favor of the government market, based on the company's turning down their orders but accepting the government's order. There must be some other explanation for at least one of those things that explains why the company is not actually shifting from one to the other.

Choice (A) is outside of the scope: We're concerned with who Primatech does business with, not who their customers work with. (B) suggests that Primatech isn't in trouble, but doesn't give us a reason why they are not shifting their business to the government market. (C) seems to strengthen the argument, providing more evidence that the company will be marketing to the government.

Choice (D) also seems to strengthen the argument a bit. It wouldn't be a strong answer to a strengthen question, but if private sector customers get a discount, perhaps the government market would be more lucrative on a per-item basis. (E), finally, is correct. The reason Primatech gave for turning down orders was a short-term materials shortage, so if the government doesn't need delivery for a year, that would explain why the company can accept a government order but not private sector orders, and can do so without reflecting an overall shift in strategy.

80 Explanations: RC: Mixed Review 2

91. **E**

The phrase "present the most serious disadvantage" signals that you're dealing with a weaken question here. Everything mentioned in the passage—additional acreage, a huge amount devoted to wheat farming, economies of scale—sounds good, but there is a wild card in the passage: "extremely high amounts of rainfall." We don't know whether that's good or bad, but if it's in the passage, the GMAT expects us to pay attention to it.

Choice (A) seems to weaken the argument: it supports the "economies of scale." Less manpower per acre would seem to reduce costs, which is generally a good thing, and it is what they're aiming for. (B) is also a positive. If wheat prices increase, Western's investment will probably pay off. (C) mentions the heavy rainfall, but it is out of scope; Western's plan seems to be to purchase the land for wheat farming. It doesn't matter what impact the rain would have on the company's ability to do things it doesn't plan on doing.

Choice (D) is an irrelevant comparison; presumably, Western's goal is profit, not to own more or less land than its competitors. (E), finally, looks good. The passage tells us that the majority of Western's land will be used for wheat cultivation in a region with heavy rainfall—this choice tells us that such a strategy can have highly variable results. Choice (E) is correct.

92. **A**

This is a sort of inference question; it is a little different than usual because so much of the conclusion ("a proper test of an executive's. . . ") is in the question itself. The passage emphasizes a balance between experience- and data-based decisions.

Choice (A) is reasonable: it suggests executives should be able to use one type of decision-making to support the other. (B) is close, but not as good, as directing data-collection efforts doesn't necessarily mean one will use the results of the data. (C) is wrong, since the passage emphasizes using both types of decision-making, not mastering one in order to ignore the other.

Choice (D), like (C), places one type of decision-making over the other— "data that supports the conclusions. . . " (E) is off-topic, as the passage is about executive decision-making, not about hiring employees and/or delegating decision-making. Choice (A) is correct.

93. **B**

To weaken the argument, we need a relevant reason why the acquisition was a good idea. Presumably it will address the complaint that the acquisition will "provide other competitors an opportunity to enter the field at a lower price."

Choice (A) is off-topic, as we don't know whether Bluecorp is located in one of those countries. What's more, it's unclear whether nearly monopolizing the market would weaken the argument. (B) illustrates why the acquisition had at least one positive effect, and it relates directly to the argument: the benefit of the acquisition will result in a lower price—presumably one that will not allow smaller competitors to enter the market.

Choice (C) is irrelevant, as the passage doesn't address differences between urban and non-urban areas. (D) tells us that smaller firms will result from the acquisition, but that doesn't address the complaint that the larger firm won't sell at a lower price. (E) is better than most of the choices, but not as good as (E). Weaker terms like "tend" can't compete with direct statements like "far lower cost" in (B), and it isn't clear that there aren't existing firms in the field that could challenge the resulting firm's dominance. Choice (B) is correct.

81 Explanations: RC: Scope-Based

101. C

The scope of the passage is the importance of her novels; the first paragraph describes how previous generations ignored her, and the following two focus on the impact of her work on future authors and its value to scholars.

Choice (A) is wrong, as it doesn't even mention Haywood, the topic of the passage. (B) is probably something the author would agree with, but the passage is more about Haywood's novels. (C) is correct: it encapsulates the topics of all three paragraphs. (D) is a comparison that the author doesn't address. (E), like (A), doesn't mention Haywood, and is much too specific. Choice (C) is correct.

102. C

The author is supporting the position that Haywood's novels are important, despite the earlier beliefs that they were not. Choice (C) accurately represents that, both including the notion that Haywood was not considered important ("underrated") and the idea that her works are of serious importance. The verb, "show," is also representative, as the passage provides many examples as evidence to support the position.

Choice (B) may be tempting, but "examine" is not as accurate as "show," since the author is clearly taking a side in this debate.

103. D

The main focus of the passage is defining post-Keynesians, specifically as regards their theory of time. Choice (A) isn't too far off, but it isn't exactly right that the passage uses time to illustrate a different view, and it is off-topic to put that in terms of its role in neoclassical economics. (B) is way off base, as equilibrium is not the main distinction in the passage. (C) is closer, but doesn't mention the fields that support those two notions, which is really the main idea.

Choice (D) is right: It emphasizes the focus on post-Keynesians and explains that the passage does so by discussing one concept. (E) is too specific, and is a position of the post-Keynesians, not necessarily the author of this passage.

104. D

The passage is most concerned with explaining the views of post-Keynesians in reference to those they disagree with, especially as they concern time and the labor market. Choice (A) doesn't touch on post-Keynesians at all, which disqualifies it. (B) overstates the importance of post-Keynesians; the passage doesn't describe how much of an effect they have had on economics in general.

Choice (C), like (B), goes beyond what the passage tells us in terms of the importance of Keynes's ideas. (D) is correct, as it emphasizes the differences between traditional and post-Keynesians, and points out that the differences lead them down different paths. (E) minimizes the role of Keynesians, which is certainly wrong when describing a passage that is about Keynesians and their theories.

82   Explanations: RC: Detail-Based

111.   A

The relevant sentence is the last one: "Most importantly, the 18th-century novel was largely concerned with domestic issues hinging on the role of women. . . " This matches up very closely to choice (A), which is correct. (B) isn't mentioned in the passage; (C) is something in Haywood's biography, not the novel; (D) is part of the novel tradition, but not the primary issue, and (E) is another tidbit from Haywood's biography, this time the target of Pope's "Dunciad."

112.   C

The relevant sentence is: ". . . 'Betsy Thoughtless' can be seen as the beginning of a tradition of novels of marriage, which culminated in Bronte's "Jane Eyre." Choice (C) is correct.

113.   B

The third paragraph holds the answer: "Haywood's 'Anti-Pamela,' a satire of Richardson's didactic novel, was as widely read as Fielding's parody of the same. . . " Choice (B) reflects the fact that both satirized the same work, so it is correct.

114.   A

The relevant sentence is the last one in the first paragraph: "post-Keynesians try to shift focus away from the 'long run"'-level analysis and analyze instead events in 'historical time,' emphasizing the real-world effect of deviations from equilibrium." Choice (A)'s reference to "practical effects of inefficiencies" is synonymous with "real-world effect of deviations," and the question tells us we're focusing on the labor market.

115.   A

The answer is contained in the second sentence of the first paragraph: "Most models of neoclassical economics utilize the notion of 'logical time,' in which markets (whether they be capital, goods, or labor markets) return to equilibrium after a disturbance is introduced and then overcome." Choice (A) just slightly rephrases the first part of the sentence.

83 Explanations: RC: Inference-Based

121.   D

The first paragraph describes only the vaccine, not any pros and cons. The drawbacks and comparison to the other vaccine come up in the final sentence: "While the first method is better established, the second may turn out be both more cost-effective and easier to use in treating large numbers of patients." In other words, the first may be less cost-effective and more difficult to use in treating large number of patients. That's choice (D), almost literally.

122.   D

The description of the viral vector vaccine tells us that it is manufactured in the laboratory (which is somewhat different from the first method), and those cells are introduced to provoke an immune system response. Further, we know that regardless of the vaccine used, each "must be created specifically" to generate a response to the patient's unique tumor.

(D) encapsulates much of that: they are created in a laboratory (we probably could guess that from the word "manufactured") and they must be created specifically for each patient. (A) is wrong, as the object isn't to weaken the immune system. (B) is wrong, as the cells are created in the laboratory to induce a response that existing cells aren't bringing about. (C) describes something more like the vaccine in the first paragraph. (E) also refers to the HSPs described in the first paragraph, which aren't discussed in reference to the viral vector vaccine. (D) is the correct choice.

123.   A

The second paragraph notes that deficit spending is something both traditional and post-Keynesians agree on as a solution to certain inefficiencies. Choice (A) doesn't represent all of that, but it does state something true, that traditional Keynesians support it as a method.

Choice (B) is too extreme, using the phrase "solves all of the problems." (C) is inaccurate, as it sounds like deficit spending is an aspect of this theory, but not necessarily a key aspect. (D) is wrong, as traditional Keynesians favor "long run" analysis. (E) is also incorrect, as deficit spending and "pump-priming" are two terms for the same concept. (A) is correct.

124.   E

Most of the passage is about time in some form or other, so rather than trying to predict the parameters of an answer, proceed through the choices. (A) is too strong, as the author doesn't tell us that post-Keynesians represent a particularly "trenchant" critique. (B) is an irrelevant comparison, as the passage doesn't discuss any other applications. We don't know it applies most directly to the labor market. (C) is another irrelevant comparison ("most?") and the author doesn't take a stance on whether it is a problem.

Choice (D) conflates theory (the level at which we talk about "historical time," for instance) and actual real-life effects, such as those brought about by deficit spending. A theoretical concept isn't what wreaks havoc with something in the real world. (E), finally, is correct. The whole reason that time is discussed is to describe where two schools of thought diverge.

125.   A

Traditional Keynesians play a large part in this passage, but their specific positions are not often defined; we may have to look for an answer that represents something different from what we know about the positions of post-Keynesians.

Choice (A) is exactly that. We know that Keynesians generally support deficit spending to solve short- and medium-term inefficiencies, and that post-Keynesians differ in that they focus on more than just those inefficiencies. Thus, it can be inferred that traditional Keynesians are not interested in other things ("That is the extent of the story for the traditional Keynesian").

(B) misrepresents the passage, in which Keynesians are said to generally support deficit spending/"pump priming." (C) gets the distinction backwards; traditional Keynesians use "logical time." (D) is up for debate, as "many post-Keynesians believe that the movement known as Keynesianism actually represents a severe divergence from the ideas of Keynes." Most of (E) is correct, but it is unclear in the passage whether traditional Keynesians are neoclassical economists.

84 Explanations: RC: Structure-Based

131.   C

The third paragraph consists mostly of examples of Haywood's influence. It could, then, be considered evidence for the claims presented earlier in the passage.

Choice (A) is incorrect, as there is no attempt to reconcile the author's positive view of Haywood with the earlier, less favorable ones. (B) is also incorrect: the third paragraph and second paragraph both support the idea of Haywood as influential. (C) is correct: the first sentence of the second paragraph is the main point of the whole passage, and the third paragraph provides examples that support the pro-Haywood view.

Choice (D) is close, but the third paragraph also discusses another work ("Anti-Pamela") and it doesn't mention "Love in Excess." (E) is wrong, as the first paragraph represents the view the Haywood is not important. Choice (C) is correct.

132.   C

The second paragraph presents the author's view (Haywood's novels shouldn't be disregarded) and evidence to support it, while the first describes the way previous generations of scholars considered her work.

Choice (A) is wrong: the second paragraph doesn't try to explain the reasons behind the earlier disregard for Haywood's novels. (B) understates what the author is doing; the argument is much more than an exception to the principle of disregarding Haywood's novels. (C) is correct: the second paragraph argues against the old view of Haywood's work.

Choice (D) suggests that the two paragraphs support the same position, which is not true. (E), again, does not reflect the fact that the two paragraphs describe almost precisely opposite viewpoints. Choice (C) is correct.

133.   A

The first paragraph describes why Haywood had not been viewed as important, and the last sentence suggests how her supporters had slightly begun to see value in her work. There is only one main perspective in the paragraph: that her works, especially her novels, were not very important. Choice (A) reflects that: the viewpoint is the position that her novels could be disregarded, and that historical evolution represents the last sentence.

The other four choices all describe much more than is contained in the one paragraph. Because there is only one main position in the paragraph, there is no room for "opposing viewpoints," something "described and refuted," "evidence provided to question" anything, or something "shown to be false." Choice (A) is correct.

134.   A

The second paragraph describes the second vaccine—the viral vector vaccine—and concludes with a sentence on the two vaccines's similarities, and another comparing the pros and cons of each. Choice (A) describes that almost perfectly.

(B) overstates the difference, as the viral vector vaccine is not described as inferior. (C) is off-topic, as the passage isn't about distribution. (D) is wrong, as it suggests that the second paragraph keeps discussing the first type of vaccine. (E) only represents the final two sentences, and misrepresents the comparison in the last sentence. Choice (A) is correct.

135.   C

There is no opinion presented in the first paragraph; it is just a description of one type of vaccine. All of the choices refer also to the second paragraph, which is a description of another type, following by some comparisons between the two.

Choice (A) is incorrect as there are not "opposing views" in the first paragraph. (B) is wrong as the focus is on the details of the method, not its importance. (C) is better: "describes a method" characterizes the paragraph, and that method is contrasted with the one in the second paragraph.

Choice (D) suggests that one method has superseded the other, which is not supported by the passage. (E) makes assumptions not warranted by the passage; we might assume that cancer vaccines would save lives, but that's outside of the scope of the passage. (C) is correct.

85 Explanations: RC: Mixed Review 1

141.   A

The author isn't presenting an argument; the passage only describes how an old system has stood the test of time, despite adjustments and competing approaches. (A) matches that characterization almost perfectly.

Choice (B) is limited to the ways in which the taxonomy has been updated. That's part of the passage, but not the primary purpose. (C) isn't even covered in the passage, which mentions that the taxonomy has been expanded, but not how that is done. (D) is very similar to (B), which describes a part, but not all of the passage. (E) unnecessarily limits the taxonomy to two specific fields, which misrepresents why those two fields were mentioned in the passage. (A) is correct.

142.   E

Cladistics is only mentioned in part of one sentence: "cladistics—the classification of species based on evolutionary ancestry—has brought about a parallel hierarchy that sometimes, but certainly not always, overlaps with the traditional Linnaean divisions." Choice (E) is very similar to the phrase between the dashes, and accurately represents what we know about cladistics. (E) is correct.

143.   C

The author uses the word "remarkably" before pointing out that the taxonomy has remained effective ("proven robust"), suggesting that it is something of a surprise. The reason given follows the comma in that sentence: "long before Charles Darwin's theory of evolution drastically altered our understanding of the natural world." Choice (C) represents that reason why the robustness of the taxonomy is remarkable.

One might defend (D), as well, but it is not as well supported. While we're told that Darwin's theory "drastically altered" scientific knowledge (and thus, taxonomies might be expected to change), we aren't told what fraction of claims made in the mid-1700s have stood the test of time. Choice (C) is correct.

144.   E

Here's the relevant sentence: "More seriously, the taxonomy has required vast numbers of additional levels of classification, especially in species-rich fields such as entomology." In other words, the uniqueness of entomology is that is covers so many species, and that number of species has led to new levels of classification even more so than other fields.

Choice (E) represents that quite well—the number of species has placed stress on a system that was originally designed for a smaller number of known species. (A) is inaccurate, as insects might be a sub-category of one of the kingdoms. (B) is true of zoology, not entomology. (C) may be true, but the passage doesn't speak to that. (D) is unsupported, as the passage doesn't tell us much about where cladistics might be better than the traditional taxonomy.

145.   A

The passage doesn't have an argument; it is purely explanatory. What it explains is an old system (Linnaean taxonomy), the adjustments that have been made to it, and one differing system (cladistics). Choice (A) represents those three aspects.

(B) is wrong, as there is no suggestion that a third method is needed. (C) is incorrect, since the traditional approach isn't really supported with evidence; the passage simply says it has held up. (D) misrepresents the passage as arguing for something, which is a very common GMAT wrong answer type. (E) is wrong, as there is no reconciliation attempted between Linnaean taxonomy and cladistics.

86   Explanations: RC: Mixed Review 2

151.   B

This is an inference question that could refer to nearly any part of the passage. Since there is no way to narrow down what the passage said about the Ming Dynasty, look at each answer choice.

Choice (A) is incorrect. The first sentence of the paragraph tells us that the Ming was more open than previous dynasties, but we don't know how it compared to those that followed. (B) is not only correct, it sums up much of the main point of the passage. The trade brought in silver, and when the silver dried up, it caused economic problems.

Choice (C) is wrong, as all we know is that the Ming suffered from Japanese piracy, and Japanese silver was brokered through a third party. (D) is impossible to tell; if anything, the Protestant raids hurt the Ming. (E) could be true, but the passage only gives us one instance of treatment of foreigners, so we can't draw a generalization. Choice (B) is correct.

152.   E

The passage doesn't tell us much about Ming-Japanese relations, other than that the Ming suffered "Japanese piracy in coastal areas," and that other countries brokered silver between Japan and the Ming. Recognizing that limitation, we can eliminate each of the first four choices. We don't know anything about the welcome granted the Japanese, whether they brokered goods from other sources, whether they were jailed, or whether they limited themselves to luxury goods. We do, however, know that they were considered illegal (that's what piracy is), and the characterization of Portuguese trade in (E) is accurate as well.

153.   D

In scope questions, start by looking at the initial verbs. The author is not arguing a side in this passage, so "arguing" is wrong. Even "suggesting" and "emphasizing" indicate more of a position from the author's perspective; I wouldn't completely rule those out, but I would focus instead on the two choices that open with "explaining."

Choice (B) is far too broad, and is only addressed by one sentence in the second paragraph. (D) is much better, and includes descriptions of content in both paragraphs. Note that (D) has much of the same description as (A), but the initial verb makes the difference. To confirm that the others are incorrect: (C) is wrong because of the word "only," and (E) is much too broad, while the passage focuses on only one dynasty. Choice (D) is correct.

154.   D

The phrase "according to the passage" signals that this is a detail question. The correct answer should closely reflect some part of the passage. The Chinese reluctance is detailed in the first paragraph, including this: "Given the contemporary Chinese experience of Japanese piracy in coastal areas, it is no surprise that authorities were skeptical of foreigners..." That's (D), which is correct.

155.   C

This is a rare occurrence in a Reading Comprehension passage: a weaken question. It isolates which conclusion we're to focus on, so we know we want a choice that explains why the inflation in silver values would not contribute to disaster for rural Chinese.

Choice (A) is incorrect, as it explains what happens after the disaster. (B) doesn't explain why silver wasn't important; if anything, it sounds as if currency would've been very helpful. (C) weakens the conclusion as, if rural Chinese didn't use hard currency (such as silver), the change in silver values would not have affected them.

Choice (D) is irrelevant, as it doesn't even tangentially address silver. (E) is also irrelevant: the question is about rural Chinese, not people anywhere else in the world. Choice (C) is correct.

87 Explanations: SC: Verbs

201.   A

One difference that appears in the answer choices is the first few words: (A) has "less," (B) and (C) have "in less" and (D) and (E) have "it took less." The event referred to in the non-underlined portion is the adoption of a method, something that would happen at a single point in time. "It took less than 15 years" is wrong—we're talking about a single moment in time, while something that "took less than 15 years" refers to a process.

It's also possible to eliminate (B) and (C) by the same reasoning, but it's much less clear. (B) can be eliminated because it creates a nonsensical meaning: The modifier has "patenting," as if it's the main competition doing the patenting. (C) has a verb problem: "15 years since" should be followed by the simple past tense, as in "In the 15 years since the system was patented," instead of past perfect. Choice (A) is the remaining correct choice.

202.   D

Phrases like "the list of countries" should sound an alarm. "Countries" is plural, but "list" is singular, so you have to determine which one "qualifies" corresponds to. As it turns out, the list is of countries "that qualify" for the rating—the list itself doesn't qualify for a rating. That leaves only choices (D) and (E).

The first difference between the remaining choices is "qualify for an investment-grade rating" and "qualify for earning the investment-grade rating." "Qualify for earning" is redundant; there's no notion of "earning" in the original sentence, so there's no distinction between qualifying for the rating and earning the rating. Further, "for earning" is not idiomatic, and because the phrase is redundant, there isn't even really a way to fix it by changing a word or two. That leaves choice (D).

203.   B

The first word of the underlined portion should not be singular, since it refers to all three items in the preceding list. Thus, (C) and (D) can be eliminated. The phrase "were an impression," which opens (E), is extremely unidiomatic, so (E) can eliminated as well.

If you focus only on the beginning of the underlined portion, (B) is preferable to (A), as (B) does not employ the passive voice. This is a subtle distinction, but the sort of thing that makes one answer superior to another on a difficult question. Also, "also was acknowledged" is preferable to "was also acknowledged," since there was no previous "was" in the sentence, and "also was acknowledged" put the entire verb ("was acknowledged") in one place. Choice (B) is correct.

204.   B

Comparing the two openings in the choices, "had expected" is correct. The emissions increased in the last year (in the past), while analysts made their prediction before that time in the past. Therefore, we need the past perfect tense: "had expected." Choice (A) or (B) must be correct.

The first difference between (A) and (B) is the missing "them to" in (B). The sentence is still clear without those two words, so not only is (B) possibly correct, it is more likely to be correct than (A), as the GMAT prefers efficiency. The second difference is the word "that" in (B), while "that" is not in (A). There's a "that" earlier in the sentence: "The study showed that" [one thing] "and that" [another thing]. This is a shorter version of saying, "The study showed that... and the study showed that..." Since the two things are somewhat unrelated, it is proper to include the "that" before the second thing the study showed. (B) is correct.

205.   A

Three of the choices end in "is," while the other two end in "are." The subject in question is "cultural psychology," which is singular, so "is" is correct. Eliminate (C) and (E). (B) is incorrect because of the extraneous (and flawed) "to them." If anything, "them" should refer to "data," which is singular. Regardless, the "to them" is unnecessary. (D) is incorrect because of the phrase "approach data." The meaning is that the practitioners "collect data" through certain approaches, which is something else entirely. That leaves only choice (A).

206.   B

To make things simpler, ignore the phrase between the dashes. So, to abbreviate: "Mann's methods and his areas of reform was as radical..." When two nouns are combined with the word "and," they become plural, so the verb should be plural. That eliminates (A) and (C).

(B)'s verbs make sense. "Were" is plural and past-tense, reflecting the reference to "his own time." "They are" is correct as well—"they" refers to the methods and areas of reform, while "are" is present tense, as it refers to "our" time.

(D) is incorrect: the past perfect tense ("had been") is only correct when there are two separate events in the past. There is only one reference to the past ("his own time") in the sentence. (E) is incorrect, since "have been" is present perfect, while "his own time" should be in the past. Choice (B) is correct.

88   Explanations: SC: Lists

211.   B

To make the sentence simpler, ignore the phrase between the commas, "presenting...primates." Next, notice that the sentence includes a list. The researcher demonstrated that he was "challenging..., comparing..., and he combed." That list isn't parallel, so there's one mistake to correct. Eliminate (A).

"Challenging" can't be changed, so unless you drastically change the sentence, the parallel verbs should be "comparing" and "combing." That eliminates (C) and (D). (E) has parallelism problems as well. Each item in the list must begin with the verb itself. "He was" doing three things: "challenging," "comparing," and "combing." It would be incorrect to say, "he was challenging..., he was comparing..., and combing." (D) is the only choice remaining, so it is correct.

212.   A

The first distinction between the choices may be the opening phrases, but it may be easier to start with the list in the sentence: "will increase..., shed..., and aid..." As is, the list is parallel, but that isn't the case in all of the choices.

(B) has an extraneous "and" before the word "shed." That's inappropriate before the second item in a three-part list. (C) has other problems ("Having translated" is the wrong verb form, and "by increasing" is more idiomatic than "in increasing") but by moving "increasing" into a modifier, makes "shed..., and aid" a two-part list. That in itself isn't incorrect, but a two-part list wouldn't have a comma, as there is before "and aid."

(D) uses "shedding" instead of "shed." If you only read the underlined portion, this may appear correct, but the form of the verb "to shed" must be parallel with "aid" later in the sentence. Finally, (E) has a similar problem, with "would be shedding." Again, this must be parallel with "aid," requiring that the verb in this position be "shed." (A) is the only remaining choice.

213.   D

There are two key differences among the choices: the opening few words, and the form of the verb "indicating." The thing that indicates "Jane Addams's desire" is "Hull House's founding" of various things. Ignoring the lengthy list for now, "Hull Houses's founding" is a singular noun, meaning that the proper form of the verb is "indicates." That eliminates (A) and (E).

Both (B) and (C) are wrong because they deviate from the list structure in the non-underlined part of the sentence. Hull House founded (a) "a public kitchen;" (b) "a sociological institution;" and (c) "schools for adults and young children." If you substitute the phrases in (B) or (C) for the final item in that list, the word "founded" or "founding" is redundant. As part of the list, it is clear that that item was founded by Hull House. Therefore, (D) is correct.

214.   E

The first list in this sentence is completely contained in the non-underlined portion, but the underlined portion has a pair of items that should be parallel as well. The policies (a) "provide cost certainty..." and (b) "make it easier for firms to recruit...." The intermediate phrase has to stay, but in such a way that makes it clear that those two items are grammatically parallel.

Start with the correct verb form of "make." "Provide" doesn't change, so the parallel verb is "make," leaving only choices (A) and (E). In (A), the "that" is extraneous; the correct form would be "provide cost certainty...and...make it easier," so (E) is correct.

215.   E

Most of the underlined portion is a three-part list. "Either" implies two choices, so it is wrong, eliminating (A) and (B). You can sort out the remaining choices by focusing on the words at the beginning of each list item.

(C)'s list items open like this: "to prevent..., for recovery..., or relieving." None of those are parallel. (D)'s open like this: "for preventing..., to aid..., also pain relief." Again, not parallel. (E)'s look much better: "to prevent..., aid..., or relieve." Those three verbs are parallel, so (E) is the correct choice.

216.   E

As usual, if there is a long phrase separated by commas, read around it. To abbreviate the sentence: "Double-blind experiments at the Sudbury Neutrino Observatory is designed..." Without the interruption, it may be clearer that "is" is incorrect, eliminating (A) and (B) because we need the plural verb.

Since each of the remaining choices have the word "and," check to see that they are parallel. In (C), they are not. Grammatically, "scientists' preexisting expectations" and "the elimination of" are both things the experiments are "designed to control." They aren't designed to control the elimination—they are designed to eliminate the bias.

(D) is closer, since both list items start with "toward," but "toward the control" and "toward eliminating" are not parallel. (E) solves the problem: "toward controlling" and "eliminating" are parallel; the experiments are designed to do those two things. (E) is correct.

89 Explanations: SC: Comparisons

221.   C

This is a tricky sentence to fix because it includes two pieces of background information about Trippe. There's only room for one between a pair of commas (such as "the founder of Pan American Airways") so the correct sentence will find a way to include both without the ambiguity of the initial sentence. Eliminate (A) because you can't "read around" the first phrase: "Juan Trippe because he planned..." doesn't make sense.

(B) is incorrect because of its use of the passive voice, "was planned by." Also, the "and" in "and so he" is unnecessary; "so he" would be sufficient.

(C) is correct: it moves one of the pieces of background information to a modifier. It is Trippe who planned to expand his airline's service; he was also the founder of the airline, and if you read around the "the founder" phrase, the sentence works: "Trippe acquired several..."

(D) has a modifier problem and incorrect parallelism. It is Trippe who was "planning to expand," not "Airways," which immediately precedes the verb. Also, by preceding "acquired" with "and," it sounds like there should be a past tense verb somewhere earlier in the sentence. There is not.

(E) moves the phrase "the founder..." too far away from what it modifies, "Juan Trippe." The modifier must be immediately adjacent to what it modifies.

222.   A

This is a textbook comparison question. The question even uses the word "contrast" before comparing two things, "rising unemployment rates in the US and Canada," and "the Chinese unemployment rate." Each of the last four answer choices fail to make an appropriate comparison. Unemployment rates must be compared to other unemployment rates. For instance, (B) is wrong because it compares "rising unemployment rates" to "China." (C) and (D) do the same. (E) compares the "rising unemployment rates" to "increasing demand abroad," which is also not comparable. (A) is correct.

223.   E

The opening word "unlike" should signal that this sentence involves a comparison. To isolate the comparison, ignore the phrase "which insist... as equals" and focus on what is being compared. The initial sentence compares "many collective bargaining agreements" with "employees at the aluminum plant," two things that cannot be compared. Since we can't change the first part of the comparison, we need some other agreement to follow the comma.

(B) has the same problem as (A), while the other three choices follow the comma with "the aluminum plant's agreement." (C) is incorrect because it suggests that the agreement itself compensates its employees. Logically speaking, the agreement doesn't do the compensating, nor does it have employees. (D) and (E) differ only in the first phrase; (D) is redundant. If the agreement treats "classes of workers as equals," it's implied that it treats them as "equal to one another." The GMAT dislikes redundancy, so (E) is correct.

224.   D

In the initial sentence, "ones" refers to "wings," but that isn't clear until the second half of the sentence. A better construction would use the word "wings" in the first half of the sentence. That leads us to (D) and (E).

Another distinction among the choices is the presence or lack of a connecting word such as "with" or "whereas." To contrast bald eagles and golden eagles, we need such a word. That eliminates (A) and (E), leaving only (D) as a likely correct answer. (D) uses the word "wings" in the first half, and word "whereas" connects the two contrasting facts. (D) is correct.

225.   C

The first difference to focus on is that between "that" and "which." As a general rule, "which" follows a comma, and since there are no commas, that leaves us with (B) and (C). (More specifically, "that" is restrictive. Since "that" specifies the sort of "approach" we're referring to, it is correct.)

The first difference between the remaining choices is "with his" versus "with that of his." The comparison is between Eakins's approach and Muybridge's approach, so "with that of his" is correct, as the "that of" stands in for "the approach of." Choice (C) is correct.

226.   A

The word "like" signals a comparison. The comparison is between "the telephone" and "the internet," so (B) and (D), which include the term "internet's representation," are incorrect.

The "As" in (C) is only correct if it is paired with a noun, as in the opening phrase of (D), "As did the telephone." (We've ruled out (D) for other reasons, but the opening phrase could be correct.) (E) has the same problem: "as" needs to be paired with "did," which is missing in this choice. Choice (A) is correct.

90   Explanations: SC: Modifiers

231.   D

The modifier "based on extant archeological evidence" is incorrect: "each hunting season" is not based on evidence. Perhaps research regarding the hunting is "based on archeological evidence." Eliminate (A) and (B). (C) has a more accurate modifier, while (D) and (E) have no modifiers at all.

(C) is incorrect: To see why, focus on the word "that." "in pursuit of game animals that would feed the tribe and that, ..., women hunting alone..." In this choice, "that" refers to the pursuit of game animals. "Women hunting alone" does not. The choice, then, creates a list that is structured around the word "that," but that makes no sense.

(D) is better. The evidence "indicates that" women and men collaborated, and that women hunting alone were not uncommon. That's a well-structured list, and both of the phrases following the appearances of the word "that" refer to what the evidence indicates.

(E) has a similar opening to (D), but is missing "that" following the word "indicates." "Indicates," like "suggests," "implies," or "points out," should be followed with "that" in order to be idiomatic. Choice (D), then, is correct.

232.   C

This is a long, complicated sentence. The first order of business is to make sense of all the commas and short phrases. One place to start might be the modifying phrase "amassing little support, collapsing within hours..." Both of those things refer to the coup's failure. That means the modifier is in the right place, but since there are no other items in the list, it would be preferable to condense both into one modifier, as in choice (C): "amassing little support and collapsing within hours..." This makes (C) a strong possibility.

(B) and (E) use "collapses" instead of "collapsing," making it seem like "fails" and "collapses" are parallel items in the same list. If the typical military coup "fails," does it also "collapse?" Yes, but that doesn't mean "collapses" should begin a parallel list item. "Collapses" would be redundant as an item of such a list; instead, it modifies the failure by further specifying what is meant. Again, this makes (C) look better, as it includes "collapsing" in a modifier.

(A) is clumsy due to the phrase "having usually gotten." With no subject (compare to "it" in choice (C)), this sentence implies that it is "the ideology" that has gotten the attention. That isn't what the sentence means. (D)'s problem is that the comma, followed by "but," implies that what follows is a complete sentence. For comparison, (C) is a complete sentence after the ", but." (C), then, is the only correct choice.

233.   E

When a modifying phrase is separated by two commas, the sentence should be grammatically correct without it. (A) is not: "The gypsy moth it has established itself." The "it" is problematic. That eliminates choices (A) and (B).

263

One key difference among the remaining choices is the verb containing the word "eradicated." (E) is only "eradicated," while (C) is "has been eradicated" and (D) is "having been eradicated." "Eradicated" is sufficient on its own, so (E) is the most likely correct choice. (C) is incorrect also because it connects the moth's eradication and its ability to defoliate in the same phrase—those are contradictory. (D) is incorrect also because of the redundancy of "Although" and "still." One or the other is fine, but both are not necessary. (E) is correct.

234.   B

You should recognize this as a modifier problem. What is "Displayed...?" It turns out that electric light is displayed, but the words "electric light" don't show up until long after the comma. (A), then, is wrong.

(D) and (E) have a different opening modifier, but they are also wrong. Who is "witnessing electric light for the first time?" Presumably the residents of San Francisco, yet those words don't show up right after the comma.

(B) and (C) are very similar until the final phrase. Read around the phrase "one hundred years...Independence," and determine what should follow the comma. "Displayed..." should modify "electric light," meaning that (B) is correct. Note that (B) is passive voice and (C) is not; answers with passive voice are often, but not always, wrong. If every other answer has more serious grammatical problems, a choice containing passive voice can be correct.

235.   A

Not only is the entire sentence underlined, but a glance at the choices reveals that there are no clear patterns to help you eliminate multiple choices at once. The initial sentence looks good: the taxon includes a number of species, which is more than the other taxons. There are multiple modifiers, and they appear to modify the right things.

(B) has extraneous language, such as "that is" following the first comma. Also, the concluding "classified in it" is awkward. (C) has a phrase you can read around, leaving you with "The Mormyridae taxon it includes..." which is clearly wrong.

(D) has an extraneous "which is," as well as the "classified in it" that was awkward in (B). Also, it implies a contrast ("While..."), though there is no apparent contrast between the number of genera and the number of species. (E) repeats the awkward "classified in it," and separates the "203 different species" from "more than all the other..." Those two facts are related (and are adjacent in the initial sentence), making this construction much less clear.

91 Explanations: SC: Pronouns

241.   D

First, notice that the sentence contains a list. The state agencies are "using," "consulting," and "studying." "Using" and "studying" can't be changed, so "consulting" (which is parallel with "using" and "studying") must remain the same. That eliminates choices (B) and (E). The three remaining choices differ in the first part of the underlined portion.

Both (A) and (C) use a pronoun, "their" or "them." While it is clear from context that the pronoun refers to the water resources, the GMAT holds you to a higher grammatical standard. In this part of the sentence, there are two plural nouns, "state agencies" and "water resources." Technically, the pronoun could refer to either of those, so "the previous rate"—which could only refer to the rate that water resources are being used—must be correct.

242.   C

The first apparent difference in the choices is between starting with "a distinctive weaving style" and starting with "with them." The latter is correct, because the phrase following the comma ("through which...") refers to the weaving style. Therefore, we want the phrase "weaving style" to be as close to "through which" as possible. That eliminates (A) and (B).

(D) is incorrect because of the present tense "maintains," which conflicts with the past tense "adapted" at the beginning of the sentence. That leaves "through which they maintained both a livelihood" and "and maintaining through it both a livelihood." The key difference is "which" instead of "it." "It" could refer to any singular noun in the sentence ("The Navajo people," "life in captivity," etc.), while "which" can only refer to the subject that precedes it. (C) is clear, so it is correct.

243.   D

The first issue in the initial sentence is the word "they." The subject of the sentence is "the company," which is singular. "It" is correct, eliminating (A), (B), and (C).

Two key differences between (D) and (E) are "being based" versus "based," and "demand for" versus "demand it had for." When in doubt, go with the shorter answer, but we can be more specific here. "Being" is almost never correct, and is certainly not correct when it isn't necessary. "It had" is vague, as "it" could refer to the company (as it does earlier in the sentence) or the distribution system. Choice (D) is correct.

244.   E

Choices (A) and (B) both have the pronoun "it," presumably referring to the newly low level of funding. While we can deduce what "it" must refer to, using the pronoun is only correct when the noun it refers to is present in the sentence. Since "it" refers to something that isn't in the sentence, (A) and (B) can be eliminated.

(C) is incorrect due to the word "would." That implies something hypothetical, whereas the sentence is referring to a decrease that has actually happened. (D) suggests that the low level will last (or has lasted) for a decade, while the sentence refers to a "recent decrease" to a certain low level at one point in time. That leaves only choice (E), which has the "lowest level" at one point in time, and no problems with a pronoun.

245.   D

The long opening phrase is a modifier, referring to "local school boards." Many of the choices have problems, but as it turns out, proper modification isn't one of them.

The construction "a recognition" is unidiomatic, so both (A) and (C) can be eliminated. Both (B) and (E) use the pronoun "they" (and "them" in (E) as well) before the subject is stated. In special cases, that's acceptable, but such cases are rare. In general, pronoun usage requires that it is clear what the pronoun refers to when the pronoun is used. (D) solves that problem. The modifier refers to something that can be true of the "local school boards" without using pronouns, so (D) is correct.

246.   A

In the underlined portion, "it" is an abbreviation for "tsunami-related property damage" and "did" is shorthand for "rose," so the underlined portion needs to communicate, "more than property damage rose ." That's correct: "considerably more than property damage rose in the previous year."

Go through the other four answers to find the errors: (B) uses "they" instead of "it" to refer to the singular "property damage." (C) and (E) use "was" instead of "did," while "did" is correct in representing an active verb. (D) has no subject, making it unclear what is greater than in the previous year. Choice (A) is correct.

92 Explanations: SC: Idioms

251.   C

The first difference between the choices is the initial word in each: Choose between "for," "to," and "that." This is one of the many English idioms governing which preposition to use along with a verb. In this case, the association "uses" something "to" do something. (When in doubt, avoid the construction that requires an –ing verb, such as "for establishing.) That limits our choices to (B) and (C).

Comparing (B) and (C), we can focus on the end of the underlined portion: "of" or "of as many, or." (B) is not only longer, but it is slightly nonsensical: "as many as" and "more than" mean different things. Since we can't take out "more than," we're stuck with that meaning. To avoid a contradiction, (B) can't be correct, leaving (C) as the correct choice.

252.   D

The opening modifier refers to something that must have been accomplished by a person or a group of people. Therefore, the words immediately after the comma must refer to a person or group of people. That eliminates (A) and (B). The differences between the other choices hinge on the word "both." When used to pair two things in a sentence, "both" is like a branching off.

For instance, in (D), there are two items paired by "both...and." Both should logically finish the phrase begun by "how the country can." In this case, the results are: "how the country can expand foreign trade" and "how the country can work effectively toward peace..." Those work, so (D) is a possible answer. The same cannot be said of the other two remaining choices.

In (C), the resulting phrases would be: "must now ascertain how the country can..." and "must now ascertain work effectively..." The latter doesn't make sense.

In (E), the word "also" creates problems. The resulting phrases are: "how the country can expand foreign trade," and "how the country can also how to make it work." Again, the latter doesn't make sense. (D) is correct.

253.   D

The first glaring error in the initial sentence is the idiom "decided of." That's wrong; among the choices, "decided that" is the only acceptable alternative. ("Decided to" or "decided on" can also be correct, depending on context.) That eliminates (A), (C), and (E).

Of the remaining choices, (B) is incorrect. That choice makes it sound that Walker and his band decided that bluegrass expanded. That doesn't make sense; if anything they would decide that bluegrass could expand, not that it had already done something. By contrast, (D) makes things much more clear. The use of "which" indicates that it is bluegrass that "has continued to expand," without suggesting that it is expanding simply because of Walker's decision. Choice (D) is correct.

254.   D

First, you can assume that (A) and (B) are almost certainly wrong, due to the phrase "of there being." "Being" is almost always incorrect. (E) also has a major flaw: "figurative significance" means something very different from "significantly figured."

The key difference between (C) and (D) is "of" versus "that there were." While "of" is shorter, whatever follows a phrase like "support the notion" must be a complete sentence. (D) connects "the notion" to the complete sentence starting with "there were many women. . ." with the word "that." (C) does not, so (D) is correct.

255.   D

Since the sentence is saying he did not seem likely to develop the reputation, we need the word "nor," limiting the choices to (B), (D), or (E). (E) is wrong because of the double negative ("nor. . . not").

The two phrases "he did not have" and "seem likely to develop" both serve to start the sentence, so both need a subject and a verb. "He did not have" has a subject ("he") and a verb ("did have"), so we need "nor did he" after the comma so that there's a subject and verb in that phrase as well. Choice (D) is correct.

93   Explanations: SC: Other

261.   E

If one thing should be clear from the sentence, it's that (A) is incorrect. As written, it's a mess. "Has been automated" is passive voice and rather awkward, it's not clear what "it" refers to in "whether it be," and "or also" is never correct.

The problem with "or also" allows you to eliminate (D) as well, while the ambiguity of "whether it be," makes (C) wrong. (B) and (E) also end with the word "but," which creates the conjunction "but also." "But also" is correct only when paired with "not only," which appears in (E) but not in (B). (E), then, is the correct choice.

262.   C

There are two places in the sentence to focus on: the area around "generating solutions," and the first few words after the semi-colon. The latter might be a bit easier. A phrase that follows a semi-colon must be a complete sentence, so (B) is incorrect: "Mainly to create a system..." is not a complete sentence.

Several other choices have problems in that area as well. (A) has the adverb "mainly" in the wrong place. "Main" should modify "aim." The sentence is trying to point out the analysts' central goal. The idea of "main creation" doesn't quite make sense, and it certainly isn't what the sentence is trying to get across. (D) is missing a word for clarity: It should read, "their main aim is the creation of." (E) also has an error here: the aim is "to create," not creating. To say that the "aim is creating" means something else, that the aim itself (the fact that analysts have a certain goal) is creating a certain system. (C) is the only remaining choice.

263.   D

The underlined phrase suggests that the poetry made way for some future developments, meaning that we must refer to the poetry as something that was created in the past. (Sometimes, as in "some critics say that it is," we use present tense to refer to works of art.) So, "pointed" is correct while "points" is incorrect, eliminating (C) and (E).

There is also a comparison issue. It "pointed the way" to a type of poetry as well as "the work of" another poet. It wouldn't be correct to say that it pointed to "free verse" and "Jack Kerouac"—those aren't grammatically comparable. Instead, "free verse" is grammatically similar to "the work of" Kerouac. Therefore, only (D) can be correct. Note as well the idiom "pointed to" instead of "pointed for." We didn't end up needing that, but it is another way to eliminate a couple of choices.

264.   E

Three of the choices open with "dangers," while the other two start with "that the dangers." By comparing the dangers posed by the snake to the dangers posed by "more mundane matters," the sentence requires "recognized that," because the traveler recognized a fact. The traveler may have "recognized dangers" (by which we would mean that he realized that dangers were present), but that's not what the sentence is about. Eliminate (A), (B), and (C).

(D) is incorrect because of the "are" at the end of the sentence. It's generally bad form to end a sentence with a verb, and it's unnecessary in this case. It is also poor style to repeat the word "dangers" when "those" would suffice. Choice (E) is correct.

265.   E

Not only is this a long, complicated sentence, but there are no patterns that jump out at you in the answer choices. Start by analyzing the sentence as written. It is incorrect due to the passive voice: "combined in it...were..." That error might recur, but the only way to find out is to analyze each of the other choices as well.

(B) is not a complete sentence. The phrase starting with "a test" is a modifier of the initial phrase, so there is no noun to pair with "combining." (C) is unlikely to be correct, as there are multiple instances of passive voice. The vaccine "was licensed," and three strains "had been combined in it."

(D), like (B), is not a complete sentence. Read around the phrase "combined...1955," and what's left still needs a verb. (E) finally solves all of these problems. There is a slight instance of passive voice ("was licensed") but nothing as bad as (A) or (C). It is a complete sentence, and it is clear that Salk did the combining of the strains. Choice (E) is correct.

266.   A

Since four of the choices start with the word "and," focus on the grammar rule governing "and" following a comma. When "and" follows a comma (and it is not part of a list), what follows "and" must be a complete sentence. That eliminates (B) and (E), neither of which have a subject after "and."

(C) and (D) have a subject ("it") but it isn't clear what the subject refers to. There is no subject in the first phrase that is the thing raising the number of countries recognized, so "it" doesn't make sense in this context. Choice (A) is correct.

94 Explanations: Additional CR

301.   D

The question is not a classic "weaken" prompt, but it is similar: we're looking for a problem with the argument. The argument compares two types of food storage, one of which leaves ecological waste; the other is biodegradable. It concludes that, despite the advantages of the first type, the more wasteful type will not be used in the future. The most immediate objection is that the advantages outweigh the environmental impact–that is captured in choice (D), which is correct.

(A) may be tempting, but "mitigating" impact does not eliminate it, and the argument is focused on avoiding environmental impact altogether. The other incorrect choices are irrelevant to the argument.

302.   B

Fill-in-the-blank questions require that you focus on the scope of the passage. The phrase the fits the end of the passage must not go off-topic.

Here, we are looking for an explanation why members leaving a commune end up in more lawsuits, and this explanation must not be related to the fact that they are in "mainstream" jobs. (A) doesn't provide an explanation, other than the nebulous "difficult time" they face. (B) is generic and acceptable: there are many changes other than getting a job. (C) may be true, but doesn't fit in the sentence. (D) links lawsuits to jobs, which isn't what the passage is doing. (E) explains why lawsuits may be low in the commune, but doesn't address life afterward.

The only acceptable choice is (B), which is correct.

303.   E

This is essentially a weaken question, only with suggestive questions for answer choices. We're looking for a choice that calls into question the validity of the claim made in the passage.

Choice is a common type of wrong answer choice: it seizes on one irrelevant part of the passage and says that "it varies." (B) is also irrelevant: the argument classifies everyone as "dehydrated." (C) is yet another off-topic comparison. (D) doesn't make any specific challenge. (E) is correct: It suggests that there may be no evolutionary advantage to this defense. If there is not, it is unlikely that the mind has "evolved" such a tactic.

304.   B

As in many CR passages, the conclusion weighs competing considerations and claims that one is superior. Here, the benefits of the student-centered curriculum ate relevance and an adequate pass rate, with the negative of decreased classroom behavior. The conclusion suggests that the classroom behavior is at least as important to the "overall learning experience" as the other considerations.

That connection is explicitly addressed in (B), which is correct. (A) digresses to a detail about the mandated tests, (C) is an irrelevant comparison to other subjects, and (D) is an irrelevant comparison across multiple years. (E) may be tempting, but without addressing the importance of the behavior and whether it will return to the pre-change levels, it would still not be very useful to know without also knowing (B).

305.   B

The argument rests on the assumption that as scientists pass information up the chain of command, it is not supplemented with any information from outside that chain. If every scientist were corresponding with colleagues or reading journals, there would be no reason for the lab director to be less knowledgeable than his or her subordinates. This assumption is captured in (B), which is correct.

306.   D

This argument is flawed in a very common way: it confuses revenues (the sale price for each item sold) with profits (revenues minus expenses). The first sentence is about revenues; the second is about profits. The first establishes that revenues are higher for name-brand products. To cast doubt on the conclusion that profits are higher for name-brand products, look for a choice that raises the issue of higher expenses for name-brand products.

(D) is perfect, as it offers a large expense that is relevant to name-brand products but not to generics.

307.   C

The argument is one of causality. It claims that a drop in local alarm system installations will hurt the business of Fire-Away and result in local job losses. A ten percent drop sounds series, but only if local system installations are a core business of Fire-Away. (C) weakens the argument by claiming that maintenance, not installing, is the primary source of annual revenue. This means that the evidence given is not nearly as important to the success of the company as the passage supposes.

(A) is irrelevant to employment levels at Fire-Away, as is (B). (D) slightly strengthens the argument, and (E) offers a mitigating factor that is not relevant to the concerns regarding job loss.

308.   C

The passage presents something of a paradox. Protected acreage is increased, yet the harvest in the area suffered for part (but not all) of the time the protection was in place. The best way to explain these paradoxes is to show some external cause that accounts for the observation.

(A) presents another data point, but does not explain anything. (B) may not be on topic, since it is not clear that all of the protected acreage was once deforested. (C) is correct: a severe drought would explain a poor harvest for three years, regardless of protection. (D) makes the paradox even stronger, since it suggests that the increase in acreage did not change when the harvest level did. (E) would explain a steady increase in harvest, but not the harvest levels referred to in the passage.

309.   D

The conclusion of this argument is set forth before it is clear that it's the conclusion. "The response...is yes" refers to "The question has been raised" in the second sentence. Since the response is "yes," that question gives us the content of the conclusion. The first sentence and the rest of the last sentence are both evidence for that conclusion. The correct choice, then, is (D), the only choice which identifies the second bolded portion as the conclusion.

310.   B

The phrasing of the question may be unfamiliar, but this is just another form of inference question–from the statements above, what can be accurately deduced?

(A) is wrong, as the passage suggests that lampshades were probably not made in the 13th century. (B) is correct–while lampshades were not manufactured in the 13th century, the manufacturing techniques are the same, validating the artisans' claim that the production process is similar. (C) is wrong; while the methods may be the same, the training might not be. (D) is not supported; in fact, it is suggested that lampshades were not made in the 13th century. (E) is an irrelevant comparison to something alien to the content of the passage.

311.   B

The proposed plan has a goal of increasing weight loss by reducing cheating. The method involves monitoring food diaries. What is required–what is assumed by the conclusion that the plan will work–is that monitoring food diaries will actually reduce cheating, which probably requires that cheaters report their cheating to their diaries.

This is described by choice (B), which is correct. For the monitoring of food diaries to be of value, the food diaries must be accurate.

312.   C

The argument has a lot of assumptions; it may be quicker to scan the answer choices and eliminate wrong ones.

(A) is not necessary to the argument; it is more about speed and ridership than manufacturing volume. (B) is close, but note that the choice doesn't specific import levels "of transit," which is its fatal flaw. (C) is correct–the argument focuses on the speed of the imported trains, and then concludes that ridership will go up, assuming there is a link. (D) may be true, but it is certainly not assumed by the argument. (E) is tempting, since the argument does seem to assume that Colbyville riders value speed, but we don't know anything about how Harpertown riders feel about speed.

313.   A
Consider what we know about the Cray microscopes, as well as what we know about Spectrum's needs.   All we know about the microscopes is that they have "exceptional magnification capacities." Spectrum needs "detailed and high-definition images." It seems like exceptional magnification would give you "detailed," but what about high-definition? That may be the weakness of the plan.
That's choice (A), which is correct.   If Crays do not produce the desired type of image, then they may not meet Spectrum's stated needs.   (C) is a disadvantage for some employees, but not necessarily for the company as a whole. (B) and (D) are irrelevant, while (E) supports the plan.

314.   D
The argument makes a small shift: the goal is to draw the largest possible audience, so if a theater has an opportunity to draw a larger audience for a specific production, it should do so. Note the adjustment to "specific production"–the first claim regarding the "largest possible audience" is to the "art of theater"–something that is far more general than simply getting more people in the crowd for a specific production.   These two goals may often coincide, but to weaken the argument, one may show that the goals do not coincide.
(A) explains why avant-garde productions are appealing, but does not weaken the argument. (B) names a challenge of regietheater, but does not weaken the argument. (C) is a fact regarding regietheater, but does not weaken the argument. (D) addresses the scope shift mentioned earlier: these productions may get audiences for a specific production, but does not attract them to theater in general. (E) is more a benefit than a downside of regietheater. Choice (D) is correct.

315.   B
The passage makes clear the benefits of the process: preventing melting and increasing shelf life are good things. Perhaps there is something that the passage has overlooked, a downside of the process. Choice (B) is the only clear-cut example of a potential downside to the process, and it is correct. (A) is a downside only if buyers must consume the ice cream at the temperature at which it is stored. (C) suggests a possible flaw, but does not state that it is the case. (D) may not be a problem at all, if the process is sufficiently effective. And (E) does not affect the argument whatsoever.

316.   D
To fill in the blank, look for a valid reason why natural grocery stores do not carry bulk or generic products, based on the previous sentences that customers want to be associated with "something healthy," which gives them a sense of moral superiority.
(A) is the opposite of what we need, as it supports carrying bulk items. (B) is bad news for grocery stores, but doesn't relate to the argument in the passage. (C), like (A), is the opposite of our goal, as it supports carrying generics. (D) is

correct, as it tells us why generics do not give organic customers what they are looking for. (E) is another choice that provides a reason to carry bulk items, not the opposite.

317.   C

The relevant combination of data is that, after receiving the vitamin tables, the parrots have no higher vitamin levels. That's a bit of a paradox – if you take vitamins, your vitamin level usually goes up. There must be some other reason why the vitamin levels did not increase.

The correct choice is (C), which explains why the vitamin level did not increase. None of the other choices resolve the issue by suggesting a reason why the vitamin tablets did not increase vitamin levels.

318.   D

The conclusion is that manufacturers are concerned with "average car buyers," as contrasted with "luxury car collectors." We're told that luxury car collectors don't care about fuel effiency standards, while presumably average car buyers do. If the conclusion is true, it is necessary (but not stated explicitly) that car manufacturers ignore the desires of luxury car collectors in setting fuel efficiency standards. That's (D), which is the correct choice.

319.   E

To explain the facts given in the passage, the correct choice must offer a reason why one group is affected by the disease while the other is not, despite the apparent similarity of their situations. (A) reports a difference, but in the wrong direction–it suggests that office workers are more exposed. (B) compares the two groups to others, which is irrelevant. (C) is similar. (D) introduces some combination of the two groups ("hotel guests who work in offices), which unnecessarily complicates the issue.

(E) is correct. It offers a reason why hotel guests are affected by an illness, even though their exposure to it is superficially similar to another group that is not typically affected by it.

320.   C

This very typical "weaken" question offers one explanation for a phenomenon, and the likely correct answer will provide an alternative explanation. The explanation given is that parents are aware of the studies, and thus prevent their children from watching as much television. There must be some other reason why children are spending less time watching television.

The correct answer is (C), which shows that TV-watching time has shifted to another medium, and the shift probably has nothing to do with parents' awareness of the dangers of TV watching. (A) may be tempting, but it does not directly address the issue of childrens' TV-watching time–it may be that families purchase more televisions for other reasons.

321.   A

The passage provides some evidence that suggests that hunter-gatherer societies should be decreasing in number, but notes that they are increasing. Four of the five choices will explain the increase; we're looking for the one that does not.

Choice (A) is correct–the validity of the predictions is irrelevant. Whether or not the predictions were based on logical premises, this choice doesn't give us a reason why the size of these societies would increase. Each of the other choices provides a reason why the size of the societies would increase.

322.   E

The argument concludes that poisoning voles is not recommended, because the poison also harms predators of the vole. The conclusion assumes that harming the vole's predators is a bad thing, but the passage does not directly say so. Thus, to undermine the conclusion of the argument, we must contradict the assumption–we must say that the harming the predators is acceptable. Choice (E) does this, saying that the predators are themselves considered pests.

323.   B

Note a subtle shift in scope between the first and second sentences. The first specifies "non-industrial means," while the second makes a broader statement: "the most effective tool." If an industrial tool is more effective than seaweed farms, the argument is invalid.

That is, indeed, the point made by choice (B), which is correct. If technological advances affecting large factories (i.e. industrial means) are more effective, then the first sentence is still true, but the second sentence does not follow.

324.   D

This is a tricky question with a very slight difference between the two pieces of the evidence. The statements are identical, except that one source uses the number 90, while the other says 70. Consider each choice.

(A) is irrelevant–it doesn't address the requesting of solar panels. (B) is also irrelevant–both statements use the same terminology of "US business owners." (C), like (A), does address the specific scope of the question. (D) is correct. If solar power companies are not the only providers of solar panels, then it is possible that solar panel providers are not aware of the entire market. In other words, the second finding is based on a different sample than is the first finding. Finally, (E) attempts to challenge the validity of the poll, but does not point as clearly to a discrepancy as does (D).

325.   C

Consider each choice. (A) is too strong of a conclusion; there is no evidence that companies do not provide workers with these tools. (B) is possible, but also unsupported; it is definitely one reason, but not necessarily a "large part" of the impetus for guidelines. (C) is correct–we'll return to that in a moment.

(D) makes an unsupported comparison; there is nothing in the statements about sitting. (E) makes another unsupported comparison.

(C) is not a particularly compelling answer, but that is part of what makes it correct. The statements suggest, but do not state, that companies adhere to these guidelines for insurance reasons. That lack of certainty is reflected in the wording of the choice: "may be able," which is vague enough to be supported by the statements.

326.   A

The question is specific: we're looking for a reason why the plan to finance the program will not work. Somehow, either the program will cost too much money, or the financing plan won't raise enough. Choice (A) is all we need. Fox hunters, apparently, aren't committed to purchasing fox hunting licenses every year; when prices go up, some will opt for other, presumably cheaper, options. If this happens, then the amount of money raised to fund the program will be less than expected.

327.   A

First, fill in the gaps. If the documentary channel accounted for 20% of ad sales and 40% of profits, then the children's channel was 80% of ad sales and 60% of profits. Since that is the extent of the information given in the passage, it seems likely that the correct choice will make a basic conclusion on the rates of ad sales and profits–that the documentary channel was more profitable relative to ad sales than was the children's channel.

Indeed, choice (A) does just that, and it is correct. The last three choices may all be true, but they all go too far, making plausible claims that are not fully supported by the data. In inference questions, be careful not to go beyond the very limited information provided in the passage.

328.   D

The passage makes a causal link: the opening of the daycare center led to more mothers entering the workforce. The most common way to weaken a causal link is to suggest that the outcome was caused by something else. In this case, that "something else" is choice (D): within these last three months, many of these mothers' husbands were laid off, eliminating each family's only income. That is a very strong reason for the women to enter the workforce, and thus suggests that the causal link between the daycare center and reentering the workforce is in doubt. (D) is correct.

329.   E

Presumably, the gauge manufacturers aim to make money, by putting sizes of gauges on the market that customers want to buy. An "excessively narrow range," then, would be so narrow that it would exclude sizes that many customers want to buy. That is summed up by choice (E), which is correct.

330.   C

A ban was enacted that forced insurance companies to accept clients with pre-existing conditions, and that caused an increase in health insurance rates. The passage suggests that this is not acceptable, so the types of plans offered must change to those with lower levels of coverage. We're looking for a reason why limiting levels of coverage is wrong.

The correct choice is (C), which tells us that the intention of the original ban was to allow those with pre-existing conditions to be insured with full or almost-full coverage. If that was the intent of the ban, changing the rules again would subvert the original ban, and no goals would be accomplished.

331.   D

As in many passages dealing with microeconomics, supply and demand is not always so simple. The passage suggests that if restrictions were lifted, more spinach plants would be available in Illinois. There must be some reason why that wouldn't be the case.

(A) is irrelevant–the question is about supply, not demand. (B) is also irrelevant, as we're concerned with the plants being produced in Illinois. Perhaps, if the Wisconsin factories are supplying plants to Illinois stores, that would have some bearing on the subject, but we don't know that. (C) explains the limit, but does not affect the argument.

(D) is correct. If there is no profit motive for selling more plants in Illinois, there is no reason to expect that the factory would do so. Finally, (E) wrongly focuses on Wisconsin, which is not within the scope of the passage.

332.   E

Despite the appeal of the free trial and discounted five-year contract, there must be a negative. (A) is the opposite of what we want, so it is wrong. (B) is possible–a five-year contract is not so appealing if you will move before the end of it. On the other hand, we don't know whether the security system can move with you, so (B) is ambiguous at best. (C) is irrelevant–it reveals Iron Man's motives, but does not make the deal any worse for the homeowner.

(D) may be tempting, but it is too far removed from the specific context of the passage. Finally, (E) is correct–the promotion by Iron Man would suggest that Hytek systems are favored by the insurance company, but if customers can get a discount for using other systems, perhaps Hytek is not such a good idea.

95   Explanations: Additional RC

333.   D

The first line of the second paragraph, that "theoretical models acknowledge none of these factors," tells you that any choice is very likely to be wrong. Look for what few things we know that the theoretical models acknowledge. The only such choice is (D); the theoretical model acknowledges this in the final sentence.

The theoretical model does not accept any of (A), (B) and (C), while only the theoretical model states (E).

334.   C

The relevant part of the passage is this: "the incentive to stay in an urban area may allow the worker to improve his prospect of high wage employment but increases his risk of unemployment." This is summarized by (C)–some workers benefit, others do not. While some of the other choices may be true, they do not capture the "fate" that is the concern of this question.

335.   A

The structure of this passage is simple: The first paragraph outlines a real-world, empirical model, while the second paragraph describes a theoretical model that is often at odds with the first model. Choice (A) describes it accurately. There is no "reconciling," "assessing" or "weakening," and there is no "ideology" as such in the passage.

336.   C

While the passage describes two types of tornadoes, the main focus on the passage is in the second passage, with its emphasis on line storms, not cell storms. The author highlights line storms to show some reasons why they have been inappropriately neglected. This is choice (C), which reflects a point of view, but not one so strong as (E). (A) is specific to the wrong sort of storm, and (B) focuses too much on the last sentence of the passage. (D) is too narrow, as the passage goes beyond simply comparing the two types of storms.

337.   D

The discussion of cell storms is in the first paragraph, and sure enough, the correct answer is in the very first sentence–cell storm-based tornadoes are relatively small compared to line storms. Choice (D) is correct. (A) is not stated in the passage, while (C) is true of line storms. (B) and (E) are both comparisons that may be true, but are not explicitly made in the passage. Be especially careful of (E)–while cell storms are more common than line storms in tornado alley, (E) does not logically follow.

338.   C

The part of the passage that makes recommendations about line storm-based tornadoes is at the end of the last paragraph. This part supports (C), pointing out that the current warning system is more appropriate for other types of tornadoes. (C) is correct.

(A) is not supported by the passage. (B) is tempting, but the passage is more specific, saying that during these months, line storms form at night. (D) is true, but is not the reason why research is important. (E) is a better description of cell storms, not line storms.

339.   C

Look for a choice that summarizes as much of the passage as possible. (A) is just one detail. (B) is true, but ignores much of the detail described in the passage. (C) is correct, capturing both the lack of understanding and the benefits of the notions of dark matter and dark energy. (D) is not supported by the passage, and (E) is a specific point only supported by the passage if we define "suggested" very broadly.

340.   A

At first glance, all of the choices appear to be supported by the passage. However, look closely at (A). While dark matter and dark energy account for the difference in observed mass and the mass supported by Einstein's theory, dark matter and dark energy do not "explain" the density of the universe any more than gravitational pull "explains" gravity. (A) is correct.

341.   D

"Anomalous gravitational effects" are listed as the first "indirect manifestation" of dark matter. The items in that list are given as phenomena that are best explained by theories that include the presence of dark matter.

(A) is wrong, as the Theory of Relativity is what gives rise to the idea of dark matter, so it is backwards. (B) is incorrect, since the passage brings up these gravitational effects because they are explained by physics. (C) refers to something in a different part of the passage. (D) is correct, as it characterizes the function of this list in the passage. (E) refers to another item in the list, which the passage does not link to anomalous gravitational effects.

342.   E

For any "primary purpose" question, aim to summarize the whole passage without choosing an option that is too broad. (A) is wrong, since there is no discussion of "leading" women. (B) is too general, as it doesn't even mention women. (C) is too specific; both education and feminism are mentioned, but the link is not the focus of the passage. (D) is also too specific; the "ideal" is just one notion described in the passage. (E) is correct, as it encapsulated the entire contents of the passage without being too broad.

343.   C

The relevant sentence is the last one: women were "no longer ... solely relegated to the kitchens and parlors of their homes." This is described by choice (C), which is correct. (A) was a common belief, but we don't know that it was true of education. We might infer (B) due to the reference to "seminaries," but that one word is not enough to deduce this choice. (D) may be tempting, since the passage tells us that education for women was primarily in the East, but notice that the question is about what is true of "education" in general, not education for women. (E) is somewhat true of education for women, but like (D), remember that the question is more broad than that.

344. A

The most relevant sentence is this one: "However, as a result of industrialization, modernization and the accompanying changes in society, women became increasingly, though gradually, more independent and empowered." This is very similar to choice (A), which is correct.

(B) is wrong–there might have been a slight difference from the "ideal," but not a stark one. (C) is probably true, but is not discussed in the passage. (D) gives too much weight to the references to academy curricula. (E) is probably true, but again, not discussed in the passage.

345. D

Choices (A) and (E) are mentioned in the first paragraph, while (B) and (C) are mentioned in the second. That leaves only (D). While the passage points out that unions may survive within government, there is no mention of the "increasing size" of government. (D) is correct.

346. E

The relevant paragraph is the second. The general statement is, "management ... [was] less inclined to accede to union demands for higher wages and benefits. Management also became more aggressive in fighting union attempts to organize workers." The specific point in the correct answer is raised in the next sentence, regarding the increasing tendency to hire strikebreakers, choice (E).

347. D

The best answer will summarize the entire passage without being so broad that it ignores the specific subject of the passage. (A) and (B) are too broad. (C) ascribes to the passage a position regarding union membership that it does not have, and (E) is too specific. (D) is correct.

348. D

Look for a choice that is supported by information in the passage. (A) is not supported by the passage, which says nothing about foreign workers themselves. (B) is a value judgment that the passage does not make. (C) is too extreme– worker mobility is seen as bringing out a decline in union membership, but "destroy" is strong. (D) is correct, as is strongly supported by the last sentence of the first paragraph. (E) mischaracterizes Reagan's beliefs, which the passage hints are not corporatist.

349.   C
Choices (A), (B), and (D) are mentioned in the first paragraph, while (E) is in the final sentence of the last paragraph. That leaves (C), which is the disputed issue described by the passage. (C) is correct.

350.   C
The influence of the Iroquois constitution is debated within the passage; the conclusion seems to be that while many people ascribe a fair amount of influence to the Iroquois, it is a minor influence compared to more classical sources.

(A) is too strong, since we know that some of the founders met with the Iroquois. (B) may be true, but is an issue that the passage does not address. (C) is correct: we know that it was familiar, but the passage concludes that it was not a major influence.   (D) grants too much power to the Iroquois constitution. (E) is completely unsupported by the passage.

351.   D
Look for a choice that covers the whole passage, but only the specific focus of the passage. (A) makes a false distinction between the two documents. (B) is too strong, both in "carefully considered" and "ultimately rejected." (C) is also too strong, with "important source" unsupported by the passage. (D) is correct, as it summarizes the degree of influence, which exists, but is not too great. (E) focuses too much on the flaws of the U.S. Constitution, which is not the focus of the passage.

352.   C
Consider each choice. (A) is too narrow; the passage is about both generalist and specialist firms. (D) repeats the mistake. (B) is also off-topic. A historical situation is described, but the passage is more focused on a business phenomenon than a particular historical situation. (E) has a similar problem. (C) is correct– there is both description and explanation in the passage, and the "pattern in the marketplace" refers to the continued existence of specialist producers.

353.   D
The only mention of "increased market penetration" in the passage is about specialist producers.   Thus, (D) is not listed as a disadvantage of generalist firms. (D) is correct.

354.   B
The relevant sentence is: "Increased concentration among generalists has had a positive effect on **foundings of specialist producers and specialist distributors**, and the specialists have been more active in the creation of new film genres." In other words, generalists are all doing the same thing ("increased concentration") which increases the need in the marketplace for new ideas.
That's choice (B), which is correct.

355.   A

The relevant part of the passage is the last few sentences. We're told that many films from before 1950 did not survive, and it is implied that this dearth of evidence is why some people believe that independent, specialist producers did not exist before 1950. The passage suggests that they did exist, though their product has not lasted.

Thus, the passage implies that specialist producers were making films back then that compared to generalist productions in the same way that the two types of filmmakers relate today. Thus, (A) is correct–it is suggested that specialists created a wider range of styles than did generalists. (D) may be tempting, but it is too strongly worded for a question like this one–generalists could probably match the artistic quality, even if they did not always do so.

356.   C

While the first half of the passage is specific to the Hypacrosaurus, the last focus on Hypacrosaurus turns out to be solely on its evolutionary strategy–that of maturing faster than predators. As the passage reaches its end, it becomes more broad, mentioning other species that do the same, and citing an authority on the frequency of the strategy. Thus, the correct answer is (C).

(A) is too specific to a single species. (B) is off-topic, as "implications" are not discussed. There is no assertion to be defended, so (D) is incorrect, and the underlying circumstances, the subject of (E), do not come into play in this passage.

357.   D

The passage explains that, while hadrosaurs were vulnerable to predators, their one advantage was quick maturation. Slower maturation would make them more vulnerable, so the correct answer must be either (A) or (D).

When looking for what the passage "suggests," be careful of strongly-worded choices. (A) is one such choice–"soon become extinct" is an extreme outcome. We may know that the species would be much more vulnerable, but we don't know enough to make such a strong statement. Thus, (D), which is more conservative, is correct.

358.   D

The passage gives us no explicit information about the Thomson's gazelle; it merits only a passing mention in a comparison: "Hypacrosaurus, which lived from 67-80 million years ago, was one of three common prey for tyrannosaurs and velociraptors, and was the most vulnerable, possessing long limbs and a soft body; it is sometimes described as the "Thomson's gazelle" of the late cretaceous era."

Something of this description of the hypacrosaurus must apply to the Thomson's gazelle, as well–perhaps the vulnerability, or the "long limbs and soft body." Those characteristics are mentioned in (B) and (D). (B) fails in that it makes an irrelevant comparison–the long limbs may be a notable feature, but nothing we know suggests that they are its "most distinctive feature." Thus the more carefully worded (D) is correct.

359.   A

The answer is given in this sentence: "Corporate leaders, facing a desperate shortage of workers because of wartime mobilization and the draft, opened their doors to black workers for the first time, particularly in the automobile industry." The question asks something very specific, and (A) gives an appropriately specific answer.

360.   C

The passage tells us that white activists worked to "wrest control over their working conditions from owners and managers," while blacks were more focused on desegregating workplaces, getting access to jobs. (C) is the correct choice. (A) and (B) are irrelevant, (D) may not be true, and (E) compares two things that black activists considered important.

361.   C

The first paragraph establishes the background, where black workers want access to jobs; the second paragraph describes a brief moment in time when they got that access, only to lose it. (A) is inaccurate, as no similarities are identified. (B) is wrong, since no evaluation is included in the passage. (C) is simple and accurate–it is the correct choice. (D) is too narrow, focusing only on World War II. (E) is too broad, since the passage is about only the single issue of black activists' priorities.

96 Explanations: Additional SC

362. C

Two things may jump out upon first reading: The awkward possessive of "emission's" and the presence of a semi-colon, which is unusual in GMAT SC items. The awkward possessive only appears in (A), so any of the other choices would be acceptable by that standard. The semi-colon is more complicated.

As written, the use of the semi-colon is correct, since what follows the semi-colon is a complete sentence. The same is true of (C), the other choice that uses the semi-colon. With that in mind, turn your focus to the verb tense. The X-ray emission originally had one function, now another function has come about. The phrase "has become," used in (C) and (D), is correct. (C) is preferable, since the use of "it" makes it clear that what has become something different is the X-ray emission, not "a means of improving air quality" from the previous clause. (C) is correct.

363. A

(A) is the only choice that begins with "whose," which is correct, as it refers to scientists, who are people. Choices (B) and (C) use "where" instead. This is incorrect, since "where" must always refer to a physical location. (D) and (E) use "extensiveness," which is non-standard. (D)'s "on ... knowledge" is not idiomatic, while (E)'s "to ... knowledge" is also not standard usage. Choice (A) is correct.

364. D

The phrase demarcated by dashes is a distraction; ignore it. Instead, read "its name ... is invoked more frequently than any visible star ...." The comparison is incorrect, contrasting "its name" with "any visible star." We should compare stars to stars, or names to names. Choices (D) and (E), in their use of "that of..." correct the issue. (D) is correct because it uses the idiom "more ... than," while (E) incorrectly compares using "more ... as."

365. C

As in any comparison, note carefully the idiom used to make the comparison. In (A), it is "between ... with," which is incorrect. The same mistake is repeated in (B). The correct idiom is "between ... and," used in (C). (D) and (E) opt for other constructions, neither of which is correct. (D) uses the passive construction "the career that Schoenberg had." (E) uses "differences of," which is non-idiomatic. Also note the idiom "so much ... as," which is used in (C) and (D). "so much ... but," which appears in the other choices, is incorrect.

366. B

The use of a semi-colon in the original sentence is incorrect, as what follows the semi-colon is not a complete sentence. Note that three of the remaining choices use the construction "that of." The sentence compares two cooling systems: "not centralized air conditioning" and "a type of individual machine." The last three choices would change this to some variation of "that of a type of individual machine." The "individual machine" is a type of cooling system, so "that of" is superfluous. The only remaining choice is (B), which is correct.

367.   D

There are a number of variations of the first several words, but none stands out as particular good or bad; focus instead on the idioms in the latter part of the underlined section. The word "both" is misused here. If it were correct, the sentence would read, "features both central to ... and [adjective] to...." While the word "and" appears later in the sentence, it is not setting up a second item in a list. We can eliminate (A), (B), and (E), all of which misuse "both."

(C) is wrong by using the construction "that centralize," which changes the meaning of the sentence. In fact, the resulting meaning is not at all easy to parse. (D) communicates the simple point that Ambleside has certain common characteristics, and it is correct.

368.   B

First, compare "when" and "by" at the end of the underlined section. The use of "was led" suggests that something happened at a certain time; only the use of "when" makes sense in the context of the sentence. Eliminate (A) and (E).

Both (C) and (D) are not grammatically correct. The construction "and when ..." begins a subordinate clause, but one that is not followed by anything else. (D) makes the whole sentence incomplete, missing a central verb to associate with "Mohenjo Daro." (B) is correct.

369.   E

Note the distinction between "much" and "many" among the choices. Since "ulcers" can be counted, the correct word is "many," limiting our choices to (D) and (E). (D)'s construction is awkward compared to (E); particularly, "from which Americans are suffering" is preferable to "Americans are suffering from," as it does not end with a preposition ("from"). Choice (E) is correct.

370.   A

In constructions like this one, an infinitive must be followed by an infinitive: "The only way ... to [do something] ... is to [do something else]...." Thus, the underlined portion must begin with "to," limiting us to choices (A) and (E).

Of the two, (A) is correct. (E) opts for the passive "have them covered," while the switch "and the bones are ruined" makes less clear the connection between the bad weather causing the bones to become ruined.

371.   A

There are no obvious problems with the sentence as written. Choices (B), (D), and (E) change the tense of "seems," which makes each of them wrong. The contrast in the sentence is between how the canal "seems" (in the present) to be valuable for certain purposes and the fact that it has nonetheless declined in importance. (C) doesn't change the tense, but the word "as" is misused; it should be followed by another "as" to form the idiom "as ... as ...." (A) is correct.

372. E
The correct idiom is "could not deny that..." not "...whether," so (A) and (B) are wrong. (C)'s verb tense is confusing, putting one "had not" later in time than another. (D) repeats the mistake of "whether" about a denial. That leaves only (E), which uses the correct idiom, does not confuse the chronology, and is correct.

373. A
First, decide between "include" and "includes." The relevant subject is "The 375 languages," which is plural, so the correct option is "include." Eliminate (D) and (E).

Next, focus on the construction of the two attributes of Semitic. As written, the sentence is correct: "Semitic, which was ... and is ...." In (B), "found" might be correct, but "...and is" is only correct if there is a "which" earlier in the sentence. (C)'s use of "finding" and "being" is non-idiomatic; "finding" doesn't make logical sense. (A) is correct.

374. E
The construction "try and" is common, but it is always wrong. Better is "try to." Next, the correct idiom is "set limits on," not "set limits for." We're now down to choices (D) and (E).

The phrasing of (D) is awkward. Additionally, "to set limits ... and ... " should be followed by another infinitive, such as "to impose," as in (E). Instead, (D) uses "imposing," which is not parallel. (E) is correct.

375. E
The construction "during all of the year's times" is grossly unidiomatic, so (A) must be incorrect. (B) repeats the mistake. The correct choice will make clear the causal relationship, that the regulations achieve a goal "by effecting" a ban. (E) is the most obvious choice that follows that pattern, and it is correct.

Choice (C) implies that the regulations are not always in place; they are only effective "when" they are in place. (D) uses the passive construction of "a rigid ban is effected" rather than attributing the effecting of the ban to the regulations.

376. E
Neither "should" nor "will" is clearly incorrect as the first word of the underlined portion, so move on to other issues. As written, the sentence contains a list, but it is not grammatically parallel. All of the choices begin with "...repaint peeling walls," meaning that all other list items must begin with a verb. That eliminates every choice but (E); in each of the first four options, the second

list item is "new flooring should/would be laid down," which is not parallel with "repaint peeling walls." (E) is correct.

377.   B

There are two mistakes in the sentence as written. First, "they" should be preceded by "that," as the clause beginning with "they" has a subject and verb. Also, "desire ... for fleeing" is unidiomatic; a preferable option is "desire ... to flee." Thus, our choices are limited to (B), (C), and (D).

The main difference between these choices is in the last few words. Since the singer has a desire "to flee," what results should be grammatically similar: "to become." The only choice that contains such parallel infinitives is (B), which is correct.

378.   A

Four of the five choices start the underlined portion with "and." Using "and" in this position implies that Pope beginning his translations and the number of translations increasing are separate things. By leaving out the word "and," the sentence implies (as it should) that Pope beginning a translation leads to the number of versions increasing. (A) is correct.

379.   C

In each choice, it may help to "read around" the clause between commas. That makes it clear that "between" must be followed by "and." For instance, (A) is wrong, as it uses the construction "between quasars ... with ...." (D) repeats the error.

Choice (B) is nonsensical; "the resembled quasar" has no discernible meaning in English. (E) uses the incorrect idiom "resemblance with," which would properly be "resemblance to." That leaves only (C), which is correct.

380.   E

First, choose between "virtual" and "virtually." The word is in the position of an adverb, modifying the adjective "endless," so the proper choice is "virtually." (A), (B), and (C) are wrong.

To decide between "all" and "each," look at the end of the sentence. "The body of the mother" is singular, so "each" is correct. For "all" to be correct, the sentence would have to end with plurals: "bodies of mothers or surrogates." (E) is correct.

381.   D

This is a long, complicated sentence, but the underlined portion is simply part of a list. The relevant part is: "the parasite ... causes ..., is moved ..., and is treated ..." The list items are not unparallel, but consider the meaning of the second item. In its original form, it uses a passive construction, as if something else moves the parasite into the lungs. It makes more sense if the parasite simply "moves" into the lungs, as in (D).

All of the other choices use a passive construction for the second list item, so (D) is correct.

382. A

The sentence is acceptable as is. (B) has no obvious error, but it is excessively wordy, using both "because" and "due" and introducing a subordinate clause. (C) uses the passive construction "has been sent." (D) opts for the unidiomatic "from," as well as the ambiguous pronoun "its" that intends to refer to the museum. (E), like (B), is excessively wordy, using "with the result that" where the structure of (A) communicates the same more simply. (A) is correct.

383. B

In the sentence as written, "exhibiting" is redundant; if physical characteristics are present, they are exhibited. This limits us to choices (B) and (D). Note also that the sentence includes a list, which must be grammatically parallel. Further, the proper idiom is "such ... as," which is incorrect in (A) and (E).

In (B), the list is grammatically parallel. In (D), the first two items are parallel nouns ("correctness," "the performance") but the third is a verb ("demonstrating"). Thus, (B) is correct.

384. E

The phrase "the writers' attempting" doesn't make sense; judging from the choices, we must opt for "the writers' instrument," and choose among (C), (D), and (E). Both (C) and (D) are wrong because "try" is redundant; it is already clear from context that authors attempt to interest readers via critics. Further, (D) is wrong because it replaces the correct idiom "try to" with "try and." (E) is correct.

385. E

The sentence begins with a comparison, and the second item being compared is "the liver." The first should be grammatically similar, so it should be "the heart." That leaves us with (A) and (E). (E) is better; by using the word "unlike," it is clear that the attribute of the liver does not also apply to the heart. (E) is correct.

386. B

The first difference among the choice is "that" versus "of." Since what follows "that/of" is a complete sentence, "that" is correct, limiting us to (A) and (B).

Since the rest of the sentence is a prediction, it is in the future relative to 2007. A past prediction forecasts that something "would" happen, not the simple past tense like "did" happen, as in (A)'s "surpassed." (B) is correct.

387.   A
First compare "signal(s)" with a comma followed by "signaling." The comma, followed by a modifier, results in an incomplete sentence, which is missing a verb. Eliminate (D) and (E). Now compare "signal" and "signals." While "decrease" is singular, the combination of two subjects joined by "and" forms a plural subject, so "signal" is correct. Eliminate (B).

(C) contains the passive construction "as have previously been thought." The passive construction is not preferable, and "have" should be the singular "has," since it refers to "electromagnetic activity." Thus, (A) is correct.

388.   B
The first verb in the sentence is "withstand"–present tense. Thus, we're looking for present tense in the underlined portion as well. That leaves only (B), with (D) the only other choice that is not in past tense. (D)'s present perfect progressive is present, but a different verb form, where we don't need the sense that it "has been" happening.

Also, in this case, "that" is preferable to "which," since "prevented the foundation..." is modifying this particular type of "metal framework." A clue is that there is no comma; a comma usually precedes the word "which."

389.   E
"The laboratory" is singular, so the first underlined word should be "it," not "they." Eliminate (A) and (B). (C) doesn't have "it" or "they," which is a good clue that (C) is a passive construction, which should be avoided. (D) is redundant, using both "formerly" and "in the past." That leaves only (E), which is efficient and uses the proper pronoun.

390.   E
The proper idiom is "more ... than," which eliminates (A) and (B). In (C) and (D), the words "it is" are superfluous and "it" does not refer to any previous noun in the sentence. That leaves (E), which is efficient and contains the proper comparison idiom.

391.   C
The modifier "made by allowing" describes metallic glass, "this novel material." As such, it must be placed as close to the term "novel material" as possible, leaving us with (B), (C), and (E). (B) inserts the unnecessary word "being," so it is wrong. (E) confuses what is being modified; with the phrase beginning with "which," the modifier could apply to "a particular atomic arrangement," which is not the sentence's intent.

392.   E
The word "either" must be followed by "or," but "or" is not in the sentence, so (A) and (B) are wrong. Note the comparison structure: after the underlined section, technology companies are compared to "mature companies, which ...." Thus, the best choice is (E), which matches that structure with "which produce."

393.   B

As written, the word "they" clearly refers to homeless people, but logically, that cannot be the meaning of the sentence. (A) is wrong. (E) repeats a similar error; "they were thought" is just about meaningless, anyway. Both (C) and (D) are missing the word "that," which idiomatically follows "show" when followed by a claim like the one in this sentence. That leaves only (B), which is correct.

394.   A

The list at the end of the underlined portion is the same in all five choices, so focus on the first few words. Eliminate (B) and (E) because "consistent orders" is ungrammatical–the sentence refers to a single order that is always applicable. (C) and (D) use the undesirable verb "having," which the GMAT avoids whenever possible. (A) is correct.

395.   A

Since the idiom "either ... or" is underlined, make sure that the comparison is between like things. What follows "or" is "low-income working families," so look for another plural noun. The only choices that follow the format "to either [noun] or [noun]" are (A) and (B). The others move or add the word "to," breaking the similarity.

The difference between (A) and (B) is subtle. In (A), "to be rented to" modifies "housing units." In (B), "to rent them" is slightly redundant with "it will offer"–it needn't be said that they are being offered to be rented. (A) is correct.

396.   B

The first clause sets up a comparison, so what follows the comma must be of like nature to "other developing nations." (C), (D), and (E) place a mortality rate after the comma, which is wrong, leaving only two possible choices.

The second half of the underlined portion has another comparison. What is "closer to the U.S.?" It should be a country. (A) compares the mortality rate to the U.S., which is not comparing like with like. (B), however, is comparing the country to the U.S., which is grammatically proper. (B) is correct.

397.   A

Note that all the tenses are some form of past–the auto maker "pointed out," "sold," "began to favor," etc. That helps determine that "were becoming" is correct, especially in the idiom "were becoming ... as ...." (B) is incorrect, as "had been becoming" suggests that the trend stopped, which is not consistent with the contents of the sentence. (C) contains superfluous language: "that there were...." What follows "smaller cars and trucks" must be "that," as what follows is the "justification." An argument can be a justification, but a vehicle cannot be. (D) and (E) are wrong. (A) is correct.

398.   D

The sentence begins by referring to plural "department stores," so any use of "it" or "its" in referring to them is wrong. Eliminate (A) and (E).

(B) can be eliminated due to the passive construction of "by whom," compared to the active "who so christened" of later choices. (C) is wrong as it drops the connection between Bader and the christening altogether, which must be included for the sentence to make sense. (D) is correct.

399.   E

The modifier "because of their increased access..." should immediately precede what "their" refers to: the "wealthier families." It doesn't, so (A) and (B) are wrong. (D) is also incorrect, as the same modifier problem moves to a bit later in the sentence. (C) is grammatically closer to correct, but the construction suggests that the experts predicted only the 80/100 ratio, not that girls are more likely to marry supportive husbands; instead, the last part is referred to more as a logical implication. (E) maintains the intended meaning of the sentence and corrects the modifier problem by dropping "their" from before "increased access to ultrasound."

400.   A

While "students" is plural, the "cohort" of students is singular, so "has" is correct and "have" is incorrect. Eliminate (D) and (E). (B) is excessively wordy, with "that are estimated" instead of "estimated" and "to have a" instead of "at a." (C) shifts the focus of the sentence to the act of participation, while the focus of the sentence should remain on the awards and scholarships. (A) is correct.

CPSIA information can be obtained at www.ICGtesting.com
Printed in the USA
LVOW050710260512

283422LV00004B/24/P